FREEDOM OF MIND
AND OTHER ESSAYS

Freedom of Mind

AND OTHER ESSAYS BY

STUART HAMPSHIRE, 1914-

PRINCETON UNIVERSITY PRESS

PRINCETON, N.J.   1971

STUART HAMPSHIRE has spent most of his academic career at
Oxford University, where he was elected Fellow of All Souls College
in the year he completed his undergraduate studies.
During World War II he spent five years in the British Army and
an additional two years in the Foreign Service. After the war
he served as Lecturer in Philosophy, University College,
London, for three years before returning to Oxford. He subsequently
became Grote Professor of Philosophy of Mind and Logic at
University College, London; and from 1963 to June 1970
he was professor and chairman of the department of philosophy,
Princeton University. On October 1, 1970 he returned once again
to Oxford to accept appointment as Warden of Wadham College.
He has published numerous articles in philosophical journals
and other media, and his book-length publications
include *Spinoza* (1951), *Thought and Action* (1959),
Freedom of the Individual (1965), and *Modern Writers and
Other Essays* (1970). He is a Fellow of the British Academy.

This book has been composed in Linotype Caledonia
Printed in the United States of America
by Princeton University Press, Princeton, New Jersey

Contents

Preface

Written and published at different times over a period of twenty years, these essays converge upon a common topic. Broadly summarised, the topic is: What are the peculiarities of the concepts that we use to describe and to criticise the mental states and the performances of human beings, as contrasted with the states and performances of things of other kinds? What are the peculiarities of the knowledge that we may possess of our own mental states and attitudes and of the mental states and attitudes of other persons? All the essays in this volume are directed to some aspect of these questions, or to some ancillary question closely connected with them.

Two short articles, "Dispositions" and "Multiply General Sentences," do not fall under the general heading of ethics and the philosophy of mind. They are included only because they both raise issues that are unavoidable in the context of any discussion of freedom of mind or of the free-will problem. In all the other essays the main questions are never far from the surface of the argument.

Of course the questions just mentioned are too vast and too difficult to be directly answered in any summary way. But there is one suggestion of one part of a tentative answer which recurs in these essays: the suggestion is that the concepts applied in the description and criticism of the mental states and performances of men are applied in two crucially different ways. Sometimes the concepts are used in expressions of self-knowledge, and in adopting contemporary beliefs and intentions of one's own; and sometimes they occur in the descriptions and criticisms of an external observer, who reviews the beliefs, desires, and intentions of another or of his own past. The knowledge that any man has of mental states and performances comes from at least two different sources, and is of at least two different kinds. The problems of freedom of mind and of decision, as philosophical problems, arise at the points of intersection of these different kinds of knowledge. For example, if a man tries to adopt the attitude of a scientific observer to the sources of his own present beliefs and decisions, he finds himself in the odd situation of dissociating himself, to a greater or less extent, from these beliefs and decisions. Conversely, if a man tries to interpret the beliefs and decisions of a friend, exactly as his friend interprets them, he finds himself in the odd situation of having to adopt a whole system of beliefs and desires which are not his own, but his friend's. These are some of the difficulties that limit the moral, or human, sciences; they are difficulties that have no close parallel in men's understanding of other natural processes.

Every man is a student, and potentially a scientific student, of the beliefs, desires, and attitudes of people in general, including himself, and is naturally interested in their regular causes and effects. Every man is also a moralist, in so far as he thinks of himself as continually assessing, and changing, his own beliefs, desires, and attitudes, in accordance with some standard, or standards, which he chooses to apply to them, or which he happens to apply to them. In virtue of this self-criticism, he thinks of himself as the author of his beliefs and attitudes, and of at least some of his desires, and as having authority in declaring what they are —rather as a man is the author of the sentences that he writes, and has some authority in declaring what he means by them. A confusion arises when, changing our standpoint from that of the scientific student to that of the responsible author, and vice versa, we try to reconcile the explanations that we would give of the same mental state or process from the two different points of view; and this confusion is the

centre of the problem of freedom of mind, which has presented itself most acutely to those philosophers who have
combined an unlimited confidence in scientific explanation
with the preoccupations of a moralist. Among these is
Spinoza.

The two expositions of Spinoza are included because his
definition of freedom included the insight that a person's
understanding of the causes of his own contemporary states
of mind, and particularly of his beliefs, desires, and intentions, modifies these states of mind. This insight has always
seemed to me to explain the two beliefs which are naturally
held by most men and which at first seem incompatible:
that our changing states of mind are instances of lawful reg-
ularities, and are the effects of assignable causes, no less
than their physical states: but also that a person, while he
is able to think, has a peculiar power of reflection, which
modifies his states of mind, and makes them different from
what they naturally would have been if he had not thought
about them. His awareness of this power is often called his
sense of freedom of mind in the formation of his beliefs,
desires, and intentions.

But a mystery still obviously remains, even if this insight
of Spinoza's shows more precisely where the mystery lies.
Not only the power of thought, but the actual use of this
power by any individual on any particular occasion, are
naturally held to be in principle explicable by antecedent
conditions in the organism, which determine how this
power will be used on any particular occasion. But this is so
far an article of faith only, and we have no systematic
knowledge of what these determinants may be. The relation between specific organic states and specific processes of
thought is still a dark area of ignorance. Spinoza's modified
materialism, which represents a sequence of thought as embodied always in a matched sequence of physical states, is
only a hypothesis, or, it might be said, a guess. Its implica-

tions are worth reconsidering now, partly because the invention and study of artificial intelligences have made the hypothesis a little less obscure and more open to investigation: and partly because philosophers have in recent years questioned those theories of meaning which imply that any identification of physical states with processes of thought must be excluded a priori.

I think therefore that it can properly be claimed that there are common themes running through this volume. The arguments are not always presented as I would choose to present them now, and there are many points at which I now believe that the argument could usefully be carried much further. But I have made substantial alterations in the original published versions where I found what seemed to me to be obscurities or obvious inadequacies and errors.

The later essays have benefited greatly from the restraining criticisms and the encouragement that I received from my former colleagues in the Department of Philosophy at Princeton University; and I am grateful to Mrs. Pearl Cavanaugh for her continuous help in the preparation of this book.

Oxford   S.H.
January 1971

Sources and Acknowledgments

"Freedom of Mind" was presented as the Lindley Lecture at the University of Kansas in March 1965. It is copyright © 1967 by the Department of Philosophy, University of Kansas, and is reprinted here, slightly revised, with the kind permission of Richard T. De George, chairman of the department.

"Subjunctive Conditionals" was first published in *Analysis*, vol. 9 (1949), pp. 9-14, and is reprinted here with permission of the editor.

"Multiply General Sentences" was published originally in *Analysis*, vol. 10 (1950), pp. 73-76, and is reprinted with permission of the editor.

"Dispositions" is reprinted with permission of the editor from *Analysis*, vol. 14 (1953), pp. 5-11.

"Fallacies in Moral Philosophy" appeared in *Mind: A Quarterly Review of Psychology and Philosophy*, vol. 58 (1949), pp. 466-482. It is published here with the permission of the editor.

"Ethics: A Defense of Aristotle" was originally published in *University of Colorado Studies*, Series in Philosophy, No. 3 (January 1967), pp. 23-38, and is reprinted with permission of the University of Colorado Press.

"Ryle's *The Concept of Mind*" appeared in the critical notices section of *Mind*, vol. 59 (1950), pp. 237-255, and is reprinted with permission of the editor.

"The Analogy of Feeling" was first published in *Mind*, vol. 61 (1952), pp. 1-12. It appears here with permission of the editor.

"On Referring and Intending" is reprinted here with permission from the *Philosophical Review*, vol. 65 (1956), pp. 1-13.

"Feeling and Expression" was the Inaugural Lecture as Grote Professor of the Philosophy of Mind and Logic given at University College, London, on October 25, 1960.

"Disposition and Memory" was presented as the Ernest Jones Lecture before the British Psycho-Analytical Association, June 15, 1960. It later appeared in the *International Journal of Psycho-Analysis* and is reprinted with permission of the journal and the association.

"Spinoza and the Idea of Freedom" constituted the Dawes Hicks Lecture on Philosophy read before the British Academy on May 25, 1960, and was originally published in the *Proceedings of the British Academy*, vol. 46 (1960), pp. 195-215.

"A Kind of Materialism" was the Presidential Address to the Eastern Division of the American Philosophical Association, 1969. It will appear in the *Proceedings* of the Eastern Division of the APA and is reprinted with permission.

"Sincerity and Single-Mindedness" was presented in two sessions as the Howison Lecture at the University of California, Berkeley, in 1967. It is published here for the first time.

FREEDOM OF MIND
AND OTHER ESSAYS

Freedom of Mind

My thesis will be that, no matter what experimental knowledge of the previously unknown causes that determine a man's beliefs is accumulated, that which a man believes, and also that which he aims at and sets himself to achieve, will remain up to him to decide in the light of argument. Secondly, I want to point to a generally unrecognized consequence of asserting the doctrine that the physical states of the organism determine uniquely corresponding states of mind. I shall argue that when this causal dependence of states of mind upon physical states of the organism is known to hold, then the dependent states of mind become, in virtue of the knowledge of the dependence, a form of perception.

I shall not be trying to disprove, or to contradict, anything that could properly be called a thesis of determinism: e.g. the proposition "every event has a cause," or "every event is an instance of some natural law, which explains its occurrence by reference to some set of initial conditions." About these propositions I would only say that they seem to me to be illegitimately general, and for that reason vacuous. Because nothing would count as finding a negative instance to them, nothing would count as finding a good reason to believe that they are true or that they are false. Therefore they, and their negations, will play no part in my argument. But I am ready to agree that, given that we have any true statement of fact about a state of mind, e.g. that Jones believes that there is a lectern in the next room, then we can always look for, and may expect ultimately to find, an explanation of this fact by reference to some set of initial conditions, which will, in normal circumstances, constitute sufficient conditions of Jones having this belief. I am also ready to agree that this request for an explanation of psy-

3

chological fact, if pressed far enough, and pressed successfully, will always include, as one element in the whole explanation, an experimentally confirmed covering law. I am
ready to agree that there is no a priori reason why, given
that a psychological fact is specified by a description, and
given that we hold this description of the explicandum constant, we should not find an explanation under a covering
law, experimentally confirmed.

Suppose my name to be Jones and I speak. I say "It is a
fact that I believe that there is a lectern in the next room."
I can give you my reasons for believing, which, in the normal case, I believe to be good reasons, or at least not altogether bad ones. I give you my reasons, and then say "Now
you know why I believe that there is a lectern in the next
room; you have the explanation of my belief." I have not
told you all that you might conceivably have wanted to
know when you inquired why Jones had this belief. I have
not claimed to give you an explanation that amounts to
specifying a sufficient condition of the belief. I have only
claimed to mention one interesting condition which I take
to have been a necessary condition for the consequence, or
at least *a* cause, on this occasion. I have committed myself
to the assertion that, had I not recently been in the room
and seen something that looked like a lectern there (this being my reason), and if everything else in my situation had
remained the same, I would have been more doubtful of the
existence of a lectern in the next room than I in fact am, at
least for some interval of time. When I give my reason for
believing something, and claim to be accurate in this piece
of autobiography, I state another belief, and a sketch of an
argument which was in some sense present to my mind, or
which would have come to mind, if I had been challenged;
and I am committed to the hypothetical statement that, if
this belief, and/or sketch of an argument, had been shown
to be erroneous, I would in fact have reconsidered, or

4

weakened, the belief which was their consequence. I am committed to no more than this by offering you the reason for my belief. But also I am committed to no less. I am therefore implicitly denying that sufficient conditions of my holding the belief at that time about the lectern in the next room can be found in states of the organism, or of the environment, which do not include the belief, and/or sketch of an argument, that constitute my reason. I am not committed to denying that there existed in the state of the organism, and of the environment, conditions that were necessary to explain my holding the supporting belief or my following the supporting argument to its conclusion. If, for example, you were interested in the causal explanation of an error of Jones' about the objects in the next room, you might find an adequate explanation in some state of his organism. Equally if you were interested in Jones' surprising ability to form true beliefs about objects in the next room, you might find some adequate explanation in the state of his organism and of the environment. By manipulating and changing the relevant states of the organism and of the environment, you might thereby change his true beliefs into erroneous ones and his erroneous beliefs into true ones. But if Jones' account of the reason for his belief was a true one, then the states of the organism and of the environment were necessary, but not sufficient, conditions for his belief.

How does Jones know what the reason for his belief that there is a lectern in the next room is or was? Sometimes of course he does not know, and particularly in these perceptual cases; but sometimes he does know. In one simple type of case he knows the reason for his belief, just because he gives his assent to a proposition, under a certain condition or proviso, and this condition is that which he gives as his reason when he is asked. When asked whether there was a lectern in the next room, he might have answered "Yes, there is, if the room which I have just visited is the next room to this one, as I believe it to be, and if that tall thing which I saw in the corner is a lectern, as I believe it to be." Here he has spelt out in conditional form his belief together with its ground. In general we form beliefs which we are ready to revise if other beliefs that we hold are shown to be false. One belief is conditional upon another and upon a reasoning process of some kind, which at each step involves a belief. I could for some purposes present my beliefs as a chain of beliefs connected by reasoning, and therefore in conditional form, and without detachment. When I am forming my beliefs in conditions of uncertainty, they present themselves to me with some of their conditions attached. When I am asked to give my reason for a belief that I hold, and that I have detached, I am asked to reconstruct some of the chain of conditions upon which it depends. In this reconstruction I do not need to appeal to a general covering law in order to assure myself that I have found a necessary condition of my detached belief. For I know that this belief was formed conditional upon others. Exactly the same may be true when I form an intention or adopt an aim. I may form it, or adopt it, subject to certain conditions, which I could either specify in conditional form, or produce as my reasons for forming that intention or having that aim. In cases where I have the conditional intention of leaving early if it rains, the rain may be my reason for leaving early, if this is what I finally do. Similarly in cases where I will only believe something if certain observations were actually made, then these observations can be given as my reasons for believing. These are the simple cases, which illustrate the possibility of knowing the implied singular hypothetical proposition to be true without appeal to a covering law.

I am not arguing that a man cannot be mistaken in giving his reasons for a belief or for having a certain aim. He can, and often he is mistaken. An argument from parallel cases may lead to the conclusion that his alleged reasons ought to be regarded as rationalisations, which do not at all explain his belief or his intention. The argument from parallel cases might be sufficient to convince us that the supporting belief, and/or reasoning, was not a necessary condition of the ensuing belief: that he would not in this case for a moment have suspended or weakened his ensuing belief, if the supporting belief and/or reasoning had been shown to be erroneous. I am only arguing that we do not *need* inductive, experimental argument in order to be assured justifiably that so-and-so is the reason for a belief or an intention.

This rough outline of an account of "being my reason for believing *p*" can be generalized, and applies equally to my reasons for wanting, my reasons for doing, and my reasons for having a certain attitude towards an object, or for feeling a certain emotion about it. Whenever I state "This is my reason, and it is my only reason," there is a singular hypothetical proposition entailed. Suppose that my reason for an action is specified by a belief about some features of the action, e.g. its consequences: "I am doing it because it would help my friend." Then the entailed hypothetical is "If I did not believe that it would help my friend, I would become, at least for a time, more uncertain about doing it; I would reconsider." If this is given as my reason in the past ("My reason for doing it was . . ."), then the implied proposition is the hypothetical "If I had not believed that it would help Jones, I would have reconsidered doing it; that is, I would have been more uncertain, at least for a time, whether I was going to do it." This hypothetical proposition can be relevantly challenged by an appeal to inductive evidence; but the subject may be justified in claiming to know that it is true merely in virtue of his memory of his calculations at the time. So "*x* is his reason for *ϕ*-ing" entails the hypothetical "If he was shown that *x* includes a false belief, he would become more doubtful whether to ϕ or not," or "he would reconsider whether he would ϕ or not."

My becoming doubtful whether I would ϕ or not, during deliberation, and when reasons are in place, amounts to the same as reconsidering. For my becoming sure that I will do so-and-so, that I believe so-and-so, that I am frightened of so-and-so, amounts to deciding; deciding, in the sense that, if I have first been uncertain whether I will do so-and-so, believe so-and-so, want so-and-so, fear so-and-so, and then consider the matter, my becoming sure, for some reason, brings it about that I intend to do so-and-so, want so-and-so, fear so-and-so, believe so-and-so. So we get the sequence of hypotheticals: if I lose some confidence in the validity of the reasons that explain my belief, intention, desire, attitude, or emotion, I lose some confidence that this is my intention, desire, attitude, or emotion. While I lose confidence, I cease to intend, want, believe, fear, etc. The reasons for intending, wanting, fearing, believing can be entered, in these cases of deliberation, into the full characterisation of the intention, the desire, the fear, or the belief. The reason is in this sense internal to the state of mind, although it may also be a partial explanation of the state of mind. To classify my state as fear about so-and-so, or anger with so-and-so about so-and-so, is already to imply a partial explanation of the perturbed state of mind.

The claim that explanation of states of mind by reasons is a distinct kind of explanation from explanation by causes, is unclear, and, insofar as it is clear, undemonstrated. But there is a distinction between two kinds of hypothetical proposition which may be involved in explanation; the first kind does not require the support of a covering law whenever someone claims to know that there is a true explanation, although it may be challenged by an appeal to a well-confirmed covering law. The second kind of explanation does require the appeal to a covering law, or at least to the evidence of parallel cases, if a claim to knowledge is to be justified at all. Consider the following:

1. "I would not like that person, if he did not have that particular quality."

2. "I would not want to go there, if they took the casino away."

3. "I would not have gone to the opera last night, if Callas had not been singing."

4. "I would not have believed that, if I had not had his eye-witness account."

5. "I would not be frightened of going up in the elevator, if it were larger."

In each case the condition stated in the if-clause gives a reason which will serve as a partial explanation. At the same time the condition stated can be viewed as specifying more fully the intention, the desire, the fear, the belief, the state of mind. I may simply recall that my intention to go to the opera was in this way conditional. But the reason and the partial explanation may be shown to be a mere rationalisation. Inductive arguments from parallel cases may lead me to doubt whether the statement of my reason is acceptable, that is, whether the implied hypothetical is true; just as inductive argument from parallel cases may lead me to doubt whether an unconditional statement of intention is true, even though I do not need to support a statement of intention with inductive evidence that I will in fact try to perform the action when the time comes. The question "How do you know that this was your reason?," and even more, the question "How do you know that this is your reason?," are odd and require a special context; but the questions "Are you sure that this was your reason?," and "Are you sure that this is your reason?" are normal. It is worth noticing that in this context I may give what would be my reason for doing something in advance, and before I had decided whether to do it or not; and similarly for belief. Balancing the several reasons for believing or disbelieving the story that I have been told, I may say that these would be my only reasons for believing the story, even when I am not sure whether I do believe it or not. In cases of this kind the reasons for believing, or for acting, or for feeling, are incomplete explanations; we can always ask why those reasons actuated you at that particular time, while they did not influence others relevantly like you, or why they did not influence you on relevantly similar occasions.

Consider the situation of someone who has a belief when there is evidence that sufficient conditions (with the ordinary reservations that must always be attached to this phrase) exist in the state of the physical organism for his holding this belief. There are two possibilities: first, that he does not know that his belief can be adequately explained by the physical state of the organism: secondly, that he comes to know that his belief can be adequately explained by the physical state of the organism. Of the first case, a belief explicable by hypnotism would be an example, if we knew of a physical mechanism upon which the success of hypnotic suggestion depends. Let us suppose that we acquire this knowledge. Any reasons that the victim offers in partial explanation of his belief under hypnotism will be rationalisations. The reasons will be no part of the explanation of his belief, and it will not be true that, if his reasons are shown to contain error, he will for a moment reconsider, and be for a moment more doubtful about his belief. He will simply substitute another reason, clinging all the time to the suggested belief. I will leave aside the suggestion that all our beliefs, and all our intentions, might rest on rationalisations in this way, without asking whether this is a coherent suggestion. At least we know of some clear cases of rationalisation.

Turn to the case where the subject comes to know the adequate explanation of his belief. Then the question is unavoidably raised for him of whether there is a correlation between the physical state of the organism and his belief in the specific proposition in question being true; that is, he must ask himself whether there is a rational connection between his organism being in a certain state and there being in fact a lectern in the next room. In other words, he has to evaluate the discovered causes of his already formed belief as evidence of the truth of the belief. While he is evaluating the causes of his former belief as evidences of truth, his belief is suspended, and becomes only an inclination to believe. For if he says (to himself or to another), "I now know why I have believed this, but I don't yet know whether the causes are reasons for believing or not," he is not expressing a present belief. Suppose that he finds that there is indeed a correlation between the operation of these causes and his holding a true belief; then he has learnt how he knows, or why he believes, that there is a lectern in the next room, in the sense that he has learnt the mechanism which is at work. So a man might all his life have been able to judge the distances and sizes of objects seen from a great height, without knowing the mechanism that was at work, and in this sense without knowing how he knew, or why he believed, that one object was further away than another on a particular occasion. He previously was unable to give his reason for believing that the tower was further away than the bridge, and, because he was unable to give the reason, there is a sense in which he had no reason for the belief; namely, that there was no true hypothetical proposition present to his mind, or specifiable by him on request, of the form "I would have reconsidered whether the tower was further away from the bridge, if I had not believed so-and-so." We have a choice here: the language allows us to say both that he just had the belief without a reason, and also allows us to say that there was a reason which he did not know and which he has now learnt. So the connoisseur who can tell on sight the date of certain works of art, but cannot say how he tells, may be said to have a reason, which might be disclosed by interfering with clues. By suppressing some information which he was receiving, without his being distinctly aware of it and of its efficacy, we may discover the clues which he is "using," without his knowing that he was "using" them. Or he may be said to tell without having any reason at all.

But the interesting difference is the difference that is made by his coming to know how he forms his beliefs, or whence he derives his knowledge. Then he again has the evaluative question, like the man who has discovered that there exists a physical state of the organism which is a sufficient condition of his belief. Now knowing the mechanism, he must raise the question of whether there is a reliable correlation between the physical state of the organism and the truth of the relevant belief. If he discovers there is such a correlation, then he has acquired a reason for now, and henceforth, endorsing the inclinations to believe which occur when the physical state of the organism is present. If there is, as far as he can discover, no such reliable correlation, then his inclination to believe, which will now be his state of mind, will no longer be for him a reason for actually believing. The hypnotist's victim, who could be made to believe false or true propositions indifferently, was ignorant, while hypnotized, of the adequate explanation of his belief. If he had known, while under the influence of the hypnotist, that his beliefs were adequately explained by the hypnotist's suggestions, as sufficient conditions in themselves, and that these suggestions were not sufficient evidences of truth, then his beliefs would have been only inclinations to believe. For a man distinguishes "I believe p" from "I am inclined to believe p," as reports of his state of mind, precisely by the implication (not entailment) which is attached to the first-person, and not to the second- and third-person, uses of the verb—namely, "p is to be believed."

Consider the following design of an experiment. An advertiser wishes to have some scientific foundation for his attempts to influence the beliefs of a certain class of consumers. He wants to know what are the sufficient, or, under normal conditions, nearly sufficient, conditions of their believing that they are suffering from a certain physical weakness and need a certain kind of tonic. He therefore arranges an elaborate experiment to assess the efficacy of his techniques of brain-washing. He is allowed to vary the stimuli from the environment and to vary the state of the organisms, only provided that he does not bring about the state of affairs which he wishes his subjects to believe exists. My suggestion is that if he asks the brain-washed group to report changes in their beliefs, as he changes the state of their organisms and the stimuli from the environment, he must refrain from telling them what he is doing. If he tells them what he is doing, then they *can* only report changes in their "beliefs" in an inverted-comma sense, and their changing states of mind are more properly described as their inclinations to believe. The experiment otherwise cannot be carried through. The subjects are bound, by the sense of the concept of belief, to regard their belief-reports as reports of inclinations to believe, if they do not believe that the changes in their organisms and in the evironment can be shown to be means of sharpening their powers of discovery.

The presence of the clues by the use of which I unknowingly form my veridical beliefs about physical objects will be a sufficient condition, taken together with the normal state of organism, of my forming these beliefs. When I have learnt the mechanism from the scientific study of perception, I may use this knowledge to protect myself against error, and thus employ a method of inference which was not available to me before. My beliefs, even in the normal cases, will then have a different explanation from before, merely in virtue of this new precaution against error: another factor has been added. Unless I believed that the mechanism was working normally and along the standard path towards discovery of truth, I would not *now* endorse the inclination to believe which is its outcome; and this hypothetical proposition I may know to be true directly. When my belief is based on inference, and has been reached after precautions against error, there is always a hypothetical proposition that could be quoted to specify one of the necessary conditions of my belief.

One sees therefore why the phrase "the causes of the belief" sounds odd, if "causes" is interpreted as sufficient conditions (with the necessary reservations). Sufficient conditions of belief are immediately converted into sufficient conditions for an inclination to believe, when the conditions become known to the subject and are believed by him not to be reliable indices of truth; or the sufficient conditions of belief, hitherto, become reasons for belief, when the conditions become known to the subject and are taken by him to be reliable indices of truth. But this is not to say that the phrase "the causes of the belief" is improper, or that there cannot be sufficient conditions of particular beliefs, both of true beliefs and of false beliefs. *Looking back* to beliefs that have been held by me, or that are now held by others, I can indeed seek to explain them adequately, as I can seek to explain any other phenomenon. But one must always allow for the fact that an increment to the subject's knowledge of the factors that are determining, and that explain, his current beliefs will by itself change the account that will have to be given of why he believes.

A similar complexity attends the explanation of a man's intentional actions. Given that we have the specification of a man's intention at a particular time to act in a particular way, and provided that we hold this description constant, we can seek an adequate explanation of the fact in some covering law, which will correlate such an intention with some initial conditions, normally including those desires and beliefs which the subject would give as his reasons. But an increment to the subject's knowledge of the factors, other than his own specifiable reasons, which explain his intentions, must complicate his intentions in one way or another. Suppose that he learns that, in addition to the reasons that he would give to explain his intention, there are certain other necessary conditions to be observed in the state of his organism and in the inputs that explain this state of the organism. He has learnt that he would not have acted in the way that he is acting, if these conditions had not existed. In virtue of this knowledge, there is at least one account of his intention that becomes applicable, even when his original intention is not otherwise altered: namely, that he intends to allow his conduct to be determined by these factors.

If one accepts, as I do, that no limits can be set a priori on the scope of scientific explanation, one must still observe that scientific explanation requires that the description of the phenomenon to be explained must be held constant from the beginning of the inquiry to its conclusion. If a man comes to believe that his state of confidence in the excellence of his performance is wholly explained by a confidence-engendering pill which he has taken, he will no longer be so confident of the excellence of his performance. A state of tranquillity will remain, but the change in the subject's belief about its cause will constitute a change in his state of mind. The peculiarity of the explanation of intentional states—beliefs, intentions, attitudes of mind, desires—is that the subject's acquisition of knowledge about the explanation, or a change in his beliefs about the explanation, modifies the descriptions applicable to the phenomenon explained, and also modifies the explanation itself. This is not a ground for suspending, or despairing of, the search for scientific understanding of mental states of any kind. On the contrary: the more I learn of mechanisms that may explain the past occurrences of these states, the more I am in a position to anticipate, and either to modify or to reinforce them, as I choose.

We see this complexity in the explanation of intentional states most clearly if we trace the full implications of one traditional, 19th-century materialist hypothesis. Suppose that we assume that for every distinct state of mind, and particularly for every distinct emotion, marked in the common vocabulary, there exists a distinct physical state of the organism which is invariably correlated with it. It would be surprising if this hypothesis turned out to be true, or even approximately true, if only because the distinctions among emotions marked in the common vocabulary have been made, and made gradually, to serve a variety of quite different, non-theoretical purposes. But let us disregard the implausibility of the hypothesis, so crudely formulated. For it is enough to consider a single possible case falling under the general hypothesis: for example, that with the emotion of anger there is an invariably correlated state of the organism, which can be stimulated by some physical inputs, and removed by other physical inputs, with immediate corresponding effects on the emotion. These correlations are to be supposed to hold in spite of variations in the objects, and the specificable reasons, for the subject's anger. In all cases we find that subjects cease to be angry with x, and to be angry with x because of y, if the appropriate physical change is made; they only consider y as a reason for being angry when they are in the appropriate physical state; and when they are in the appropriate physical state, they always find some reason for being angry with someone. If the facts were discovered to be exactly as supposed—which is of course extremely improbable—we should have to say that the reasons which men had previously given in explanation of their being angry were really rationalisations. For we should have discovered that the implied hypothetical propositions—"If such-and-such an injury, as I considered it to be, had not occurred, I would not, at least for a time, have been so angry"—were false; I would have been just as angry, if, and only if, the appropriate physical state existed, and I would have immediately found some other reason for being angry. We will implausibly suppose, for the sake of the hypothesis, that being angry consists merely in having certain feelings and being disposed to behave in certain ways, and does not entail a certain belief of the subject in a specific reason for the disposition. So it has been discovered that the state of anger, whenever it occurs, does not in fact co-vary with any variation in the subject's *independently* established beliefs about the situation, but is varied only by a change in his physical state.

Neglect, if you will, the vast accumulation of evidence from experience which we have and which tells against this hypothesis: the evidence from experience that our anger does sometimes change as a result of an argument that convinces us that there is nothing to be angry about, and change in such a way that we have good grounds for believing that a belief was a necessary condition of the anger occurring. If the implausible hypothesis were verified, we should say that the state, which we had been calling anger, was a perception of a certain physical state; when we are angry, we are really perceiving a modification of our body in its interaction with the environment. We are perceiving, or feeling, this state, in the same sense that we feel a bruise or that we feel a heavy object on our back; and a feeling of this kind counts as a perception, in so far as we are able immediately and reliably to infer the change in the state of the body from the experience. We could speak of perceiving an

17

external object, in so far as there was a physical cause of the change in the bodily state, the presence of which was immediately and reliably inferred from an inner feeling. In so far as smelling the flowers in the room counts as perceiving that the flowers are there, any similar immediate and reliable inference from a sensation to the external physical cause, which affects the body by an understood, regular process, will count as a perception of the cause. If we found that a certain feeling, which we had previously associated with certain beliefs and had distinguished as one of the emotions, was in fact reliably correlated with a certain physical stimulus from a certain kind of physical object, we should say that we are perceiving that kind of object, when the feeling occurs: perceiving it, in the extended sense in which smelling it is perceiving it. When we understand the physical mechanism by which the effect is produced, we have a reliable method of immediate inference to the presence of the cause; and the inference in time becomes a habit to such a degree that it is no longer thought of as an inference.

I dwell on this Spinozistic consequence of taking one version of the materialist hypothesis seriously because it brings out the consequences of *learning*, and of *coming to know*, the mechanisms upon which the occurrence of the state of mind depends. One is liable to be persuaded that the consequence of such discoveries would be a helplessness, or a sense of helplessness: as if men would have depressingly discovered that their ability to modify and control their own beliefs, desires and sentiments, as they think fit on reflection, was in fact zero, or near to zero. This is a mistake. The coming to know about the mechanism, about the cause of a certain distinguishable type of state of mind, opens the way to a method of inference which can proceed from the state of mind to the external cause. Knowledge of a causal mechanism is converted into knowledge of a reality external to the mind. A person is an instrument that records the effects of stimuli, and the consequent changes of bodily states, in the experience of psychical states; but a person is an instrument that also reads, and interprets, its own recorded results, and, in reading and interpreting them, in a sense changes the result. For the recorded result in a psychical state, as interpreted by the subject in the light of new knowledge of the explanation of the state, has for the subject a different significance, and therefore constitutes, because of his accompanying thought, a different state; just this is the intentional component in psychical states. The state that began as anger with Jones for something he had done, has now become an awareness of a changed physical state, in relation to which Jones' action was merely an inessential occasion. Since the subject no longer believes Jones' action to be a necessary element in the explanation of his state, there is a good sense in which he is no longer angry with Jones for what he has done; in this sense the knowledge of the explanation has changed the state of mind. But a scientist may regard the state of mind simply as an experience, abstracting from the subject's own beliefs about the explanation of it; and he may have shown by experiment that *this* experience, so identified as the experience that the man had when he ignorantly took himself to be angry, is to be explained by a clearly identifiable physical state. The subject, once convinced of the truth of the scientist's explanation, will determine his attitude to Jones' action all over again.

There is for this reason an unclarity, or even an ambiguity, in the otherwise acceptable statement that the occurrence of any state of mind can in principle be explained like any other natural phenomenon, by reference to an experimentally confirmed covering law, which correlates such an occurrence with some set of initial conditions. This statement may be true, when a proviso is added that is uniquely applicable to intentional states: that the subject's knowledge of the explanation by covering law will by itself change the state explained, even though the lawful connection does continue to hold between the initial conditions and the same state of mind, as identified under the original description used in the relevant science; but the intentional description, which incorporates the subject's thought of a cause, will have to be changed, as the subject's beliefs change. The discovered physical causes of anger are the causes of that independently identifiable state which the subject previously classified as anger, thereby explaining the state in a way which he now knows to have been erroneous. The causes of *that* state which he has previously classified as anger will no longer be causes of anger. This is the reason why the causal explanation of intentional states and processes is not a simple matter. The reflexive knowledge of the causal mechanism constitutes a change in the effect. And this is the complexity which makes a place, as Spinoza suggested, for freedom of mind.

Subjunctive Conditionals

"If Hitler had invaded in 1940, he would have captured London." Statements of this kind have constituted a problem for three overlapping classes of philosophers: (a) those who wish to insist that all complex statements must be truth —functions of their constituent statements; (b) those who wish to insist that saying that an empirical statement is true is equivalent to saying that it corresponds to a fact; (c) those who wish to insist that to understand a sentence as being an empirical statement involves being able to prescribe how it might in principle be, directly or indirectly, verified or falsified.

I shall not discuss the perplexities of the truth-functional or correspondence-theory philosophers, partly because these philosophers seem to me wrong in principle, apart altogether from the special case of conditional sentences in the subjunctive mood. I shall assume that it is one of the characteristics of ordinary languages, distinguishing them from constructed languages, that they are not truth-functional; and I shall assume that we do not need to invent special categories of facts so that true statements may correspond to them. But it does seem to me that when we are considering whether a sentence can be interpreted as a significant empirical statement, we are always and necessarily asking a question about the possibilities and appropriate procedures of verification and falsification; that is, "I understand this sentence as an empirical statement" is equivalent to "I know how this might in principle be verified or falsified"; and if I cannot answer the question "What tests would lead the assertor to withdraw this sentence?," then it follows logically that I do not know what is being asserted.[1]

[1] Of course there are degrees of vagueness in understanding. I may

Subjunctive conditional sentences present a problem because it looks as if they are often used to make statements which, though intelligible, cannot be said to be in principle either verifiable or falsifiable.

Consider the following dialogue. A: "If this family had been on either the third or the first floor, they would not have been killed by the bomb." B: "You mean that when bombs of this kind hit houses of this kind, the first and third floors are generally safe?" A: "No, I do not mean that; I do not want to commit myself to any statement about what generally happens in these cases; I do not know what generally happens, but I do feel certain about this particular case." B: "But I can show you that you are wrong, by showing you other houses similar to this in which people have not survived on the first or third floors." A: "But whatever evidence you produce about the effects of bombs on houses, it is still logically possible that *these particular* people would not have been killed in *this particular* house; and that is my firm conviction; it may be irrational, but it may be nevertheless true, as many irrational beliefs are." B: "Of course, I agree that you may make irrational statements; you may gamble and guess; but my objection is, not that your statement is irrational, but that it is in principle undecidable, and so not a genuine statement, just as a bet which is admitted to be in principle undecidable is not a genuine bet." A: "But you cannot deny that I have made a genuine statement: for suppose (what I do not in fact expect) that we later find this family alive somewhere, and find also that they were on the third floor and not (as we had thought that they were) on the second, then you will admit that what I said was true." B: "No, I will not; if that is the possibility of verification you had in mind, the form of your statement was misleading, because it suggested that you

know only *roughly* what tests are to be taken as decisive, in which case I know only *roughly* what is meant.

were making a causal statement. If you were not, you ought not to have used the subjunctive form."

Two connected points emerge from this dialogue. The first is that the use of the subjunctive conditional form usually suggests that some causal and therefore general proposition is being asserted. It is natural to try to interpret a subjunctive conditional sentence as (at least in part) a disguised general statement; whenever they can be so interpreted, we can always prescribe a method for establishing their falsity (i.e. we can look for a negative instance); and of course sentences of the subjunctive conditional form are often used to express general statements—e.g. "If you had had no faculty of sight, you would have no conception of distance," which can properly be used in place of "Men without sight have no conception of distance, and you are a man."

That a singular hypothetical statement should *in fact* be unverifiable or unfalsifiable, because its antecedent is *in fact* unfulfilled, presents no problem for upholders of the verification principle. The problem arises when we are presented with putative statements, the grammar of which explicitly suggests that they are intended to be in principle undecidable; and singular subjunctive conditionals, in any context in which they cannot be replaced by a combination of general statements and statements of particular conditions, are of this kind; for the force of the subjunctive is usually to suggest a statement of the form "If p, then q, but not p," which, unless (as normally) it is a causal and so a general statement, is explicitly undecidable in principle.

When and why do we use sentences of the subjunctive conditional form, without being willing to replace them by general statements and statements of particular conditions? Suppose we replaced them entirely by statements of the form, "If anything is a ϕ, it is always as a matter of fact a ψ," and "this is (or is not) a ϕ," and never used the form,

23

"If this had been a ϕ, it would have been a ψ," what would we lose? Theoretical scientists would lose nothing; they can state their laws without using subjunctive forms. But judges, juries, historians, and moralists would certainly be embarrassed, if challenged to replace all their singular conditional sentences—"If he had not acted as he did, the disaster would not have occurred"—by a combination of general statements and singular categorical statements. The judge, jury or moralist needs to be able to say that if a *particular individual* had not acted in a *particular* way in this *particular* situation, the disaster would not have occurred. Experts supply the falsifiable general statements of the form, "All arsenic-takers die, and this man took arsenic," but the final decision must be formulated in the form— "If this man had not taken arsenic, he would not have died." There is a sense in which the final judgment goes *beyond* the experts' scientific statements; for it is logically possible to accept the scientific statements, and yet to disagree with the final decision. (And this is perhaps part of the justification of the employment of juries.)

Similarly the historian is professionally expected to make judgments of the form "If Hitler had invaded in 1940, he would have captured London." If challenged to translate this judgment into a set of falsifiable statements, he would be unable and unwilling. He might justifiably reply "History is not science," meaning precisely that the historian is not primarily concerned to establish general statements falsifiable by experiment, but that his conclusions (if any) are judgments about particular persons and particular events, judgments which may be more or less reasonable, but which cannot in principle be verified or falsified.[2] It is to be noticed that, both in referring to the sentences that express a jury's conclusion and to the sentences that express a his-

[2] One problem of historical method, or of the nature of historical judgment, *is*, in logical terms, the problem of subjunctive conditionals.

torian's conclusion, we are normally inclined to speak of "judgments" (reasonable and unreasonable) rather than "statements" (true or false); the dissenting juryman would not normally say "It is not true that if he had not taken this drug, he would not have died," but rather "I do not agree with your interpretation of the facts." Similarly historians admit that their disagreements about hypothetical conditions are disagreements of "interpretation" or "judgment," using these words to discriminate them from the decidable disagreements of scientists.

Certainly the distinction between a judgment (reasonable or unreasonable) and a statement (true or false), or between an interpretation and a scientific theory, is one of degree and admits a multitude of border-line cases. The language of science (by definition) consists wholly of decidable statements. When we ask "Is economics a science?" we are in effect asking whether sentences like "If the rate of interest had been lowered in January the level of unemployment would have fallen in March" are intended to be taken as in principle conclusively refutable by experiment, or whether they are to be taken as judgments or interpretations, justified as plausible by reference to general statements and statements of particular conditions, but not reducible to them. So *A* in the above dialogue could have defended himself by saying that he was offering only his judgment (plausible or unplausible) in a matter in which no decision by experiment is possible. A rigid application of the verification principle—in so far as it involves a refusal to admit the gradations of difference between practical and historical judgments and decidable statements—amounts to a recommendation that all discourse should be scientific discourse.

The elimination from our language of subjunctive conditional sentences would not only remove the possibility of expressing ordinary practical and historical judgments, but would also compel philosophers to abandon the phenomenalist analysis of ordinary statements about material objects. It is an odd paradox that phenomenalism, which has been generally represented as the logical consequence of strictly applying some form of verification principle, is the doctrine that even the most innocent categorical statements are more clearly expressed by a set of conditional sentences, many of which are contrary-to-fact conditionals expressed in the subjunctive mood. It seems perverse, if one is concerned to maintain that all genuine empirical statements must be in some sense verifiable or falsifiable, to convert them all into singular hypothetical sentences in the subjunctive mood. Phenomenalists are in fact recommending a move away from a language which is logically clear, or which approximates to the language of science.

I am also inclined to think (but I am not certain) that we should have some difficulty in talking about "dispositions" (now a favourite word of logical empiricists) in a language which excluded subjunctive conditionals. Do we not want to say that "he knows" or "he understands" means more than that whenever he has a certain stimulus, he in fact always or generally responds in the appropriate way? We are certainly inclined to say that, in conditions which cannot be fulfilled, he always *would*; certainly the subjunctive form suggests itself as part of what we mean by attributing a disposition to someone. Statements about dispositions do not seem replaceable by causal statements (general statements plus statements of particular conditions); they have the irreducible indefiniteness and undecidability which is the point of the subjunctive conditional form. When we make statements about people's characters or dispositions we can be said to be *interpreting* their behaviour; disputes about such statements are naturally described as differences of interpretation, to be distinguished (though only as a matter of degree) from disputes which can be settled by discovery of the negative instance which upsets a general statement.

CONCLUSION

Singular subjunctive conditional sentences are sometimes used in contexts in which they are not intended to be replaceable by falsifiable general statements plus statements of initial conditions. When so used, they can be described as expressing judgments, or interpretations, of the facts, to distinguish them from their use in strictly scientific discourse in which they are wholly replaceable by falsifiable general statements and statements of initial conditions. It is the distinguishing characteristic of practical and historical judgments (as opposed to statements of fact and scientific statements) that the conditions of their falsification are not exactly prescribed. Certainly we can indicate under what conditions they will be held to have been shown to be so unreasonable as to have been in effect falsified. But, where the subjunctive conditional form is irreplaceable, we cannot in principle prescribe tests which are final and decisive.

27

Multiply General Sentences

There is a logically peculiar class of sentences, some members of which have played an important part in philosophical arguments, without their logical peculiarities being generally noticed and labelled. My purpose is simply to indicate in what respect they are logically peculiar, and to attach a label to them; unless their peculiarity is recognised and labelled, they are always liable to mislead. I cannot define this class of sentences, which I shall call "multiply general sentences," in the sense of providing formal or syntactical rules for recognising any sentence as being a member of the class, since their logical peculiarity is not constantly reflected in their form or syntax. Precisely this makes them a philosophical problem worth investigating.

1. Consider two sentences which might be used as primitive formulations of the uniformity of Nature.

(a) Every event has a cause.

(b) Every event is an instance of some natural law.

Both these sentences look like general statements which can be confirmed or falsified by the methods which logic books prescribe as appropriate to the confirmation or falsification of statements of the form "All X's are Y's"; and they have often in fact been accepted as true or as probably true, or rejected as false or probably false, on the assumption that the normal recognised methods of confirming or falsifying sentences of the form "All X's are Y's" are in principle applicable to them; and many of those who have accepted these sentences as true, or probably true, statements, would not have so accepted them, had they reflected further on the method of their confirmation or falsification, and not simply assumed that they are in this respect indistinguishable from other sentences of the same grammatical form.

28

Of course many, and perhaps most, users of these sentences have for a variety of reasons not intended them to be taken as confirmable or falsifiable general statements, or as empirical statements of any kind; but some certainly have, and even those who have not, have not generally recognised their peculiarity as multiply general sentences among their other peculiarities.[1]

2. By a multiply general sentence I mean a sentence beginning with some sign of unrestricted generality[2]—"all," "every," "no," "nothing," "nobody," etc.—which is so constructed that no singular statement can be formulated which entails or is incompatible with it. By "singular statement" I here mean any statement which (a) does not contain any sign of unrestricted generality and (b) does contain either a demonstrative expression (e.g. "this," "that," "there," "now," or a personal pronoun) or a proper name. It is a characteristic (but not a sufficient defining characteristic) of a multiply general sentence that, in addition to the initial sign of generality, it will contain some second sign of unrestricted generality and at least one sign of negation. The effect of such combinations within a single sentence of two signs of unrestricted generality and a sign of negation is to preclude the construction of any singular statement which entails either the truth or falsity of the multiply general sentence.

Consider as a second example the multiply general sentence, "All men are mortal," so often wrongly cited in logic-books as a typical general statement, and so often accepted as a true empirical statement, on the grounds that no nega-

---

[1] That they contain only semi-formal or logical expressions—"cause," "event," "natural law," etc.—is another, more widely recognized and (I think) independent peculiarity of these sentences, distinguishing them from the standard cases of empirical general statements.

[2] The sign of generality is unrestricted when it is not used to indicate a closed or finite class of things, persons or events.

tive instance which refutes it has in fact been discovered. How in principle could the truth or falsity of this dictum be established? What singular sentence (i.e. sentence not itself containing any sign of unrestricted generality) can be constructed which would entail either that it is true or that it is false? The answer is that no such singular statement can in principle be constructed, and that this dictum cannot in principle be either verified or falsified in the sense in which any general statement not of this peculiar pattern can be either verified or falsified. Those who accept this sentence as a true statement, on the grounds that no negative instance refuting it has in fact been discovered, are in error, the victims of a logical confusion; for it is *logically* precluded that any such a negative instance should ever be found, whatever the nature of our experience or the longevity of men. On the other hand the sentence "all men are immortal" is a general statement which can in principle be falsified, in the sense that we can construct a singular sentence, i.e. "this man has died," which is logically incompatible with it; "all men are immortal" is therefore a general statement of the normal recognised pattern—"normal" in the sense that, presented with any sentence of the form "All X's are Y's," we tend always to assume that a negative instance is in principle discoverable. I am arguing only that this assumption, encouraged by text-books of logic, is unsound and needs to be restricted.

But I cannot state any general and formal restriction which would enable one infallibly to distinguish the normal from the abnormal cases; and I am inclined to believe that no such general and formal restriction can in principle be stated. One reason is that the multiple generality is not sufficiently disclosed in the form or grammar of these sentences, but emerges only from considering the use of the particular descriptive words involved. The negative instance which would falsify "All men are mortal" cannot be constructed, because, following the ordinary rules of syntax, we obtain as the negative instance the sentence "this man is immortal"; but to say of a man that he is immortal is to say that he will never (unrestrictedly) die, and this is a general statement and not a singular statement in the sense required. As "This man is immortal" is itself a general statement, and is therefore falsifiable but not conclusively verifiable, it follows that "All men are mortal" is not in principle conclusively falsifiable by the discovery of a negative instance.

What is philosophically interesting is that most people, if asked, would probably say that they believe that it is true that all men are mortal, and would justify the assertion by appeal to observation and experience; they would take themselves to be holding a belief about a matter of fact and to be making an empirical statement. But they would not be able to say, if asked, what it would be like to observe or recognise an immortal man; they would admit, if challenged, that they had not indicated what possible experience they were excluding when they claimed to believe that all men are mortal. Probably many people, when so challenged, would decide that the belief which they are expressing when they say "all men are mortal" is more clearly and less misleadingly expressed as "all men decay" or "all men are senescent"; that is, they would agree that they would withdraw their statement, and abandon their belief, if and perhaps only if, they discovered a man who showed no signs of senescence or decay; they might *decide* that this is the possible observation which (perhaps without realising it) they were excluding. Compare here the multiply general sentence "There are no perpetual motion machines," which probably means what would be more clearly expressed by the sentence "All machines dissipate energy"; more clearly expressed, if, when I assert that there are no perpetual motion machines, the only possibility which I intend to exclude is the observation of a machine which does not dissipate energy. But I might not have realised, or made clear and explicit to myself, that this is the possibility which I intend to exclude, until I am challenged. In this legitimate but strict sense I may often not know what (if anything) I am asserting when I use a multiply general sentence; and thus I am likely to mislead others, who, in order to understand me, must infer from the context what possibility I am excluding, and therefore what I am asserting. In this artificially restricted, but now familiar and useful sense, multiply general sentences may legitimately be described as vacuous or as not genuine empirical statements; "vacuous," not implying that they are not often intelligently and intelligibly used, but that they are always inexplicit and ought to be replaced by a sentence showing explicitly what definite assertion (if any) is actually intended.

3. Each of the uniformity of Nature sentences has the same quasi-syntactical peculiarity as "All men are mortal"; no singular statement (i.e. statement containing no sign of unrestricted generality) can in principle be constructed which either entails or is incompatible with either of them. Each of them involves the double occurrence of the sign of unrestricted generality, the second being implicit or half-concealed in the words "cause," "law," and "predictable." But the involutions of generality are here even more complicated. For the putative negative instance "This is an uncaused event," which entails "There is *no* other event which *never* occurs without this event occurring," is itself a multiply general sentence, for which in turn no negative instance can be constructed; so if "All men are mortal" is a doubly general sentence, "Every event has a cause" is trebly general.

Multiply general sentences occur in several other metaphysical theses or arguments,[3] i.e. in theses or arguments

---

[3] The assertion or denial of a First Cause or First Event is another

which look as if they were empirical or factual, but, when probed, turn out not to be. The trick or snare of the un-recognised multiply general sentence is a trick of *language*, and depends on the interpretation given to particular ex-pressions (not purely logical or syntactical expressions) in particular contexts; and it is for this reason that I have not appealed to any logicians' symbolism, in which such sen-tences or formulae either are, or can easily be, excluded.

---

example of an old metaphysical dispute, which involves the use of a multiply general sentence.

Dispositions

Statements about dispositions, and descriptions of character, are often said to be, or to involve, hypothetical or quasi-hypothetical statements. This seems to me false.

Examples of forms of sentences normally used to make statements about dispositions are: "X is intelligent," "X is ambitious," "X is generous," "X is honest," where "X" is replaceable by an expression referring to an individual. These are to be distinguished from expressions of the occurrence (narrative) type, such as "X is angry now," "X is jealous now," "X is embarrassed now," "X is suspicious now," "X understood what you said." One can convert expressions of the occurrence (narrative) type into dispositional expressions by such devices as: "X is an irascible man," "X is of a jealous disposition," "X is easily embarrassed," "X has a suspicious nature," "X understands English." Although contexts providing borderline cases can certainly be found, there is an essential difference in the appropriate methods of challenging and confirming the two types of statement; one can distinguish the pure case of a dispositional expression from the pure case of a narrative expression. A statement which refers to a disposition will satisfy all or most of the following overlapping criteria:

(1) It is a statement that summarises what tends to happen or is liable on the whole to happen; and it does not state what happens on a particular occasion, and therefore it is not a proper part of a narrative or story. It could not be entered in a logbook of the day's events opposite some time of the day, or in the annals of someone's life opposite some definite date.

(2) There are short-term and long-term dispositions, but a disposition cannot come into being, then pass away and

34

then come into being again very rapidly. Character may change suddenly; but it must not change suddenly too often, or it ceases to be character.

(3) A disposition must be manifested and must show itself in actual incidents; there must be at least some cases or instances of it dispersed over some period of time. One cannot normally say that someone is ambitious and generous, while denying that he has ever either acted or calculated in a generous and ambitious manner, In default of actual manifestations, one could only say that he is potentially generous, or that he would be a generous man if circumstances allowed.

(4) The risk of error in description of character is the risk of over-simplification; one may be accused of not having taken account of a variety of incidents which might be quoted as evidence of some contrary disposition. When the truth of a statement about someone's disposition and character is disputed, the final and conclusive argument must be a balancing of one set of actual incidents against another set of actual incidents. It follows that

(5) one can properly claim to know that someone has a certain disposition when (a) one has had occasion for prolonged and continuous study of the conduct and calculations of the person in question, and (b) when one can quote many incidents in which the disposition manifested itself and can quote virtually no incidents which would count as instances of any contrary disposition. Under such conditions one could say, "He is certainly and indisputably generous"; what is claimed as certain and beyond dispute is that the word "generous" is so far the right word to summarise the general trend or tendency of his conduct and calculations.

(6) There is no necessary connection between disposition and behaviour; one can have a disposition to think in a certain manner and also to react emotionally in a certain

manner. Most ordinary character-descriptions refer compendiously to a tendency discernible equally in the behaviour, and in the thought and in the feelings, of the subject.

(7) It is characteristic of many words normally used to refer to dispositions, and of expressions which summarise trends and tendencies, that they are not in general polar terms. The denial of any statement of a trend or tendency may be, not an implied assertion of a contrary tendency, but an implied assertion that there is no trend or tendency in either direction. The situation is not like that of the man who is neither short nor tall, but is of medium height; for the man who is neither ambitious nor not ambitious is not necessarily a man of moderate or normal ambitions. It may be that no sufficiently constant tendency in any direction is discernible in his conduct and calculation; he may be simply erratic and have no settled disposition in this sphere; and, as Aristotle remarked, a disposition must be to some extent a settled disposition.

(8) To attribute a disposition to someone is never to preclude that he may on some occasion act, or have acted, in some way contrary to his general tendency or disposition. That this is always possible is part of the force of calling statements of disposition summarising statements; statements describing what in general tends to happen are in this respect very unlike universal statements. It is typical of human character (as we actually conceive and describe it) that it allows of lapses, and that people sometimes behave in a way which is not in accordance with their character. One may apply dispositional expressions also to material things ("This river tends to overflow its banks" or "The English climate is changeable"); for one may often choose, or may be compelled by ignorance, to summarise the general character of some physical things, rather than to describe their behaviour in terms of their physical constitu-

tion and of the laws which govern the behaviour of objects so constituted.

But such plain categorical statements about tendencies and dispositions should be distinguished from descriptions of the causal properties of things. There is a particular range of expressions referring to the causal properties of things—e.g. "electrically charged," "magnetised," "soluble in aqua regia"—which have sometimes been misleadingly called dispositional expressions, and descriptions of human character and disposition have been assimilated to them. The full meaning of such expressions as "electrically charged," "magnetised," "soluble in aqua regia" might perhaps in principle be rendered in a set of paraphrasing sentences of the "if . . . then" form; these paraphrasing sentences would state that if certain specific operations were performed upon the objects in question, certain specific reactions would be the effects of these operations. There are at least three closely connected grounds for distinguishing the use of expressions which describe the causal properties of things from the use of expressions which describe dispositions. (1) A statement to the effect that some particular thing is soluble in aqua regia plainly does not carry the implication that this particular thing has ever in fact been dissolved in aqua regia. But a statement to the effect that someone is generous does carry the implication that the person has on occasion actually acted or calculated in a manner which was a manifestation of generosity. (2) The property of being soluble in aqua regia is not a tendency to dissolve which must manifest itself more or less continuously over some period of time; being electrically charged is a property which may be switched on and off. A particular thing may change and change again in this respect, very much as it may change and change again in respect of colour. (3) Such causal properties of things, as being magnetised and being soluble in aqua regia, manifest themselves, if at all, in specific and definitely statable reactions, which can be produced under specific and statable conditions. The incidents which may count as manifestations of human dispositions—of intelligence, ambition, generosity, honesty—are *essentially* various, and these words are essentially vague, summary, interpretative and indeterminate. The way in which statements about character and disposition fit, and fail to fit, the facts is different from the way in which normally specific statements fit, or fail to fit, the facts; the canons of accuracy applied to them are correspondingly different.

When one writes a testimonial, summarising in a few character descriptions the trend of a person's performances, one does not commit oneself to conditional predictions of the form: "if he has such and such opportunities, he will perform in such and such a manner." One provides the *grounds* upon which such a prediction can be based, but one does not, in using the present tense, actually make a prediction. If these specific predictions, based on one's testimonial ("He will, or would, do such and such, since he is an ambitious man") turn out to be false, it does not *follow* that the character description, originally expressed in the present tense, was false. There are two other possibilities open—either that his character has changed ("He used to be ambitious but he no longer is"); or that on this particular occasion he acted out of character. From the premise "he is a generous man" ("he has a tendency to act generously") one can *infer*, but not *deduce* that, if certain demands were made upon him, he would probably give some money. If one wishes to predict, either conditionally or unconditionally, the future course of a person's conduct, one must use the appropriate grammatical forms, e.g. "he will show himself to be generous if the opportunity comes," or "he will act generously." One may describe someone's character and dispositions as they are, one may state what someone's character used to be, one may predict what it will be, and one may say what it would have been under other conditions. When one makes a statement about a disposition in the present tense, one is understood to be summarising the trend of someone's behaviour and calculations up to the time of speaking, together with the normal implication that his character is so far continuing the same. The difference between "he is generous" and "he has been generous up to now" is the same as the difference between "his hair is yellow" and "his hair has been yellow up to now."

Observations subsequent to the assertion count as evidence for or against statements of the type "X's hair is yellow," and they count to the same degree as evidence for or against statements of the type "X is intelligent." But from the fact that observations subsequent to the assertion may be relevant as evidence for or against a statement, it does not follow that the statement itself was a prediction.

There is a familiar method of analysis by which almost any normal categorical statement—even a statement to the effect that someone's hair is yellow or that the grass is wet—may be represented as necessarily involving the assertion of a set of conditional predictions; and this method of analysis has been applied to categorical statements about dispositions. One may plausibly re-express almost any categorical statement in the "If . . . then" form by writing into the protasis some favourable conditions for testing the original statement, and making the apodosis roughly equivalent to the original statement, but with the addition of some verb of observation ("look," "feel," "appear," "show," etc.): so for "Jones was in my room at 11 o'clock," one may say, "If you, or any normal observer, had come to my room at 11 o'clock, you would have perceived Jones there"; a statement made in the form "The grass is wet" may be said to entail a statement of the form "If any normal observer were to touch the grass, he would feel it to be wet." This method of showing that plain categorical statements necessarily involve conditional predictions may appear successful in every case, provided that some standard conditions of testing the truth of the categorical statements are stated in the protasis, and provided that the apodosis specifies some observations which would count as sufficient evidence of the truth of the categorical statement. The identification of the meaning of a statement with the method of its verification strictly requires this trivialisation of the hypothetical form, since it requires that one should always write into the statement itself the conditions under which it would be conclusively confirmed. But when I assert that S is P, I do not assert that if such-and-such specific conditions of observation were realised, such-and-such specific evidence that S is P would be obtained. One would only have shown that S is P conveyed a disguised, hypothetical statement, if the apodosis of the hypothetical, offered as a paraphrase, mentioned specific phenomena not mentioned in S is P, and if the protasis specified the conditions of the occurrence of these phenomena (cf. "magnetised," "soluble in aqua regia"). But when I say that someone is generous, I do not thereby commit myself to saying that if certain demands were made upon him, he would respond in certain specific ways; and if I do believe this hypothetical statement, I probably believe it *because I believe that he is generous,* that is, as an inference from his generosity. Similarly if I say of someone that he understood what I said, I do not assert that if such-and-such questions were put to him, he would respond in such-and-such a manner; and if I do accept this conditional statement, my grounds for accepting it are that he did understand and *therefore* if. . . .

I conclude therefore that statements about human dispositions and character are not, *as such,* hypothetical statements and do not, as such, entail hypothetical statements. The distinction between expressions referring to occur-

40

rences (e.g. the occurrence of a state of mind) and expressions referring to dispositions ("he is intelligent," "he is musical," "he understands English") is a distinction *of a different kind* from that between categorical and hypothetical statements. Philosophers may distinguish descriptions of material objects from descriptions of subjective impressions, the discussion of abstractions (Soul, State, Economic Man, Numbers) from the discussion of concrete entities, and similarly one may distinguish narrative statements from character descriptions; but the distinction categorical-hypothetical occurs *within* these varieties of discourse. Distinctions of logic are sometimes confused with these type-distinctions by a play upon the multiple uses of the word "fact"; for the word "fact" occurs as one term in a number of different antitheses, some of these antitheses involving logical, and others nonlogical, distinctions: fact versus supposition, matter of fact versus matter of opinion, fact versus generalisation, fact versus interpretation, fact versus logical necessity—these are a few of the familiar antitheses in which "fact" may occur; and no one of these oppositions is reciprocally and necessarily connected with any of the others. If it is true that any statement about character and disposition is a summary and interpretative statement of a tendency in human behaviour and calculation, it still does not follow that such a statement entails any supposition about how the subject will, or would have, performed or calculated under certain conditions. This consequence will only seem to follow if some *simple* antithesis is supposed between fact-stating statements, taken as a single class on the one hand, and all non-fact-stating statements on the other. But disposition, style in movement and gesture, expression of the face—descriptions of these are no more out of place in categorical and existential statements than are descriptions of the shape of a man's nose or of incidents in his career.

41

Fallacies in Moral Philosophy

In 1912 there appeared in *Mind* an article by H. A. Prichard entitled "Does Moral Philosophy Rest on a Mistake?" I wish to ask the same question about contemporary moral philosophy, but to suggest different reasons for an affirmative answer. Most recent academic discussions of moral philosophy have directly or indirectly reflected the conception of the subject-matter of moral philosophy which is stated or implied in Prichard's article; and this conception of the subject was in turn directly derived from Kant. Kant's influence has been so great that it is now difficult to realise how revolutionary it was; yet I think that his main thesis, now generally accepted without question by philosophers as the starting-point of moral philosophy, had not been advocated, or even seriously entertained, by any philosopher who preceded him. I shall suggest that the *unbridgeable* separation between moral judgments and factual judgments, which Kant introduced, has had the effect, in association with certain logical assumptions, of leading philosophers away from the primary and proper questions of moral philosophy.[1]

What I shall summarily call the post-Kantian thesis, now so widely accepted without question, is: there is an unbridgeable logical gulf between sentences that express statements of fact and sentences that express judgments of value and particularly moral judgments; this absolute logical independence, ignored or not clearly stated by Aristotle, must be the starting-point of moral philosophy, and constitutes its peculiar problem. Post-Kantian philosophers of different logical persuasions have, of course, given very different accounts of the logic and use of value judgments;

[1] Hume never denied that our moral judgments are based on arguments about matters of fact; he only showed that these arguments are not logically conclusive or deductive arguments.

but they have generally agreed in regarding the logical independence of moral and empirical beliefs as defining the main problem of ethics.

If one reads the Nicomachean Ethics after reading the works of (for example) G. E. Moore or Sir David Ross or Professor Stevenson, one has the impression of confronting a wholly different subject. The first point of difference can be tentatively expressed by saying that Aristotle is almost entirely concerned to analyse the problems of the moral *agent*, while most contemporary moral philosophers seem to be primarily concerned to analyse the problems of the moral *judge* or critic. Aristotle describes and analyses the processes of thought, or types of argument, which lead up to the *choice* of one course of action, or way of life, in preference to another, while most contemporary philosophers describe the arguments (or lack of arguments) which lead up to the acceptance or rejection of a moral *judgment about actions*. Aristotle's Ethics incidentally mentions the kind of arguments we use as spectators in justifying sentences that express moral praise and blame of actions already performed, while many contemporary moral philosophers scarcely mention any other kind of argument. Aristotle's principal question is—What sort of arguments do we use in practical deliberation about policies and courses of action and in choosing one kind of life in preference to another? What are the characteristic differences between moral and theoretical problems? The question posed by most contemporary moral philosophers seems to be—What do we mean by, and how (if at all) do we establish the truth of, sentences used to express moral judgments about our own or other people's actions?

The difference between these two approaches to the problem of moral philosophy emerges most clearly from the analogy between aesthetics and ethics to which allusion is made both in Aristotle's Ethics and also in most modern discussions of so-called value judgments (e.g. by Sir David Ross in *The Right and the Good* and by A. J. Ayer in *Language, Truth and Logic*). For Aristotle (as for Plato) the aesthetic analogy which illuminates the problem of moral philosophy is the analogy between the artist or craftsman's characteristic procedures in designing and executing his work and the similar, but also different, procedures which we all use in designing and executing practical policies in ordinary life. For contemporary moral philosophers, largely preoccupied with elucidating sentences that express moral praise or blame (moral "judgments" in the sense in which a judge gives judgments), the relevant analogy is between sentences expressing moral praise or condemnation and sentences expressing aesthetic praise or condemnation. As aesthetics has become the study of the logic and language of aesthetic *criticism*, so moral philosophy has become largely the study of the logic and language of moral criticism.

No one will be inclined to dispute that the processes of thought which are characteristic of the artist or craftsman in conceiving and executing his designs are essentially different from the processes of the critic who passes judgment on the artist's work. It is notorious that the processes involved in, and the gifts and training required for, the actual making of a work of art are different from those that are required for the competent appraisal of the work; the artist's problem is not the critic's problem. An aesthetician may choose—and in fact most modern aestheticians have chosen—to confine himself to an analysis of the characteristic arguments involved in arriving at a judgment about a work of art (e.g. theories of aesthetic emotion, of objective standards of taste). Alternatively he may analyse and characterise the creative process itself (theories of imagination, the relation of technique to conception, the formation of style, the nature of inspiration). He may decide that the two inquiries, though certainly distinguishable and separable, are in some respects complementary, or at least that there are some questions contained within the first which cannot be answered without a prior answer to the second. However complementary they may be, the first inquiry certainly does not include the second. Those who wish to distinguish more clearly the peculiar characteristics of artistic activity will learn little or nothing from the typical aestheticians' discussions of the objective and subjective interpretations of critical aesthetic judgments. But it seems now to be generally assumed that to ask whether sentences expressing moral praise or blame are to be classified as true or false statements, or alternatively as mere expressions of feeling, is somehow a substitute for the analysis of the processes of thought by which as moral agents we decide what we ought to do and how we ought to behave. Unless this is the underlying assumption, it is difficult to understand why moral philosophers should concentrate attention primarily on the analysis of ethical terms as they are used in sentences expressing moral praise and blame; for we are not primarily interested in moral criticism, or even self-criticism, except in so far as it is directly or indirectly an aid to the solution of practical problems, to deciding what we ought to do in particular situations or types of situation; we do not normally perplex ourselves deeply in moral appraisal for its own sake, in allotting moral marks to ourselves or to other people. The typical moral problem is not a spectator's problem or a problem of classifying or describing conduct, but a problem of practical choice and decision.

But the aesthetic analogy may be misleading, in that the relation of the value judgments of the art critic to the characteristic problems of the artist or craftsman cannot be assumed to be the same as the relation of the sentences expressing moral praise or blame to the problems of the moral agent.[2] To press the analogy would be question-begging, although the validity of the analogy between the problems of ethics and aesthetics is so often assumed. Leaving aside the analogy, the issue is—Is the answer to the question "What are the distinguishing characteristics of sentences expressing moral praise or blame?" necessarily the same as the answer to the question "What are the distinguishing characteristics of moral problems as they present themselves to us as practical agents?"? Unless these two questions are identical, or unless the first includes the second, much of contemporary moral philosophy is concerned with a relatively trivial side-issue, or is at the very least incomplete. My thesis is that the answer to the second question must contain the answer to the first, but that, if one tries to answer the first question without approaching it as part of the second, the answer will tend to be, not only incomplete, but positively misleading; and that the now most widely accepted philosophical interpretations of moral judgments, of their logical status and peculiarities, are radically misleading for this reason. They purport to be logical characterisations of moral judgments and of the distinguishing features of moral arguments, but in these characterisations the *primary* use of moral judgments is largely or even entirely ignored.

SUPPOSE (what probably occurs occasionally in most people's experience) one is confronted with a difficult and

[2] In so far as we now distinguish between the creative artist and the mere craftsman, a work of art by definition is not the answer to any problem; the artist is only said to have problems when conceived as a craftsman, that is, as having technical problems of devising means towards a given or presumed end. Where there is no problem posed, there can be no question of a right or wrong solution of it. Therefore the critic of poetry cannot be expected to show how the poem should be re-written; he describes, but he does not prescribe or make a practical judgment, as does the critic of conduct or technique. So the aesthetic analogy misleads in at least this respect; the valued critic of art excels in description and classification; he is not the artist's adviser, while moral or technical criticism is normally the giving of practical advice.

46

untrivial situation in which one is in doubt what one ought to do, and then, after full consideration of the issues involved, one arrives at a conclusion. One's conclusion, reached after deliberation, expressed in the sentence "x is the best thing to do in these circumstances," is a pure or primary moral judgment (the solution of a practical problem). It is misleading to the point of absurdity to describe this sentence, as used in such a context, as meaningful only in the sense in which an exclamation is meaningful, or as having no literal significance, or as having the function merely of expressing and evoking feeling. It is also misleading to describe it as a statement about the agent's feeling or attitude; for such a description suggests that the judgment would be defended, if attacked, primarily by an appeal to introspection. It is surely misleading to describe the procedure by which such a judgment or decision is established as right as one of comparing degrees of moral emotion towards alternative courses of action. I am supposing (what is normal in such cases) that the agent has reasoned and argued about the alternatives, and am asserting that he would then justify his conclusion, if it were attacked, by reference to these arguments; and a statement about his own moral feelings or attitudes would not be, within the ordinary use of language, either a necessary or sufficient justification. Therefore the characterisation of such judgments as purely, or even largely, reports of feelings or attitudes is at the least incomplete, and misleadingly incomplete, because in this characterisation the typical procedures of deliberation on which the judgment is based are suppressed or ignored. It is also paradoxical and misleading to introduce the word "intuition," as another group of post-Kantian philosophers have done, in describing the procedure by which such a judgment is arrived at, or by which it is justified and defended; for the force of the word "intuition" is to suggest that the conclusion is not established by any recognised form of argument, by any ratiocinative process

47

involving a succession of steps which are logically criticisable; the word "intuition" carries the suggestion that we do not, or even cannot, deliberate and calculate in deciding what we ought to do. But we always can and often actually do deliberate and calculate.

If the procedure of practical deliberation does not conform, either in its intermediate steps or in the form of its conclusions, with any forms of argument acknowledged as respectable in logical textbooks, this is a deficiency of the logical textbooks. Or rather it is a mistake in the *interpretation* of textbooks of logic to assume that they provide, or that they are intended to provide, patterns of all forms of reasoning or argument which can properly be described as rational argument. Arguments may be, in the ordinary and wider sense, rational, without being included among the types of argument which are ordinarily studied by logicians, since logicians are generally concerned exclusively with the types of argument that are characteristic of the a priori and empirical sciences. There are other patterns of argument habitually used outside the sciences, which may be described as more or less rational in the sense that they are more or less strictly governed by recognised (though not necessarily formulated) rules of relevance. If one criticises a sequence of sentences by saying that assertion or denial of the earlier members of the sequence is irrelevant to acceptance or rejection of their successors, then this sequence is being regarded as constituting an argument. Aristotle at least remarks that not all arguments are theoretical arguments, terminating in a conclusion which is intended as a statement, either factual or logically true; there are also practical arguments—he naturally says "syllogisms"—the form of which is similar in many respects to some types of theoretical argument, but which are also characteristically different in their form. In particular they differ in the form of their conclusion, which is not a theoretical or true-or-false statement, but has the distinctive form of a practical judgment, e.g. "this is the right action" or "this is the best thing to do," or "this ought to be done."

Even when sentences containing moral terms are used by spectators (not agents) in contexts in which they seem to be in fact associated with a purely emotional reaction to a decision or action, it is misleadingly incomplete to characterise them as having the logical force only, or largely, of expressions of, or statements about, the speaker's or writer's feelings or attitudes. If a purely critical and apparently emotional moral judgment of this kind is challenged and needs to be defended and justified, it will be justified by the same kind of arguments which one would have used as an agent in practical deliberation. If I am not prepared to produce such practical arguments, pointing to what ought to have been done, I shall admit that I am not making a genuine moral judgment, but merely expressing or reporting my own feelings; and I shall admit that it was misleading to use the form of sentence ordinarily associated with moral judgments, and not with expressions of feeling. Doubtless many sentences containing moral terms are ambiguous, and may be normally used both as expressions of practical judgments and as expressions of feeling. But the important point is that, if challenged about our intentions, we are required to *distinguish* between such uses; and our languages, by providing the distinctive quasi-imperative form of the practical judgment, enable us to distinguish. But moral philosophers, tacitly assuming that moral judgments must be descriptive statements, have represented a moral problem as a critic's or spectator's problem of proper classification and description.

If, following Aristotle, one begins by describing how moral problems differ both from technical and theoretical problems, one will have begun to answer the question about the distinctive nature of moral judgments, even in their purely critical use. But if one begins by separating them from their context in practical deliberation, and considers them as quasi-theoretical[3] expressions of moral praise and condemnation, the resulting characterisation of them must be misleadingly incomplete.

THE FACT that moral judgments, in spite of the peculiarity of their form as practical judgments, are established by familiar patterns of argument, has been under-emphasised by post-Kantian moral philosophers as a consequence of three connected logical doctrines: (a) the doctrine that so-called value judgments cannot be derived from factual judgments: (b) the doctrine that, although we deliberate and argue about the facts of moral situations (e.g. about the probable consequences of various possible actions), no further argument is possible when once the facts of the situation have been determined; we are thus left in every case of practical deliberation with (c) an ultimate moral judgment, which cannot be replaced by any statement of fact, or by an empirical statement of any kind, and which cannot itself be defended by further argument. From no consideration of facts, or accumulation of factual knowledge, can we ever deduce a moral judgment of the form "this ought to be done" or "this is the right action in these circumstances." Therefore all appeal to the procedure of deliberation is irrelevant to the real problem, which is the analysis or characterisation of these *ultimate* moral judgments.

The fallacy in this position, as I have stated it, emerges in the words "derive" and "deduce." It is only in limiting cases that, in describing the logic of any class of sentences of ordinary discourse, one can reasonably expect to find another class of sentences from which the problem-sentences

---

[3] To pose the problem of ethics as the problem of "ethical predicates" or "non-natural characteristics" is at the outset to suggest that moral judgments are to be interpreted as a peculiar kind of descriptive statement.

are logically deducible. Statements about physical things cannot be deduced, or logically derived, from statements about visible properties; statements about people's character or dispositions cannot be deduced, or logically derived from, statements about their behaviour; yet in both cases the truth of the first kind of statement is established by reference to the second kind. In general, one kind of sentence may be regularly established and defended by reference to another kind, without the first kind being deducible, or logically derivable, from the second. When as philosophers we ask how a particular kind of sentence is to be categorised or described, we are asking ourselves by what sort of arguments it is established and how we justify its use if it is disputed; to explain its logic and meaning is generally to describe and illustrate by examples the kind of sentences that are conventionally accepted as sufficient grounds for its assertion or rejection. So we may properly elucidate moral or practical judgments by saying that they are established and supported by arguments consisting of factual judgments of a particular range, while admitting that they are never strictly deducible, or logically derivable, from any set of factual judgments.

Certainly no practical judgment is logically deducible from any set of statements of fact; for if practical judgments were so deducible, they would be redundant; we could confine ourselves simply to factual or theoretical judgments; this is in effect what strict Utilitarians, such as Bentham, proposed that we should do. Bentham recommended the removal of distinctively moral terms from the language, so that moral problems would be replaced by technical problems, or problems of applied science. He made this proposal quite self-consciously and deliberately, wishing to introduce a science of morals, in which all moral problems would be experimentally decidable as technical problems. The distinctive form in which moral problems are posed and moral

conclusions expressed disappears in his usage, precisely because he makes arguments about matters of fact *logically
conclusive* in settling moral problems; and it is precisely to
this *replacement* of moral terms that critics of strict Utilitarians have always objected (e.g. G. E. Moore in *Principia
Ethica*). They have argued that Utilitarians confuse the
reasons on which moral judgments may be based with those
judgments themselves; and this confusion arises from supposing that the reasons must be logically conclusive reasons,
so that to accept the empirical premises and to deny the
moral conclusion is self-contradictory. But it does not follow from the fact that moral or practical judgments are not
in their normal use so deducible that they must be described as ultimate, mysterious, and removed from the
sphere of rational discussion. All argument is not deduction,
and giving reasons in support of a judgment or statement
is not necessarily, or even generally, giving logically conclusive reasons.

Once this assumption is removed, it is possible to reconsider, without philosophical prejudice, what is the difference and the relation between ordinary empirical statements and moral judgments as we actually use them when
we are arguing with ourselves, or with others, about what
we ought to do. It is important to consider examples of
practical or moral problems which are neither trivial in
themselves nor abstractly described; for it is only by reflecting on our procedure when confronted with what would
ordinarily be called a genuine moral problem that the characteristic types of argument can be seen clearly deployed.
A simplified variant of the situation presented in a recent
novel[4] may serve the purpose. Suppose that I am convinced
that if I continue to live, I cannot avoid inflicting great and
indefinitely prolonged unhappiness on one or both of two
people, and at the same time on myself. By committing

[4] *The Heart of the Matter,* by Graham Greene.

suicide without detection I can avoid this accumulation of unhappiness; I therefore decide, after careful deliberation, that the right or best thing to do is to commit suicide. This is a moral judgment of the primary kind. (Having reached this conclusion, I may of course in any particular case fail to act in accordance with it; as Aristotle points out, deciding *that* x is the best thing to do and deciding *to* do x are both distinguishable and separable.) Suppose that in this case the moral judgment, which is the conclusion of my deliberation, is challenged by someone who at the same time agrees with me in my assessment of all the facts of the situation; that is, he agrees with me about the probable consequences of all the possible courses of action, but does not agree with my conclusion that it is right to commit suicide. An argument develops: we each give our reasons for saying that suicide under these circumstances is right or wrong. However the argument may develop in detail, it will generally exhibit the following features. (1) Although it is assumed that my disputant agrees with me about the facts of this particular situation (probable consequences of various actions etc.), he will in his argument appeal to other facts or beliefs about the world, which are not strictly describable as beliefs about the facts of this particular situation. For instance, we might both recognise as relevant a dispute, partly empirical and partly logical, about whether there is life after death, and whether the Christian dogmas on this subject are true or significant; or we may become involved in a largely historical argument about the social effects of suicide; and it would be recognised as pertinent to produce psychological arguments to the effect that intense unhappiness is often preferred to mere loneliness and *therefore* (and this "therefore" is not the sign of an entailment) it would be better not to desert the other two people involved. *The point is that it does not follow from the fact that two people are in agreement about the facts of a par-*

ticular situation, but disagree in their moral judgment, that their disagreement is ultimate and admits of no further rational argument.

Hence (2) our disagreement about the moral or practical conclusion, which is not a disagreement about the facts of the particular situation, is nevertheless, a disagreement to which empirical arguments, beliefs about an indefinitely wide range of matters of fact, are recognised to be relevant. If we are deliberating or arguing about whether suicide is right or wrong in these particular circumstances (or in any circumstances), then our psychological, historical and religious beliefs are always taken to be relevant parts of the argument. By representing so-called value judgments as ultimate and logically divorced from ordinary factual judgments, philosophers have implicitly or explicitly suggested that such sentences as "suicide is always wrong" or "suicide is wrong in these circumstances" cannot be defended or refuted by appeals to facts or to the empirical sciences. This paradox is a legacy of Kant's anxiety to underline as strongly as possible the difference between practical problems which are moral problems and those which are purely technical problems. Almost all previous philosophers—and most people without Kantian or other philosophical prejudices— have assumed accumulating knowledge, or changing beliefs arising out of the study of history, psychology, anthropology and other empirical sciences, to be relevant to their moral judgments; to be relevant, not in the sense that the falsity of moral judgments previously accepted as true can be *deduced* from some empirical propositions of history, psychology or any natural science, but in the sense in which (for example) propositions about somebody's conduct are relevant to propositions about his character; that is, previous moral judgments are shown to be groundless, the empirical propositions on which they were based having been contradicted as scientific or historical knowledge increases.

The conflicting moral conclusions of a Marxist and a Christian Fundamentalist, or the differences which may arise even between two contemporary and similarly educated liberal unbelievers, will generally (but not always or necessarily) be shown in argument to rest on different empirical, or at least corrigible, beliefs about the constitution of the universe. Whenever we argue about any moral question which is not trivial, our beliefs and assumptions, however rudimentary and half-formulated, about psychological, sociological and probably theological questions are recognised as relevant, and as involved in the nature of the dispute.

The result of the supposed argument about my judgment that suicide is the right policy in this particular circumstance might be that I am convinced that my judgment was wrong, and am persuaded that suicide is not the right policy. I might be persuaded to withdraw my original judgment, either because I have been made to recognise a fault in the logic of my previous argument, or because I have been persuaded to abandon admittedly relevant beliefs about matters of fact, or because my attention has been directed to new facts as being relevant to the decision, facts which I had known but the relevance of which I had previously overlooked. To direct attention to further known facts as relevant to a judgment is perhaps the most important effect and function of moral arguments or practical deliberation and of giving practical advice. It is misleading to speak of "the facts of a situation" in such a way as to suggest that there must be a closed set of propositions which, once established, precisely determine the situation.[5] The situa-

---

[5] The word "fact," here as always, is treacherous, involving the old confusion between the actual situation and the description of it. The situation is given, but not "the facts of the situation"; to state the facts is to analyse and interpret the situation. And just this is the characteristic difficulty of actual practical decisions, which disappears in the textbook cases, where the "relevant facts" are preselected. So

tions in which we must act or abstain from acting, are "open" in the sense that they cannot be uniquely described and finally circumscribed. Situations do not present themselves with their labels attached to them; if they did, practical problems would be conclusively soluble theoretical problems, the philosopher's dream; but ἐν τῇ αἰσθήσει ἡ κρίσις—the crux is in the labelling, or the decision depends on how we see the situation.

For these reasons the logical divorce between so-called judgments of value and factual judgments is misleading; for arguments about practical conclusions are arguments about facts. Our moral or practical judgments—"x is the right or best course of action (in these or in all circumstances)"— are corrigible by experience and observation; we feel certain about some, and very doubtful about others.

CERTAINLY there may (logically) be cases in which we cannot attribute conflicting solutions of practical moral problems to conflicting beliefs about matters of fact; that is, two disputants, in giving their reasons for conflicting moral judgments, may be unable to find among their reasons any empirical proposition which is accepted by one of them and rejected by the other. It is logically possible that A and B should agree entirely, e.g. about the effects of capital punishment, and furthermore should find no relevant differences in their general psychological or sociological or other beliefs, and yet disagree as to whether capital punishment should or should not now be abolished. However rare such situations may be (and I believe them to be much more rare than is commonly allowed) such so-called "ultimate" moral differences may occur. Both A and B, if they can claim to be making a moral judgment and not merely expressing their own feelings about, or attitudes towards,

the determining arguments are cut out of the textbook, and the gap is filled by "intuition" or feeling.

capital punishment, will be able to give the reasons which seem to them sufficient to justify their conclusion; but what is accepted by A as a sufficient reason for a practical conclusion is not accepted by B as a sufficient reason and vice versa. They may then argue further to ensure that each does recognise the reason which he is claiming to be sufficient in this case as sufficient in other cases; but, when this consistency of use is once established, the argument must terminate. How is such an "ultimate" or irresoluble difference about a moral judgment properly described?

Compare this ultimate difference about the practical judgment with a similar ultimate difference about a theoretical judgment: if A and B were to disagree about whether somebody is intelligent, and yet find that they did not disagree about the facts (actual behaviour) or probabilities (how he is likely to behave under hypothetical conditions) on which their judgment is based, they would describe their difference as a difference in the use of the word "intelligent"; they would say "you use a different criterion of intelligence, and so do not mean by 'intelligent' exactly what I mean."[6] Similarly when it has been shown that A and B generally apply wholly or largely different tests in deciding whether something is morally wrong, they might perhaps describe their so-called ultimate difference by saying that they do not both mean the same, or exactly the same, thing when they say that something is morally wrong; and in most such cases of ultimate or irresoluble moral differences this is in fact what we do say—that different societies (and even different individuals within the same society) may have more or less different moral terminologies, which are not mutually translatable. But of practical judgments one can-

---

[6] "What do you mean by saying that he is intelligent?" is ordinarily interpreted as the same question as "What are your reasons for saying, or why do you say, that he is intelligent?" Similarly, "What do you mean by saying that that was a wrong decision?" is the same question as "*Why* do you say that that was a wrong decision?"

not say that differences which are in principle irresoluble are *simply* terminological misunderstandings and in *no* sense genuine contradictions; for it is the distinguishing characteristic of practical judgments that they also have a prescriptive or quasi-imperative force. They can only argue about which of their prescriptions is right if they can agree on some common criteria of rightness. A, following the practice of all reforming moralists and many moral philosophers, may try to influence B's actions by giving moral reasons for preferring his own criteria of use to B's use; but in his advocacy of his own use of moral terms, he will be using his moral terms in his own way. The argument might have shown B that his conclusion was wrong in A's sense of "wrong" or even in his own sense of "wrong"; but no argument can show that B *must* use the criteria which A uses and so must attach the same meaning (in this sense) to moral terms as A. Between two consistently applied terminologies, whether in theoretical science or in moral decision, ultimately we must simply choose; we can give reasons for our choice, but not reasons for reasons for . . . *ad infinitum.*

WE MAY find that many people do not deliberate and so can scarcely be said to make moral judgments, but simply act as they have been conditioned to act, and, when challenged, repeat the moral sentences which they have been taught to repeat, or merely state or express personal feelings and attitudes. A second, and much smaller class, act generally, and even wholly, on impulse, in the sense that they do not propose practical problems to themselves or choose policies, but simply do whatever they feel inclined to do—and such people are to be distinguished from those who have *decided that* to act on impulse, or to do what one feels inclined to do, is the right policy; for this is to make a moral judgment. But the great majority of people for some part

FALLACIES IN MORAL PHILOSOPHY

of their lives are thinking about what is the best thing to do, sometimes reaching a conclusion and failing to act on it, sometimes reaching a conclusion which, in the light of corrections of their empirical beliefs or their logic, they later recognise to have been a wrong conclusion, and sometimes reaching a conclusion which they are prepared to defend by argument and acting in accordance with it.

"Thinking what is the best thing to do" describes a procedure which it is unprofitable, if not impossible, to analyse, or find a paraphrase for, in general terms without constant reference to specific cases. Aristotle begins by describing it as calculating means to a vaguely conceived end (happiness or well-doing), the nature of the end being more precisely determined by the means chosen as involved in its realisation. But he progressively qualifies and complicates this schematic account in such a way as to suggest that to make a moral decision is not to choose means to an already decided end, but to choose a policy of means-to-end which is judged right or wrong as a whole. Practical problems are (as Kant emphasised and over-emphasised) sub-divisible into moral and purely technical problems; the choice of the most efficient means to an already determined end is not called a moral choice. It is the defining characteristic of a moral problem, that it requires an unconditional decision, the choice of an action or policy as a whole.

THERE IS another and related logical fallacy, often implicitly assumed and not explicitly stated, which has led philosophers to describe moral or practical judgments as expressions or reports of feeling or as established by a priori intuitions, and to neglect their normal occurrence as the corrigible conclusions of arguments involving the facts of a particular situation and our general beliefs about the world. This is the fallacy of assuming that all literally significant sentences must correspond to something, or de-

59

scribe something. As ordinary empirical statements were said to correspond to facts, so some philosophers have introduced the word "values" in order that there should be something to which moral (and aesthetic) judgments can be said to correspond. We are said to "intuit" or to "apprehend" these values, these words being used to suggest an analogy with sense-perception. Other philosophers, wishing to define the world as the totality of facts, or as the objects of sense and introspection, have inferred that, as moral judgments cannot be said to correspond to anything in the external world, they must either correspond to something in the internal world (i.e. to feelings) or, failing that, that they cannot be admitted to be literally significant. The question "What do moral judgments correspond to?" or "What do they describe?" suggests itself particularly to those who are preoccupied with the critical use of these judgments as expressions of retrospective praise or blame. In so far as we relate them to practical deliberations and decisions, we come to recognise them as not descriptions of, but prescriptions for, actions. Practical judgments, no less than theoretical or descriptive statements, are in the natural sense of the words, literally significant, although they do not in the normal sense describe. If I say "this is (or would have been) the right action in these circumstances," this judgment can be significantly denied; but, as it is not a descriptive statement or statement of fact, the denial is not normally expressed in the form "it is *false* that this is the best action in these circumstances"; "true" and "false" are more naturally used with theoretical judgments and statements of fact.[7] Of course this distinction between true or false descriptive statements and right or wrong practical judgments is not absolute and clear; many sentences are partly de-

[7] Although we can speak of believing that this is the right action, we cannot speak of evidence that it is right. "Evidence" is tied to statements which are true or false.

scriptive and are partly expressions of practical judgments. But there is a distinction which emerges clearly in simple cases of pure moral judgments and purely descriptive statements. One *can* describe somebody's behaviour or character without making any moral judgment (i.e. prescription), even if in fact prescriptions and descriptions are often almost inextricably combined.

THERE IS (I think) a widespread impression that the concentration of academic moral philosophers on the attempt to *define* ethical expressions—"good," "right," "ought," etc., —as being the principal problem of moral philosophy has tended to make the subject sterile and unenlightening. One is inclined to say that it does not *matter* whether "right," as ordinarily used, is definable in terms of "good" or not. There is the feeling that the clarifications that one expects from the moral philosopher cannot be answered by verbal definitions or the discovery of paraphrases. And I think this apparently philistine impatience with the search for verbal definitions or equivalences has good grounds. If we wish to clarify our own or somebody else's use of moral terms, the discovery of verbal equivalences or paraphrases among these terms is not an answer, but, at the most, a preliminary step towards an answer. What we want to know, in clarifications of differences in our use of moral terms, is—What kinds of reasons are sufficient to establish that this is the right action? There is no reason to expect a simple answer in terms of a single formula, e.g. "it is likely to increase happiness." But to search only for definitions or verbal equivalences is to assume that there must be a single sufficient reason from which I always and necessarily derive my judgment. This is another expression of the fundamental fallacy of thinking of analysis or clarification of the standard use of words or sentences as necessarily a matter of exhibiting deducibilities or entailments. If I am asked what

61

I mean by saying of someone that he is intelligent, I explain my use of the word by describing specimens of the type of behaviour to which I apply the word; I give some specimens of the types of statements about his behaviour which would be taken as sufficient grounds for asserting or denying that he is intelligent. Similarly, one can only clarify one's own use of the principal moral terms by describing specimens of conduct to which they are applied, and by quoting the different characteristics of actions which one normally and generally takes to be sufficient grounds for deciding that they are the right actions. The type of analysis which consists in defining, or finding synonyms, for the moral terms of a particular language cannot illuminate the nature of moral decisions or practical problems; it is no more than local dictionary-making, or the elimination of redundant terms, which is useful only as a preliminary to the study of typical moral arguments. An informative treatise on ethics —or on the ethics of a particular society or person—would contain an accumulation of examples selected to illustrate the kind of decisions that are said to be right in various circumstances, and the reasons given and the arguments used in concluding that they are right. An uninformative treatise on ethics consists of specimens of moral sentences, separated from actual or imaginable contexts of argument about particular practical problems, and treated as texts for the definition of moral terms; and many academic textbooks follow this pattern.

SUMMARY

The four logically related fallacies underlying the typical post-Kantian approach to moral philosophy are (a) The assimilation of moral or practical judgments to descriptive statements, which is associated with concentration on the use of moral terms in sentences expressing a spectator's praise or blame; (b) the inference from the fact that moral or practical judgments cannot be logically derived from statements of fact to the conclusion that they cannot be based on, or established exclusively by reference to, beliefs about matters of fact; hence theories that moral judgments must be ultimate and irrational, that they are established by intuition or are not literally significant; (c) the assumption that all literally significant sentences must correspond to or describe something; moral judgments do not correspond to or describe anything, but they may, nevertheless, be said to be rational or irrational, right or wrong.[8] (d) The confusion between clarifying the use of ethical terms with discovering definitions of, or verbal equivalences between, these terms. The search for definitions is another expression of the old obsession of philosophers with entailment and deducibility as the only admissible relation between sentences in rational argument. To interpret "rational argument" so narrowly is, although misleading, not in itself fallacious; but if, on the basis of this arbitrary restriction, moral judgments are relegated to a logical limbo, labelled "emotive," the study of the characteristic logic of these sentences, and of the types of argument in which they occur, is obscured, and suppressed.

[8] "I decided that x was the right thing to do" is a descriptive statement, true or false; but "x was the right thing to do" is a practical or moral judgment, right or wrong, and is less naturally characterised as true or false.

Ethics: A Defense of Aristotle

The methods of linguistic analysis have suggested to us that we may often seesaw between one theory and another in philosophy because we have not been sufficiently patient and plodding in surveying the field: the field being the full range of uses to which some problematical and central word or phrase may properly be put. The usual story is that first one range of examples is chosen, and a theory of the standard use of the examined phrase is erected upon them: then a critic points to another range of examples, and erects another theory of proper use upon them. Thesis and antithesis, dialectic indeed, but no synthesis, and therefore no progress.

The more general in its applications a word or phrase may be, the greater the need of patience and plodding caution: the greater also the risk of partial, selective, and therefore finally unenlightening, theory. The work is not done, the word or concept is not fully exposed and seen through, until the connection between the more disparate uses is explained. We have therefore to roam about for some time in the apparent open field before trying to erect tidy fences. When a single word has been traditionally and responsibly used in ways that admit of quite different characterizations, we must still presume an underlying connection, one that is so far undiscerned. Certainly we cannot rest with the partial and rival characterizations. Something has gone wrong and we have not yet concluded.

One might take these remarks to be an exordium to something further about the word "know," still only partially characterized. They are not, but rather to something further about an equally general and indeterminate, and equally discussed and maltreated word: "good." But this lecture can only be a bare outline.

64

Philosophy has always been concerned with the five words: exist, know, same, cause, and good: indeed a concern with these five most general notions might be used to define, or to give the essence of, a philosophical interest. Surprisingly, in respect of the word "good," we seem to be still on the seesaw of rival and partial theories, supported by selected examples. Surprisingly, because I think that some of the elements of an impartial characterization of the full range of its uses (not the details) are there for all to see —in Aristotle. But Aristotle is sometimes misrepresented: as if his account of the word was inextricably in terms of essences, and of an impermissible notion of function: but I think his account can be largely purged of these taints, real and alleged.

But perhaps it would be better at this stage to forget Aristotle and descend to cases.

A MAN says "I have just heard good news." The same man says on another occasion "I have just seen a good play." He has used the same word twice, and in the same grammatical construction. Yet the uses are different, and the claims made are different. It looks as if we do not simply have a homonym here. What is dissimilar in the two uses of the word? And what is the connection between them? To begin with the dissimilarities:

A. To both statements, the socially rather crude challenge is possible "What is good about it?" or (rather less crude) "What makes it good news (a good play)?" or, more tentative still and a slightly different question, "Why do you think it is good news (a good play)?" I am assuming that these questions are asked by someone who already knows what the news is, and what the play is; he has heard the one and seen the other. Whichever form of words he uses in asking his question, and in making his challenge, he is asking for reasons to be adduced in support of the statements

65

just made: reasons, that is, for calling the news good news, and for calling the play a good play. For the original speaker announced that he had heard some news, and he called it good news; he announced that he had seen a play and he called it a good play. We are here concerned only with the "calling good," not with the announcement of biographical fact. And I am content with the word "calling" in this context, because, as far as I know, no philosopher has yet run up a theory of "calling expressions," as of descriptive, prescriptive, grading expressions and so on. We do, quite generally, call things good and we call them bad: just as we do, quite generally, think, or consider, them good or bad, without actually calling them anything. We call things good, or bad, just as we call things red or green. And the calling is in both cases a conventional sign of thinking or considering. I shall be discussing reasons for calling good, which are at the same time the speaker's reasons for considering the thing good, or thinking it good. There could of course be reasons for the linguistic act of calling something good which would not be the speaker's reasons for considering it either good or bad. But here reasons for calling something good will also be reasons for considering something good.

The first dissimilarity between the two examples of calling something good: it does seem that the reasons for calling the play a good play must be wholly found in the qualities, or features, of the play, and of nothing else. We should be convicted of talking nonsense, or of speaking inaccurately, if we adduced, as supporting reasons, the lighting of the theatre, or the comfort of the seats, or the height and bearing of the actors. If it is a play that we are calling good, then we must (as a conceptual necessity) admit at least the pertinence of saying something about the dialogue and language, about the dramatic action, about the development of themes, and about the convincing representation

66

of some aspects of human experience. This list of the relevant types of feature is not supposed to be exhaustive and complete, and it is a disjunctive set of types. Given that we know what a play is, and that we can specify the distinguishing properties of plays among other forms of art and entertainment, we know that the main reasons adduced, if they are to count as reasons, must fall, more or less roughly, under these headings. We have specifically praised the play, and singled this out from the complex happening of which it, and its performance or reading, were part; and a play necessarily has speeches and some literary form, some kind of action on stage, some theme or themes, and normally also some reference to human experience. This is how a play works. Admittedly an original writer might introduce a new form of dramatic art, which may lead us to extend our present concept of a play. The concept is not static and closed, and for this reason, among others, there are no final and definite canons of dramatic art. But if we are praising a play, then, however original and unexpected its qualities may be, we are attending to some literary and thematic qualities of something that works, and produces its effects, in a peculiarly dramatic way. The concept has some continuity in its history.

It is certainly not true that the reasons for calling some news good news must be found within the concept news. The suggestion is not even intelligible to one who reflects on the meaning of the word "news." Nor is it true that we can specify the several headings under which the reasons must fall, if they are to be intelligible as reasons for calling it good news. The features of the news that make it good news, and the reasons that may intelligibly be adduced for calling it good news, may in different cases be drawn from a vast and indefinite range of different human interests. This is the first dissimilarity between our two examples of calling something good.

B. When the man calls the play a good play, he is speaking as a critic of the play as well as praising it. His praise of it is taken to be reflective praise, in the sense that, if the critical judgment is disputed, he must refer to the intrinsic qualities, or features, of the play in supporting his judgment. It will not be in place for him to speak, solely or principally, about the relation of the play to his own desires and interests. Nor will it be in place to refer to the particular desires and interests of any particular group of persons, unless it be the class of persons who are interested in plays.

When the man called the news just heard good news, it would be in place (although it is not necessary) for him to refer to his own desires and purposes in adducing reasons for calling it good, and he must refer to the desires or interests or purposes of some sentient being or beings in giving his reasons.

C. Instead of saying "I have just heard good news," my man might have been heard to say "That's good" or "That's a good thing to have happened," when the news was told to him. The man who said that he had just heard good news has said that he had just heard of something that happened and that it was a good thing that it had happened. About anything that happens or that is done, a reflective comment, favorable or unfavorable, can be made; that it should happen, or be done, may always be considered a good or a bad thing, or a matter of indifference. If it is a change in the world, the question may always be raised of whether it is a change for the better or for the worse, or is neutral, neither the one nor the other. There is at least no linguistic absurdity or impropriety in commenting "That's a good thing," or "That's a bad thing," when some statement of fact is made, although it is easy to think of cases in which any such comment would be very strange and surprising, and when we should find it difficult to see what lay behind the comment, and in this sense difficult to interpret what it meant.

In calling the play that he had seen a good play, my commentator is not so far committed to the statement that, everything considered, it was a good thing that it should be performed, or that, taking into account all the circumstances, it was a good thing that he went to see it. It is not difficult to think of circumstances in which he would reject both these suggestions. The most that might be said to follow along these lines from calling it a good play is that, everything else being equal, it is a good thing that it was performed. And this is a very weak and vague implication indeed.

These are some of the obvious, superficial dissimilarities between the two statements, involving the word "good," from which I started. Allow me, for the sake of convenience and without any full explanation of the terms, to call the phrase "a good play" an example of an attributive use of the word, and "good news" an example of a predicative use. Wherever we can substitute for a phrase like "good news" the unqualified, indeterminate, and blank phrase, "It is a good thing that so-and-so has happened, or was done," then we have so far a merely predicative use of "good"; this is at least a sufficient condition. But I am not claiming that this distinction can always be applied with clear results. For example, if I say that person A is a good influence on person B, is this an attributive or predicative use? If it only means that the things which A causes B to do, or to feel, are on the whole good things to do or to feel, it is so far a predicative use. I am only claiming that there are certain clear cases, as in my two examples.

Given that there are at least these differences in the supporting reasons, and in the implications, attached to the two uses of the word exemplified, one may next look for some of the connecting links between the two uses. Here the difficulties begin. There must be connecting links: the word does not just have different uses. There is the institution of appraising, and of evaluating, things as there is the institution of identifying things. But the institution is not a simple one.

IF A MAN says that the play X, which he has seen, is a good play, then it may seem that he is committed to the proposition that, if anyone specifically wants to see a play and must choose among plays, this play X is the very thing he wants, and should choose. But much amplification and qualification is needed, if this alleged implication is to be anything like acceptable. First, the statement of what a man wants is not always, or even usually, a simple matter. The subject himself may be confused about his wants in a variety of complicated ways, which certainly cannot be adequately examined here. It may turn out that the man who has said that he wants to see a play in reality only wants an evening's light distraction of some kind, and that he thinks that a play would serve this purpose. Or perhaps he wants to see some acting, and has for some good reason, connected with the context, expressed this desire as a desire to see a play. For these reasons it does not necessarily follow from the fact that X is a good play that X is the very thing that he wants or is looking for. But if he has avoided the manifold difficulties of knowing and stating, explicitly and exactly, what he wants—and Aristotle thought this a difficult feat and the main problem in moral thinking,—"This is a good play," does at least seem to imply "If anyone specifically wants, or is looking for, a play, and is not looking for it mainly as a means to something else, and if this is an overriding interest for him, then this is one of the things that he particularly wants." "This is a good play," implies that, in the circumstances in which a man is choosing among plays, and while this interest overrides other interests that he may have, this is conspicuously one of the things for him to try to get. The implication holds, if the description of that which is wanted is the preferred and essential description of that which is wanted, and is not just a contingent means of identification of the thing wanted. How we determine whether a description is the preferred and essential description is a whole subject for philosophical inquiry in itself. But at least we can segregate the cases in which the description is clearly accidental: for example, where it is derived as a mere means to a distinct end, or where it is merely a contingent means of identification of the thing wanted.

But, even with these qualifications, it may be doubted whether we have a clear form of implication connecting the attributive and predicative uses of "good." There are other complexities: from the fact that someone very much wants, and is looking for, food, it does not necessarily follow that, if we have found something correctly called good food, we have found the very thing that he wants and is looking for. Evidently there are two things that a man could want food for: as a biological-physical need, that is, for the sake of nourishment, and for the sake of the pleasures of taste. At least in the language of the bourgeoisie, "good food" ordinarily takes its connotation from the second interest, and to show that a substance is not nourishing does not by itself show that it is not good food. Since there are two things that we want food for, in the sense that there are two normal interests, distinct from each other, which food satisfies, there are two quite distinct canons of excellence, two criteria of choice, in food, which are sometimes, though perhaps unnecessarily, regarded as yielding distinct senses or uses of the phrase "good food."

In the light of this example, and considering the notion of what things are wanted for, it becomes plain, I think, that the notion of want, or desire, is rather too narrow for our purpose. The concepts of interest and purpose are, I think, what we are looking for, although being more vague, the implications into which they enter are less explanatory. When the news is called good news, the judgment at least entails that some human interest or purpose has been to some degree satisfied or promoted. The questions "What is good about it?" or "Why is it good news?" ask that the interests or purposes satisfied or promoted should be specified. Nothing would count as an intelligible answer to these questions unless it drew attention to some interest or interests, purpose or purposes, which are to some degree served by the reported happenings, whether the interests are those of the speaker or of others. As for the attributive uses, a good play is something that the critic who so judges is particularly recommending to anyone who is particularly interested in plays, and who must choose among them. In the extreme case of an emphatic and confident judgment of the merits of a play, the critic would take himself to be committed to the implication that anyone not satisfied by it would not really have an overriding interest in plays, but rather an interest in something else which he had confused with an interest in plays. We accord at least this degree of objectivity to critical judgments, whether in aesthetics or elsewhere.

It seems to me that these implications, involving interest, choice, and satisfaction, do hold for both the predicative and the attributive use. But at this point there is a fundamental objection to be met: namely, that the so-called predicative, or absolute, use of the word "good" is not an intelligible, distinct use of the word at all. On this view such phrases as "It is a good thing that so-and-so has happened," are not to be interpreted as conveying a complete and intelligible judgment, which can be considered and either accepted or rejected, as it stands; the phrase has always to be interpreted as elliptical. We must look to the context to supply the missing empirical concept, which will show in what respect, or respects, the event is being judged to be good. And "in what respects" is interpreted to require that the form of sentence "It is a good thing that so-and-so happened," should be replaceable by a form of sentence that specifies a particular interest, or set of interests, that were satisfied by the happening.

That every apparent absolute, unqualified, and predicative use of the word "good" is reducible, within a context, to a qualified and attributive use, or that it requires the specification of a particular interest, seems to me a false doctrine. It is an old doctrine, and has been revived recently. Its consequences are important; for it confines the range of intelligible argument about the goodness and badness of things within specific and narrow limits. In inquiring on a philosophical level, whether or not there is a distinct, non-elliptical, absolute, and predicative use of "good," we are inquiring into the possible range of rational argument about questions of value; can we look for a thoroughgoing consistency in our judgments of value, as Aristotle supposed that we could? That is, is there a possibility of arguing about the relative value of different human interests and purposes, and of systematically relating this argument to the canons of excellence employed in evaluating particular kinds of things? Those who reject the unqualified predicative use altogether are extruding any assessment of the ultimate ends of action from intelligible and rational discussion. They are cutting off one half of the Aristotelian inquiry, that half which allows him to speak of ethics as the finding of a general target to be aimed at; and without that half, some of the grounds for clinging to certain specific criteria of choice and canons of excellence are missing.

This is the issue. But what are the arguments that will vindicate the intelligibility of an absolute, predicative use of the word "good," in judgments that are complete in themselves and not elliptical? It is not clear what kind of argument could be decisive here: certainly not an appeal to established habits of speech, since the dispute arises from the fact that these habits vary, and that there is a choice. One might try an argument from the way in which the use of the word "good" is normally introduced in our experience.

We primitively, in childhood, encounter the words "good" and "bad," as an element in speech, principally as marking wanted or unwanted happenings or actions, or wanted or unwanted features of these. Happenings that we observe, or that are reported, are wanted or unwanted, fulfill or frustrate our desires, and those of others; and, against the background of this experience, we learn to think of them as, and to call them, good or bad. The wanted or unwanted, the good or bad, happening may primitively be discriminated egotistically and from a single standpoint, a standpoint that may gradually be enlarged, generalized, and modified by reflection. Or the primitive situation might be that practices are labelled good and bad in accordance with rules whose justification is not to be questioned: a bad practice just is one of these ruled out practices, for a child and perhaps in some types of primitive society. But this is not our use, or the use of Aristotle's friends. "Is this a good thing to happen?" involving the absolute predicative use, may become a very complicated question; admitting the partial answers "good in some respects" and "good from some standpoints," but "bad from others." But still an unqualified answer can be called for, one that balances these various partial views. And if a possible action in the future is under discussion, such a balanced answer must finally be given. However reflective and qualified we become in applying "good" and "bad" in this absolute and predicative way, the original reference to desires and purposes, to the targets of action, is not eliminated in these uses. How indeed could it be? We have learned the terms in this way, and some continuity is naturally preserved. "Good" and "bad," from the beginning to the end, in primitive and in sophisticated uses, have a target-setting, choice-guiding function. This is one of the threads upon which the different uses are strung. When we speak of some happening or action as a bad thing, we are representing it as frustrating some purposes or interests, without so far stating whose, or which, purposes or interests. That we should lack the means to react positively or negatively to events in the world, as affecting our interests, is quite unimaginable; no less unimaginable than that we should lack the means to call suggested future courses of action wholly good or wholly bad.

I am making no claim that this predicative use of good (It is a good thing that . . .) can be analyzed, in Moore's sense, in terms of some sentient being's interests or purposes; the notion of analysis, that is, the reduction of a complex sense to its simple elements, is quite out of place here. Nor am I proposing a universal criterion for the correct application of the word in this predicative way, as Mill seems to have done. In wondering whether it is a good or a bad thing that so-and-so should happen, I do not necessarily, on pain of logical or linguistic absurdity, have to ask myself whether it would be in accordance, or in conflict, with my already existing interests, or with most people's ascertainable desires, or with God's will, or with any one conjunction, or disjunction, of these. I can always either be egotistical, or democratic, or pious, in setting my targets for action, without running into any conceptual embarrassments. And I am, in my absolute, unqualified, predicative judgments, setting targets for possible action, and not reading off what the targets in fact are from my desires and interests, taken as ascertained facts.

Suppose that I finally decide, for whatever reason, democratic or pious, that an event is, everything considered, a good thing: the happening might still be disagreeable to me personally and in conflict with my present interests and purposes. It follows, as Aristotle would remark, that my already existing interests are, if my conclusion is correct, directed towards bad objects, or at least not towards good ones. If I am sincere in my conclusion, there is a conflict between my present interests and purposes and my final reflective conclusion about that which is desirable. It cannot be in general true of me either that deciding that something is a good thing to happen is a mere theoretical conclusion, and is logically independent of what I want to happen; or that that which I want to happen is somehow settled for me, as a given natural fact, independently of that which I consider on reflection to be, all things considered, a good thing. On the contrary it must be true that, in a reflective person, there are many occasions of conflict between his previously formed desires and interests and the conclusions that he reaches by further thought—conclusions of the form "that so-and-so is, or is not, a good thing to happen." If he is a reflective person at all, he is necessarily criticizing and revising his interests and purposes at any time: certainly not taking them as facts to be accepted. I, like many other people in England, remember being asked, at the time of Chamberlain's shameful mission to Hitler at Munich, whether they wanted the mission to succeed or whether they wanted war. There was no simple answer to the question. In so far as one wanted the mission to succeed, and knew that one would be relieved if it did, one was ashamed of wanting this, and thought that one ought not to want this. Reflective, or deliberative wants, as Aristotle called them, are not merely given facts about oneself that one ascertains. In such cases one often comes to know what one wants by just that type of inquiry by which one decides that it would be a good thing if Chamberlain failed. "I want this to happen," (in the present tense) implies that I am disposed to

76

try to bring it about, if an opportunity presents itself and in the absence of any countervailing interest. I would not be believed, if my statements of that which I wanted to happen had no relation to my behavior on occasions of opportunity. Equally "This is a good thing to happen," implies that there is a reason for a person to try to bring this about in the relevant circumstances, even if I foresee that from weakness or tiredness or some other defect, I will fail to act in the required way myself. My judgment of the form "So-and-so is a good thing," will not be taken as a sincere expression of opinion if I have not the smallest inclination to act accordingly in relevant circumstances (if any).

So much for the argument from the primitive introduction of the distinction between good and bad, in their unqualified, predicative uses. The second argument is of a different character; roughly, that we unavoidably have the institution of weighing one human interest against another and of asking which is the more worth pursuing. This institution is sometimes disguised as a consideration of the relevant "importance" of different interests and activities. But the word "importance" is here an evasion.

Consider the predicative-type judgment: "Play-going is a good thing," and suppose that I am required to give some account of it, of why it is, and what makes it so. I have so far only suggested that any answer to this question must mention the purposes and interests of sentient beings. Aristotle went further than this; he argued that, in explaining why such-and-such an activity is a good thing, I must finally indicate its relation to other activities in a whole system of activities, which taken as a whole, constitute a good, or the best, form of life for a man. This allows Aristotle to give a clear and connected rational reconstruction of the type of arguments appropriate both to predicative judgments and to attributive judgments of value. More than that: it explains how the more reflective and critical uses of the word "good" in the attributive sense develop from those predicative uses which were originally unreflective. Within this scheme, to explain why play-going is a good thing is to explain the wider interests that it uniquely serves. It shows how play-going fits in, as a contributory means, or as a by-product, or concomitant, of activities that are essential to excellence in men and to some form of life that is to be desired. So it becomes possible to explain, by reference to the part that play-going, or the enjoyment of drama, plays in the whole scheme of a way of life, why the criterion of excellence in plays is what it is. The connection is neat and clear—more clear, I think, as an approach to a rational reconstruction of moral argument than anything else in the literature. But it has familiar difficulties.

It is notorious that Aristotle gives no convincing reason why there must be, as a matter of conceptual necessity, something that is identifiable a priori as the best form of life for a man. Aristotle argued that there must be such a discoverable norm, because otherwise our desires would be empty and vain, and our reasoning in support of judgments of the goodness of this or that would never be conclusive. The norm is easily discoverable a priori: the standard and normal form of life must be one that is the perfect development of human potentialities, rather as the life cycle of a species of plant is the realization of the essential potentialities of that species. We only need to inspect the concept of the human soul in order to draw the bare outline of the kind of life, the system of activities, which constitute the norm for an intelligent living being; the moral philosopher's secondary skill is to fill in this bare outline with concrete illustration and detail. If the best and standard form of life is the full expression of the potentialities specific to human beings, as it must be, in Aristotle's philosophy, it follows that it must be the form of life that a good man wants. For a good man is simply a man who conspicuously possesses, and manifests in action, the potentialities that, taken together, distinguish human beings from other creatures. Thus the circle is conveniently completed.

But the circle has some notoriously dubious arcs. We cannot suppose that there must be some one form of life, called "the good for man," identifiable a priori, merely because it is a condition of conclusiveness in practical reasoning that there should be such a norm. Nor can we argue that our desires and interests are empty and unintelligible, if wanting, or being interested in, something cannot always be shown to be, at one or two removes, a case of wanting, or being interested, in some single all-inclusive and final thing. That ends of action should be stated in a conjunctive form, and should permit conflicts that cannot always be settled by one overriding criterion, which is sufficiently definite to count as a criterion, is not in itself an unintelligible suggestion. To admit an irreducible plurality of ends is to admit a limit to practical reasoning, and to admit that some substantial decisions are not to be explained, and not to be justified as the right decisions, by any rational calculation. This is a possibility that cannot be conceptually excluded, even if it makes satisfying theoretical reconstruction of the different uses of "good," as a target-setting term, impossible.

It seems plain to me that we cannot identify a priori the good for man, as the one final norm, from the grounds of our classification of intelligent living beings as a distinct species. We cannot both interpret the expression "a good (or virtuous or praiseworthy) man" as an example of an ordinary attributive use of "good," and ascribe an architectonic role to the judgment that a good man is one who has interests X and Y rather than interests A and B. The judgment "A is a good man," interpreted as involving an ordinary attributive use of "good," is unlike all other critical judgments of similar form in one important respect: namely, that the interests of men cannot determine the appropriate standard, or criterion, to apply in discriminating good men from bad men: for this would surely be circular, and a begging of the question at issue. The conditions of application of the phrase "good man" cannot be elucidated by reference to the satisfaction of the normal interest, or interests, that men have in other men. We would need independently to decide what these normal interests are. We are interested in men as friends and as fellow-citizens, as partners in work of various kinds, as parents and as children: a good man is perhaps required to be at least a good friend and a good citizen, and not to be dishonest or unjust. But can we determine what constitutes excellence in these roles without a prior decision about the activities and interests characteristic of a good man? How can we determine an order of priority among them? We are going round in a circle. Secondly, the interests that could be taken to be essential to men, as the ground of their distinction from other things, are too many and various. There is no sufficiently definite fixed point, or independent authority, in the concept of an intelligent living creature: why, for example, should there be a stress on intellect rather than on imagination?

Aristotle may have had too simple a conception of "the good for man" as a unitary end or target. Different things may be good in the predicative sense, and absolutely, and yet they may not, taken together, constitute anything that can be called "the obtainable good for man"; the ends may constitute a mere list, and the pursuit of some may be in fact incompatible with others. Some interests that a good man manifests in his actions may be incompatible with the realization of others. Therefore a systematic moralist's idea that all the most praiseworthy men are very alike in their manner of living may be mistaken. There may be, as far as a priori argument can show, a number of radically different forms of human excellence, and of radically different desirable forms of life, between which some men sometimes have to make a choice, without the aid of an over-arching standard.

To SUM UP (so far):

(1) There are two roughly distinguishable uses of "good," each of which has been seized upon by theoretical moralists who have neglected the other. They are typically exemplified by the phrase "good news" and "It is a good thing that people should go to the theatre" on one side (the predicative): on the other side (the attributive), by "It is a good play" and by "He is a good soldier."

(2) Both these uses of the word are indispensable.

(3) They are not different and detachable senses of the word, but connected uses.

(4) In both uses, the implication of calling anything good is that it satisfies, or would satisfy, some purpose or interest.

(5) In the purely attributive uses, the accompanying concept specifies, or at least indicates, the nature of the purposes or interests, and thereby specifies, more or less vaguely, the range of characteristics that must be mentioned in supporting the judgment and so, more or less vaguely, the criterion that is in place. In the purely predicative uses, there is so far no restriction placed on what may intelligibly be said in support of the judgment: no criterion is so far implied.

(6) The criteria appropriate to judging plays (or food) as good or bad are derived from the purposes and interests which plays and food serve: "derived" in this sense: that a good play must to a conspicuous degree satisfy the interests that make play-going a good thing.

So we arrive at this rather paradoxical position: when we praise, and reflectively criticize, things of various kinds, the more or less vague criteria of our judgment are ultimately derived from the normal, or standard, interests that things of this kind have for us. But these normal, or standard, interests are themselves subject to reflective criticism. Therefore unavoidably we confront the problem of evaluating these human interests, and of deciding upon some order of priority among them. When we reflectively evaluate human interests and decide upon some order of priority among them, we are necessarily considering also the grounds upon which human beings are to be praised and criticized as human beings. We are inquiring what human interests ought to be pursued before all others, and what ends a man who is to be praised typically has in view.

The converse is also true: if we inquire into the characteristics that distinguish a man who is to be praised from others, we are necessarily looking for an order of priority among human interests. It must be a distinguishing characteristic of a man who is to be praised that his principal interests, as revealed in his activities, are a model of what a man's interests and purposes should be. If these two inquiries are in this way inseparable, it follows that the inquiry into the grounds upon which human beings are to be praised and criticized as human beings is relevantly unlike an inquiry into the principles of criticism applicable to plays; the first inquiry, unlike the second, cannot be settled by reference to normal human interests, and to some already presupposed order of priority among these. Human interests are the very subject matter that one is here considering and evaluating. If it is characteristic of a good man that he is interested in X and that he acts accordingly, it follows that it is a good thing that men should be interested in X and should act accordingly. The converse entailment also holds. For this reason the distinction between the attributive and the predicative use of "good" breaks down when it is applied to the judgment "He is a good man": the form of the judgment is the attributive form, but a judgment involving the unqualified predicative use of "good" is entailed by it. Therefore the dissimilarities, previously noted, between the supporting arguments appropriate to the two uses are not to be found here. The argument needed to support statements of the form "X is to be praised as a human being," will be of the form "X does so-and-so and is primarily interested in so-and-so, and it is a good thing that so-and-so should be done."

The conclusion that evaluation of human beings, and their lives, dispositions, and actions, is uniquely problematical does not entail the conclusion that there are no conceptual restrictions upon what can count as praise of a human being as a human being, as opposed to praise of him as a soldier and as an administrator. Not just anything can intelligibly be said to be a supreme human virtue, or a satisfying form of human life. But there is a wide range of choice, an unmarked area of different ideals that may be incompatible in practice, and that are all plausible as ideals of an admirable, or praiseworthy, or completely satisfying, form of life.

There are several grounds on which I would claim that this Aristotelian-type reconstruction of the uses of "good" in contexts relevant to ethics is superior to any other reconstruction so far proposed by moral theorists: first, that it does reconstruct, in very general terms, but without distortion, the order and arrangement of the argument which does in fact break out when the conduct, feelings, attitudes, purposes, and interests of persons are criticized, whether in self-criticism or in criticism of others, and also in the discussions that precede decision. It is not restrictive; for instance, it does not unrealistically confine moral discussion to discussion of actions, and exclude emotions, feelings, and attitudes. Secondly, an Aristotelian-type reconstruction is more faithful to the actual order of discussion that is raised around any large issue of social policy or of private morality than other familiar moral theories are, just because it does not separate the self-criticism of a man deciding his own future, and judging his own past, from the criticism of others: because it does not separate comment from decision: because it allows that moral evaluations, which are evaluations of a man's activities and interests and of his manner of living, taken as a whole, are different in topic, but not in subject-matter, from evaluations of other kinds: because it shows clearly that the evaluation of possible forms of social life, and of the virtues and vices that they engender, is properly inseparable from the evaluation of policies in private life. From all these points of view the Aristotelian-type reconstruction seems to me to be more accurate in not concealing the range and variety of moral judgments, as we know them, and the type of justification for them that we actually expect, when the comments or decisions are challenged. We do in fact expect some considered order of priority among human interests, constituting some ideal of a praiseworthy way of life, to lie behind the variety of moral judgments that a man makes, and that he has to justify to himself and to others; this is generally the topic of argument, when serious argument is pressed beyond a first stage, and when the participants do not appeal to a supernatural authority, as a stopping-point. The Aristotelian-type reconstruction shows the requirement of consistency in a man's policies, and therefore in his critical judgments, as they bear on public issues and on his personal relations. If one thinks of intuitionism, as an example of an alternative reconstruction of moral judgments, one sees how blank and unreal this type of account is; discussion of fundamental political issues, which may be thought the center of morality, is scarcely reconstructed at all, in this philosophy of bourgeois individualism.

Lastly, Aristotle's account of moral judgment permits other moral theories to be stated within its terminology and to be intelligible as moral theories. It is in this sense the most general, and the least restrictive, of the classical moral theories, most of which place narrow restrictions on what counts as a moral theory. Each of the other classical moral theories can be represented as singling out one human potentiality and interest as the supreme distinguishing feature of the human soul. Kant may be interpreted as representing disinterested respect for rational principle in action as the distinguishing human potentiality, which sets men apart from every other natural object. Mill represented the discovery of new forms and kinds of pleasure, and the liberty to make these discoveries, as the distinguishing potentiality of men, to which overriding value should be attached. The positive morality of these philosophers is in each case statable in Aristotelian terms, just because Aristotle's scheme requires one to ask—"What is the activity of the human soul which constitutes the highest merit, or excellence, of men, considered merely as human beings, and apart from any excellences or merits they have in subordinate roles? And what organization of society, and ways of life, are required for the realization of these excellences?" And any moral philosopher, who is not a pure meta-ethicist and has some first order morality, necessarily commits himself on at least the first of these questions. There are indeed pure meta-ethical theories, though they are rare. Professor Stevenson's reconstruction of the order and arrangement of moral discussion does not commit him to singling out the activities that constitute the supreme virtues, or virtue, of human beings; he does not tell his readers what criteria men actually do invoke, or ought to invoke, or must invoke, in making

85

decisions about the conduct of their life. But he originally achieved this moral neutrality by concentrating attention, not on the process of practical decision, but rather on the rhetoric, as he takes it to be, of moral comment.

Ryle's *The Concept of Mind*

The Concept of Mind has the radical incoherences natural to a book written in transition, the transition being from one conception of logic and philosophical method to another. Not Two Worlds, but One World; not a Ghost, but a Body; (people are not) Occult but Obvious. Professor Ryle has been betrayed into using the weapons of his enemy. It appears that the arguments which are fatal to the assertion in each case must be no less fatal to the counter-assertion: for they are *logical* arguments directed against the form and generality of such philosophical statements, irrespective of whether they are affirmed or denied; and these logical arguments are often used and implied by Professor Ryle himself as part of his attack, only to be neglected again in the polemical form of his conclusions. Thus there is (I think) an ambiguity of purpose confusing the argument from its beginning.

THE MYTH, ITS NATURE AND ORIGINS

A polemic requires an enemy. The difficulty is to pick out the Enemy in actual historical shape; it is Cartesianism (not simply and solely Descartes himself, p. 23), also "the official doctrine" and "the para-mechanical hypothesis." But precise historical identification, and even more the historical order of responsibility, are not relevant to Professor Ryle's purposes. He holds it enough that the false doctrine is known to have been held by at least one person (the author) in order that by its public destruction the true may be imparted. But the first cardinal mistake pervading the book is just this assumption that the *origin* of the conception of the mind as a ghost within a machine is of purely historical and of no philosophical interest. Had Professor Ryle pressed the inquiry into the origins of the conception (there is a half-page Historical Note on p. 23, which is particularly inadequate on the Greeks, who are here all-important), he must have realised that, so far from being imposed on the plain man by philosophical theorists, and even less by seventeenth century theorists, the myth of the mind as a ghost within the body is one of the most primitive and natural of all the innumerable myths which are deeply imbedded in the vocabulary and structure of our languages. The plain fact is that in many (perhaps most) European languages the words for mind, soul or spirit are the same as, or have the same roots as, the words for ghost, and were the same long before Descartes or modern mechanics were conceived. Apart altogether from the actual myth of detachable minds surviving as ghosts, which extends continuously from early epic into Christian literature, there is the traceable history of such words as ψυχή, πνεῦμα, anima, and many others, from which our vulgar concept of mind is descended. Such a philosophically relevant word-history would show the ghost and the two-substance conception of persons as the natural, vernacular mode of description existing before, and developing in part independently of, the attempts of Plato and of Christian theorists to systematise it as self-conscious doctrine. Professor Ryle throughout represents philosophers as corrupting the literal innocence of common sense speech with alien metaphors. In this he not only greatly exaggerates the influence of philosophers, and particularly of Descartes, on the forms of common speech, but (more seriously) neglects the fact, or rather the necessity, that the forms of common speech and its modes of description should be permeated with such metaphors, most of which can ultimately be traced back to underlying myths and imaginative pictures. In his suspicion of metaphor and of graphic representations in language he is himself a follower of Descartes. It is characteristically a philosopher's complaint (e.g. Bradley, Bergson, and many others) that we normally describe mental processes and conditions in terms which have been transferred from an original use in application to physical objects. As transferred terms are, by definition and etymology, metaphors, most commonplace psychological descriptions may therefore be said to be ultimately metaphorical. How otherwise can language develop?

Professor Ryle is here protesting not (as he believes) against a *philosophical theory* of mind, but against a universal feature of ordinary language itself—namely, that most of its forms of description have been and are being evolved by the constant transfer of terms from application in one kind of context to application in another, and in particular by the transfer of what were originally physical descriptions (e.g. "wires and pulleys," "impulses," "pushes and pulls," "agitations," etc.) into psychological descriptions. A typical instance of this Fallacy of Literalness comes in the discussion of the common and ancient phrase "In my head" (p. 35); the underlying assumption is that the "primary" or "real" sense of the word "in" is the spatial sense, and that other senses or uses must be metaphorical. In fact there are tens and perhaps hundreds of established uses of "In" in a non-spatial sense which can no longer be described as metaphorical (e.g. "In the English constitution," "in the spirit of the Act"). Even if some of these uses ultimately originated as spatial metaphors, their significance does not now depend on their being given any spatial or physical interpretation. Again, Professor Ryle distinguishes (p. 37) the tune which is only metaphorically in my head from noises which are *literally* in my head *by the use of a very significant criterion*; the *"real"* head-borne noises are those "which the doctor could hear through his stethoscope"—(cf. p. 199, "A special sense of 'in,' since the surgeon will not find it (sc, a sensation) under the person's epidermis"). These are only two instances of a fallacy that largely vitiates the discussion of impulses, motives, volitions, and mental conflicts, and to a less extent, of images and sense-impressions (consider the history of the words εἴδωλον, φάντασμα "species," "idea" and many others). It seemed as natural to the Greeks and Romans as it still does to us to describe the experience of mental conflict in terms of pushes and pulls, to describe themselves as *moved* to action, and to speak of images as mental pictures. The so-called para-mechanical hypothesis is no more than the very general fact that we naturally think and describe diagrammatically (e.g. about God, Time, and the English constitution), even when we are not talking about objects in space, or (the same fact differently expressed) we transfer terms originally used to describe visual or other sense-experience into other contexts, unconnected with sense-perception (most cognitive verbs are so derived). Another example—unphilosophical man had naturally talked of "the inward eye" (in the Bible, for instance) hundreds of years before introspection became "a term of art" (p. 163); the inner-outer "metaphor" was incorporated in the verbs and adjectives of ordinary speech long before it was formulated as explicit theory by modern epistemologists. Lastly, common-sense language is in fact, for better or for worse, firmly dualistic, in the sense that we do operate—and have operated since the earliest known literature—a distinction, or rather a whole set of distinctions, involving various and shifting criteria, between mental and physical states and events. We constantly ask, and are beginning to answer, various more or less general questions about the relation between a person's body and his mind, questions which cannot therefore be dismissed as "improper" (p. 168) if ordinary usage is to be authoritative. It is Professor Ryle, and not only Descartes, who displays an a priori theory of language involving a conflict with established usage, when he rejects (p. 22) the dogma that "there occur physical processes and mental processes; that there are mechanical causes of corporeal movements, and mental causes of corporeal movements" and argues that "these and other analogous conjunctions are absurd," his cryptic reason being "that the phrase 'there occur mental processes' does not *mean the same sort of thing** as 'there occur physical processes' and therefore that it makes no sense to conjoin or disjoin the two" (p. 22). Certainly when, outside philosophy, we habitually distinguish between the mental and physical causes of bodily conditions or movements, we are often confused, and would almost always find difficulty in formulating the very various and also historically changing criteria of distinction which we apply in different contexts; and certainly Descartes in his rigid formulation deliberately over-simplified the distinction in the interests of his programme of science (p. 21). But just because Professor Ryle has from the beginning confused a general feature of common language with a particular metaphysical theory, it is never clear precisely whom he is attacking when he attacks the Ghost and therefore what weapons are appropriate. His own explanations of his method (pp. 8, 16, 17, 21-23) unfortunately involve such notoriously obscure expressions as "logical category," "logical type" and "the sort of thing which is meant by . . ."; obscure, because they at first look like distinctions in actual grammar (see p. 101) but, where attacked with counter-examples, turn into some ideal, "Logical Grammar" (p. 244). In fact behind this ideal grammar there is implied the literalist theory of language, which betrays itself in many of the arguments used.

WHAT DO OUR PRINCIPAL MENTAL CONCEPTS
STAND FOR?

This is the fatal question in terms of which much of the argument proceeds; take any psychological verb, and ask

---

* The asterisk throughout indicates that the italics are my own.

whether it "stands for," "names," "denotes," "signifies," or "designates," either an occurrence (episode) or a disposition, two processes or one process, a relation ("such transitive verbs do not signify relations" p. 209), a thing ("the phrase 'my twinge' does not stand for any sort of thing or 'term,'" p. 209) ("the objects proper to such verbs are things and episodes"), a performance or a manner of performance. "Liking and Disliking, Joy and grief, desire and aversion are not. . . . episodes, and so are not *the sorts of things** which can be witnessed or un-witnessed" (p. 109). "The verb and its accusative ('Feel a tickle') are two expressions *for the same thing*" (p. 101). Do such verbs as "minding" and "migrating" stand for single processes or for a complex of processes? (pp. 136-38). Many of the arguments in the book seem to turn on these Categorical distinctions descried in reality, so reminiscent of earlier philosophers' distinctions between Substances, Qualities and Relations, as though there were *natural* or real accusatives and adverbs to be found behind the vagaries of actual grammar. On what grounds does Professor Ryle decide that there are no acts "answering to" such verbs as "see," "hear," "taste," "deduce," and "recall" in the way in which familiar acts and operations do answer to such verbs as "kick," "run," "look," "listen," "wrangle" and "tell"? (p. 151). The grounds suggested in this particular passage are insufficient, namely, that certain adverbs which can in English be combined with the second class cannot be combined with the first; for it is always easy to find many exceptions to such generalisations about English idioms, even apart from the idioms of other equally adequate languages. Yet the counter examples will always be dismissed as special cases (e.g. as not "the dominant sense" of the word) precisely because Professor Ryle, in common with all other serious philosophers, here lays emphasis on a particular English idiom, only as a *pointer* to something other than itself, namely, to necessary *logical* distinctions. Words such as "act," "event," "performance," "episode," "occurrence," "disposition," "achievement" and, derivatively, such words as "mood" and "agitation," function in this book mainly (but not consistently) as logical words, in the special sense that to say that an English verb is the name of an achievement or a disposition, and not of an episode, is *primarily* to say something about the kind of evidence or argument which is relevant to any statement in which it occurs. So on p. 83—"The word 'emotion' is used to designate at least *three or four kinds of different things*,* which I shall call 'inclinations' (or 'motives'), 'moods,' 'agitations' (or 'commotions') and 'feelings,'" and "feelings are occurrences"—but "Inclinations and moods are not occurrences. They are propensities, not acts or states."—These sentences can be understood when taken together with later statements such as (p. 244) "Words like 'distress,' 'distaste,' 'grief' and 'annoyance' are names of moods." To say of a particular word that it is the name of, or designates, a mood and that moods are not occurrences, amounts to saying (misleadingly) something about the kind of evidence or tests of truth which are appropriate to any statement in which this word occurs. But the non-logical terminology of "different kinds of things designated" sometimes leads Professor Ryle into uses which are inappropriate to such category-terms. He asks (p. 138) whether the same verb "minding" stands for two processes or one—and this is a form of argument which occurs repeatedly. If "process" is here marking a logical distinction, and is a logical or category word and not a descriptive expression, the question as it stands must be meaningless. It is surely only this naive correspondence theory of language which leads to the remark (p. 142) that only one thing need be going on when a bird is described either as "migrating" or as "flying south." Is it to be expected that there should be a visibly separate proc-

93

ess corresponding to each verb, each perceptible process being uniquely named by its own verb? Because words like "activity" and "process" are category-words, it is equally meaningless to say (p. 139) that minding or the brow-knitting associated with it are the same activities or that they are different activities, unless this is a question about the conventional rules of use of the two verbs, that is, the question whether any statement containing the second entails, or is entailed by, some statement containing the first; the answer to the question so interpreted is simple—"No." But for Professor Ryle the answer is difficult (pp. 138-41) because his terminology of "standing for," "designating," and "naming," here leads him to write as if there were a real answer, independent of the conventions of a particular language, to such questions as "Does the verb 'mind' or 'try' designate a single, distinct activity or a complex of activities?"—as though the world consisted of just so many distinguishable Activities (or Facts, p. 140, or States or Things) waiting to be counted and named.

In this crucial passage (pp. 138-41) the underlying confusion in the use of these category-terms emerges on the surface; for it suddenly becomes clear that there must be many verbs (e.g. "concentrating," "dying," "being anaesthetised" and countless others) which stand for an occurrence as opposed to a disposition in some of the many senses given of this central distinction, namely, that they name incidents that can be significantly dated or clocked, or that certain adverbs are applicable to them, but which in another and predominant sense of the distinction are dispositional verbs, namely, that any statement containing them can be accepted as true only if some testable hypothetical statements about the future are accepted as true. Yet the *general* thesis of the book—that there are no such things as "mental happenings" (p. 161), that to speak of a person's mind is to speak "of certain ways in which some of

94

the incidents of his one life are ordered" (p. 167)—largely hinges on this distinction between occurrences and dispositions. The core of the argument is that to talk of a person's mind is "to talk of the person's abilities, liabilities and inclinations to do and undergo certain sorts of things, and of the doing and undergoing of these things in the ordinary world" (p. 199). So the original plan of the book seems to have been to re-interpret most of the statements that have generally been construed as categorical statements about "ghostly" (= invisible, intangible, inaudible) events, as hypothetical statements about events in the so-called "ordinary" world, where "ordinary" strangely means (literalism or correspondence theory again) whatever can be perceived by anyone (not "Privileged Access") by the use of one or more of five senses (also stethoscopes, cameras, gramophones, and other accredited instruments). So putative statements, whether biographical or autobiographical, about immaterial and imperceptible occurrences must in each representative case be exhibited as disguised hypothetical statements about perceptible behaviour.

The argument about occurrences and dispositions, therefore, at first looks like one further application of the old high empiricist Hume-and-Russell method of "analysis," the logical construction method, whereby impalpable and oppressive substances, the Mind no less than the State, are shown to be logically reducible to less pretentious material. But such a simple design is never in fact executed, Professor Ryle himself indicating (e.g. p. 117), not only where in particular such reductions or rules of translation cannot be provided (e.g. for statements about emotional agitations, hankerings, pangs and thrills, silent calculations and imaginings), but also hinting in various places that to look for translations of categorical statements about mental states and activities into hypothetical statements about perceptible behaviour is, as a matter of logic, a pure mistake. The

95

double distinction, occurrence versus disposition, categorical versus hypothetical, in fact breaks down in application, because almost any statement, even the most evidently simple, may be said to be, in Professor Ryle's confusion of senses, *both* categorical *and* hypothetical (e.g. p. 228 " 'He espied the thimble' has a considerable logical complexity"; p. 141 "Most of the examples ordinarily adduced of categorical statements are mongrel categoricals"; and see p. 220 on the logical complexity of "The field is green" or "This bicycle cost £12"). But if this distinction is shown to be unworkable, and cannot be clearly formulated, the whole account of the relation between mind and body—"Overt intelligent performances are not clues to the workings of minds; they *are* those workings" (p. 58)—collapses with it. It must be re-formulated.

Occurrence versus Disposition as a Pseudo-Logical Distinction

There are three traditional enquiries that issue in distinctions between types of expression in a language; grammar, logic in the strict or textbook sense, and theory of knowledge, sometimes called "logic" in a loose sense. In grammar individual words may be classified into types by the forms which they may assume, or the positions which they may occupy, in various typical sentences of a particular language. In logic *sentences* are classified into types by the positions that they may occupy in typical formal or deductive arguments and, derivatively from this, certain individual words (e.g. "all," "if," "or," etc.) may be singled out as logical words because of their formal inference-grounding functions. A sentence is classified as hypothetical in textbook logic if and only if it is explicitly of a form which indicates that certain deductive inferences or transformations are allowed in respect of it, irrespective of the topic discussed in the sentence or the particular occasion of its use.

Clearly Professor Ryle's occurrence—disposition distinction is wholly different from a strictly logical distinction in at least two all-important respects: (a) it is generally applied (the analogy of grammar here misleads him) to *individual words* or *phrases* (e.g. "believing," "understanding," "knowing," "trying," "thinking"), taken apart from the various forms of sentence in which they may occur: (b) it is designed to mark, not solely or primarily the *deductive* inferences arising from the rules of use of particular expressions, but chiefly the *tests* that are appropriate to the sentences in which the expressions occur. "To rectify the logic of mental conduct concepts" (p. 16), Professor Ryle's own description of his aim, is to correct what other philosophers have said about the *methods of verification* of statements involving mental concepts (i.e. not Introspection, not Privileged Access); "roughly, the mind is not the topic of sets of *untestable** categorical propositions, but the topic of sets of *testable** hypothetical and semi-hypothetical propositions" (p. 46). He is throughout trying to show, taking each of the main mental concepts in turn, that any statement involving these concepts can be impartially tested, its truth or falsity decided, solely or primarily, or at least in part, by reference to the overt and perceptible performance and reactions of the person concerned. So the "logic of a description" (p. 104) or "sentence" here means "the standard tests appropriate to" or "the method of verification associated with" —which is logic in the wider sense, also sometimes called epistemology, that is, characterising in very general terms the kind of reasons that we normally give in accepting or rejecting statements about the mental activities of persons. I suspect that one of the main confusions of the book comes from the use of distinctions, such as the hypothetical-categorical distinctions, which are borrowed from logic in the strict sense, in order to mark distinctions which (I shall argue) cannot be strictly logical.

97

Professor Ryle is not really arguing that all or most statements involving mental concepts are (or are expressible as) hypothetical statements about overt behaviour, but (and it is very different) that to give reasons for accepting or rejecting such statements must always involve making some hypothetical statements about overt behaviour. Typical mental concepts are called dispositional and typical statements in which they occur are called "law-like propositions" (pp. 167 and 169) only because it is claimed that their application or assertion must in general be supported by observation of patterns of overt behaviour. See particularly pp. 167 ff. "The *test** of whether you understood it. . . ." "How we *establish** and apply certain law-like propositions about the overt and silent behaviour of persons. . . ." "I *discover** my or your motives in much, though not quite the same way as I discover my or your abilities. . . ." (See also p. 136 on "minding.") So the force of this analysis of the main mental concepts in terms of the distinction between disposition and occurrence is that almost all statements about mental states and activities are confirmed or rejected as tenable or untenable *interpretations* of overt behaviour. They are denied the status of reports or of narrative of incidents (p. 125) (and therefore misleadingly denied the status of categorical propositions) only because evidence drawn from a variety of overt behaviour is always, or generally, relevant in deciding whether they are true or false.

Proving Too Much

But Professor Ryle himself indicates (pp. 239 and 317) the fallacy which undermines any attempt so to generalise epistemological ("How do we test?" "How do we discover?") distinctions and to convert them into distinctions of logic. He suggests that for any given statement, whether involving mental or other concepts, there are an indefinite number of possible answers to the questions "How do you know?" or "What are the reasons for saying?" *depending on who made the statement, when and in what circumstances.* Such epistemological distinctions—("what kind of test is appropriate?") can never be applied to any sentence or class of sentences *without specification of the particular occasion of use of the sentence in question.* If one takes either the sentence "I am in a state of panic" or the sentence "He was in a panic" apart from any particular context or occasion of their use (see p. 97), and considers them simply as *sentences of the English language*, one can only explain their meaning and use in the language by bringing out their strictly logical relations to other sentences in the language, that is, by showing what they entail or what else *must* be true if they are true. But unless a particular occasion of use is specified, one cannot answer, *a priori and in general*, the epistemologist's question "How can these statements be tested and their truth established?"; for, as Professor Ryle self-destructively says (p. 239), there are any number of ways in which we may legitimately confirm or refute the statements conveyed on different occasions of the use of these sentences, and a great variety of different kinds of reason may in different circumstances be accepted as sufficient justification of them. The answer to the question will generally be altogether different in kind if I am testing my own statement about my panic and not someone else's statement about theirs, and very different again if I am making the statement contemporaneously with the experience which it describes. Professor Ryle's *general* thesis, no less than its rival, rests on this confusion much between (a) showing the truth-conditions of a given sentence, that is, what is entailed by the sentence as part of the rules of its use as a sentence of the language: this can be shown quite

99

generally and without mentioning particular contexts of use,[1] and (b) describing a range of typical conditions under which someone (not anyone, but someone in a particular situation) might properly claim to know, or to have established beyond reasonable doubt, that the statement in question is true. This is the confusion which either comes from, or leads to, *identifying* the meaning of a statement with *the* method of its verification, and therefore identifying the statement itself with what would (in some specified conditions of use) be taken as sufficient evidence for it. Because overt behaviour often constitutes for most people the best, and, in some conditions of utterance, the sole available evidence for statements about mental activities and states of mind, such statements come to be *identified* with hypothetical statements about behaviour—e.g. "Even to be for a brief moment scandalised or in a panic is, for that moment, to be liable to do some such things as stiffen or shriek" (p. 97); sometimes, but not *necessarily* and always. Again, "In ascribing a specific motive to a person we are describing the sorts of things that he tends to try to do" (p. 112); usually, but again not *necessarily*: we might discover from his diary, or by overhearing a soliloquy, exactly what moved him to action on this single and quite exceptional occasion. Again (p. 136) we *usually* test a child's concentration by testing his performance, but we do not *identify* the performance and the concentration, precisely because although the first may often (not always or necessarily) be properly accepted as sufficient evidence for the other, it is not a *necessary* condition in the sense of being in *all* circumstances the *only* kind of relevant evidence available, either to the child himself or to the teacher. But

[1] Analysis in this sense of what is necessarily involved in being in a panic must disregard the words (pronouns, demonstratives, proper names, etc.) which can only be interpreted in a particular context of use: it only elucidates the predicate "is in a panic." The case of tenses is more complicated.

it is the mark of dispositional terms in the *strictly logical sense* of the word—e.g. of things "brittle," of persons "irritable"—that *any* transparent statement involving them, whatever the occasion of its utterance, can (as a matter of correct English) be accepted as true only if some hypothetical statements about the perceptible actions or reactions of the thing or person concerned are accepted as true. Thus "He is an irritable man but never shows it in his behaviour" is (as normally used) a contradiction in terms, while "He often feels irritable but never shows it" (see p. 203 for sentences of this pattern) is not self-contradictory or meaningless, although often to observers other than the subject himself no means may be available of testing the truth of the statement; whether any test is possible, and what kind of test, must depend on the particular circumstances. A statement only becomes void, if it is *logically* precluded, by the rules of use of the words involved, that *anyone* should *ever* under *any* conditions establish its truth or falsity beyond reasonable doubt.

It follows that the *same* logical mistake is involved whatever *general* account is given of the logic of statements containing mental concepts, where "the logic" means "*the* method of establishing the truth of . . .*"; the too-general thesis of the solipsist (Privileged Access)—"I know about my own states of mind directly or by introspection, but I must always infer what your state of mind is and I can never in principle check my inference"—Professor Ryle effectively undermines by showing that conditions can always be described in which the observable behaviour of the subject would properly be quoted as sufficient reason for rejecting any autobiographical statement, whatever the statement may be; the possibility of obtaining relevant behavioural evidence is never excluded, *as a matter of logic or of the meaning of the words involved*, although on *many occasions of the use of such sentences* as, "I was thinking of . . ."

"I dreamt of . . . ," "I felt . . . ," no such tests of the truth of the particular statement made may be available to the audience.

But Professor Ryle, at the same time proves too much by proving, apparently as a *general* thesis of logic, that (p. 155) "The sorts of things that I can find out about myself are the same as the sorts of things that I can find out about other people, and the methods are much the same": and again the odd but revealing statement (p. 114) "In fact they (people) are relatively tractable and relatively easy to understand" (see also p. 172 about "familiar techniques of assessing").[2] This is open paradox because (if any general statement is to be made) people notoriously *are* occult in at least one very important sense, namely, that in comparison with animals and inanimate things, it is difficult to establish the truth about them, if only because there is more to be known from more sources of information. They are occult and are said to have inner lives, just because, and in the sense that, in establishing the truth of many kinds of statements about them (about their thoughts, feelings, day dreams, night dreams, stifled impulses, imaginings, concealed hopes and plans), I am often (but not always) concerned in weighing and comparing two different kinds of evidence—what they themselves confess or report and what I can observe independently of their avowals. Just because they alone of natural objects are language-users and therefore are potential reporters, they are (unlike stones and dogs) liars, hypocrites, and suppressors of the truth about themselves. It is just this conflict between what they report

[2] In fact all the familiar techniques of assessing people are constantly questioned even by the most philosophically innocent. The *criteria* of assessment are disputed in a way which has no parallel in the assessment of the properties of physical things. About moods, motives, desires, fears and ambitions we feel a general and constant dissatisfaction with our methods, however complacent we may be about skills and competences. We are always ready for new suggestions, e.g. from Freud.

(and fail to report) and how they behave which distinguishes them as occult relatively to animals and even infants who, because they make no disclosures, allow no contrast between inner and outer life. Most "mental" concepts therefore are used in application to animals (and hesitantly to infants) *solely* and always as interpretations of observable behaviour.[3] We peer at people and wonder what is going on "inside" them occultly, the wonder having point and significance just because there is always a possibility of disclosure and therefore always a possibility of non-disclosure or lies. It is this puzzlement, peculiar to the description of the states and activities of human minds, which is paradoxically omitted in Professor Ryle's polemic. His counter-theory leads him to say, what is certainly false (p. 168) "Where logical candour is required from us, we ought to follow the example set by novelists, biographers and diarists, *who speak only of persons doing and undergoing things.*"* In fact, very many, perhaps the majority of novelists and diarists, and some biographers, find comedy or tragedy precisely in the contrast between the narrative description which an observer reasonably gives of a person's life, with no data other than his own and other people's observations, and the missing confession or avowal which the person himself, if suitably gifted, may supply; and some novelists, and even more diarists, have been exclusively concerned with the provision of the missing data, that is, with that uncommon kind of autobiographical description which, in a universal and natural metaphor, is called the description of inner life. Professor Ryle himself admits (p. 58) that Boswell's description of Johnson's mind was incomplete, "since there were notoriously some thoughts which *Johnson kept carefully to himself** and there must have been many

[3] Do dogs dream? We hesitate as to what kind of question this is, because we are uncertain whether we may not one day obtain better evidence; the possibility of evidence beyond their visible twitchings is not definitely and finally excluded.

103

dreams, day dreams and silent babblings,[4] which only *John-son could have recorded*[*] and only a James Joyce would wish him to have recorded." But here lies no less the novelists' than the philosophers' problem; for we ask—since the story *must* always be incomplete unless told in the first person singular, with the hero also the narrator, must each character be his own centre of narration in order to construct the complete story involving them all? Or is there no such single story, but as many stories as there are characters?

PRIVILEGED ACCESS

On this crux of the use of mental concepts with the first person singular Professor Ryle again approaches, but (I think) falls short of, a solution (see pp. 60-61); there is the same ambiguity of purpose (pp. 183-84). Will he say that first person reports of mental activities are reducible to statements about perceptible behaviour? Nearly, but not quite. "We eavesdrop on our own voiced utterances and our own silent monologues. On noticing these we are preparing ourselves to do something new, namely, to describe the frames of mind which these utterances disclose. . . . I can pay heed to what I overhear you saying as well as to what I overhear myself saying, though I cannot overhear your silent colloquies with yourself. Nor can I read your diary, if you write in a cipher, or keep it under lock and key." The impossibility (logical) of my hearing you think (silent colloquies), if you refuse to utter or even whisper your thoughts[5] is radically unlike an unfortunate incapacity to

[4] Surely "silent babblings" (cf. "silent colloquies" on p. 182) is metaphorical in Professor Ryle's sense if anything is: also "operations" with propositions (p. 30). Yet such phrases (e.g. "silent monologues") enter into his analysis of thinking.

[5] Compare "He cannot think without talking to himself" with "He cannot think without pencil and paper." If talking to oneself is a way of thinking, as drawing diagrams or scribbling are ways of thinking, then it ought not to be identified with thinking.

decipher and unlock (empirical); I often fail simply because there is nothing to hear, even with a stethoscope. I may *see* you thinking—"I saw him sitting in the corner thinking." But if I am asked "How do you know that he was thinking?" the answer "I saw him" is by itself insufficient, while it is normally a sufficient answer to a similar question about your sitting or your talking[6]; and this (an epistemological or "How-do-you-know" distinction) leads us to say that I always have to *infer* that you are thinking, and also that thinking, unlike sitting and talking, is ("strictly") invisible (= ghostly). But you yourself always know both whether you are thinking and also of what you are thinking, and never have any need of inference in the matter; that is, if you declare "I am thinking of climbing Helvellyn," it is pointless and silly to ask "How do you know?" or "Are you certain?"; and the first question seems equally inapplicable when you avow your sensations (p. 209), or a momentary mood or frame of mind, which leads Professor Ryle desperately to assimilate avowals of the last kind to gestures and mere expressions of mood rather than to statements (p. 103). But an avowal, unlike a yawn, may be false and may be discovered to be a lie or mis-description by a careful collection of evidence. There is no *logical* difference between your avowal ("I am thinking of . . .") and my diagnosis, interpretation or guess ("You are thinking of . . ."); two people have made the same categorical statement; but my justification for making it, if any, is naturally very different from yours in these circumstances. The point becomes clearer as soon as it is noticed that the challenges "How do you know?" or "What is your evidence?" are inapplicable

[6] But would Professor Ryle as a literalist say that I only "strictly" hear the sounds of the words, and not what you say, your statements? Do I "strictly" see only the movement of your pen, and not the signing of the cheque? And are these two processes or one? At the cinema I really literally see only an illuminated sheet of linen: the prairies are "a certain sort of dreaming" (p. 255).

to avowals of thoughts and sensations (e.g. "I am in pain"),
only when these are expressed in the present tense. If you
make the statement about your thoughts or sensations a
year later, or an hour before, you, no less than I, might reasonably be required to produce evidence that these were
or will be your thoughts and sensations; but whoever makes
it and whenever it is made, the possibility of finding sufficient evidence against it is never in principle, though often
in practice, excluded. For any avowal, whether of thoughts,
feelings, even dreams,[7] conditions can always be described
in which it would generally be withdrawn, in the face of
further evidence, even by the subject himself, however rare
such conditions may be ("You could not have been in pain;
you were anaesthetised." "You did not dream of peacocks:
you were awake at the time and read about them in this
book"). Privileged Access ("Only I can ever know about
my own states of mind") *cannot* be true, generalised as a
point of logic: nor, for precisely the same reasons, can Professor Ryle's Open Access.

AVOWALS VERSUS BEHAVIOUR AS EVIDENCE

But of course there are great and also subtle differences, to
some of which Professor Ryle alludes, between (*a*) *pure
descriptions* of sensations (p. 209), also of dreams, of momentary moods, and impulses (p. 103), of mental distresses,
thrills, qualms and agitations, in which the autobiographer
generally exposes himself to the fewest possibilities of correction, by describing in a way which is essentially figura-
tive, indefinite and imprecise; and (*b*) the official diagnoses
in standard terms of emotions, attitudes, intellectual efforts

[7] Dreams, about which Professor Ryle says little, are important (e.g.
in Descartes) because they are the archetype of ghostly occult experiences: they admit no avowals in the present tense; I cannot normally ask you what you are dreaming about and you cannot say—
almost logically cannot. But some trance mediums and other seers try
to make the best of both worlds.

and achievements, inclinations, and motives, diagnoses which are sometimes in part based upon such subjective descriptions of symptoms, but which are themselves relatively definite and therefore more precisely testable. But because his theory leads him to deny in general the peculiar occultness of persons, that is, the characteristic conflict between what people say of themselves (their avowals) and how they behave, Professor Ryle neglects the all-important and revealing function of the word "really" in combination with mental concepts. "You do not *really* enjoy gardening (avowal), because when it rains . . ." (behaviour). "He does not *really* believe in the coming Revolution (as he declares) because . . ." "His *real* fears, hopes, and ambitions (as opposed to his declared) motive. . . ." "He was not *really* in love (though he said he was), because. . . ." The force of the word is generally to impose more than normally stringent conditions for the use of the mental concept by stressing one kind of evidence at the expense of another, namely, the subject's behaviour in contrast to his avowals, the implied opposition being "He declares this, and there is no reason to suppose that he is lying, but he behaves. . . ." So "He does not *really* believe in life after death" has a different use, and (in one sense) therefore a different meaning, from simply "He does not believe in life after death," the implied antithesis, what is denied, being different in the two uses; and to assess one's own or somebody else's *real* motives, fears, desires, ambitions etc. is to make a statement which has a different purpose, and which generally involves attending to a different kind and quantity of evidence, than is involved in the corresponding straightforward and unqualified assessment. The "really" statements, even when they are autobiographical, are always intended more as interpretative diagnoses in the sense that they draw attention away from declared symptoms to a wider range of patterns of behaviour. Because a wider range of evidence is involved, there are more occasions for saying "I think this is my *real* attitude, motive or feeling, but I am not certain," than there are for saying "I think this is my attitude or motive or feeling but I am not certain." Since his thesis compels him to overstress the evidence of perceptible behaviour Professor Ryle is often—e.g. pp. 107-109 on "enjoyment," and pp. 134-145 on "belief"—in fact describing how we generally test statements about what someone really enjoys or really believes, when he claims to be describing the tests we apply to the corresponding straightforward statements. Having included "unstudied talk" or self-expression under the heading of behaviour, he has destroyed the characteristic opposition (avowal versus behaviour, words versus deeds) which constitutes the peculiarity and the difficulty of assessments of people—even autobiographical assessments.[8]

WILL, SENSATIONS, AND IMAGES

(*a*) *Will.* It has been my argument that Professor Ryle has not decided whether he is saying (a) that no mental concepts "stand for" imperceptible (= ghostly) processes or states: all "designate" some perceptible or nearly-perceptible (e.g. "silent colloquies") pattern of behaviour: or less drastically (b) that all statements involving mental concepts are in principle testable, directly or indirectly and in various degrees, by observation of the behaviour of the person concerned. The mountaineer may pause to think what to do next, the chess-player to plan his moves; someone asks, "What are you doing?" "I am planning

[8] Professor Ryle takes simulation and hypocrisy (p. 173) in addition to deliberate lying (miscalled insincerity on p. 102) and deliberate reticence, as the primary forms of human deceit or occultness. But there are more complicated cases—e.g. of *general* insincerity, self-dramatisation and self-deceit, the analysis of which would (I think) involve this important contrast between "feeling" and "really feeling," "believing" and "really believing," etc.

my next move." In every sense these are incidents in the narrative of the day, clockable episodes, acts ("you ought to have planned your next move"), and such a report of them is logically independent of any hypothetical statements about overt behaviour. But they are worrying to Professor Ryle—they are not *strictly* visible (although one can sometimes see people thinking) or audible incidents; so he tries to convert them either into just-not-audible incidents ("the trick" of thinking so quietly that no one except the subject can eavesdrop) or into dispositions to climb or play thoughtfully and in a planned manner. Equally "resolving or making up our minds," "making an effort of will," "trying," "concentrating" are recognisable and dateable activities, but not *strictly* visible, audible, or otherwise open to inspection by witnesses, who must therefore guess or infer their occurrence or simply wait to be told. Professor Ryle admits that these peculiarly human and mental occurrences do occur (pp. 68-69), although he also mistakenly thinks that if he can show, as of course he can, that observation of behaviour may provide evidence of such an occurrence, he has thereby shown that it is not really or wholly an occurrence, but also a propensity to behave in certain ways (p. 72 and pp. 138 ff.). But having admitted the irreducible concepts of "trying" or "deciding," which many philosophers would take as the defining activities of the human mind (see p. 129), it is odd to dismiss "the will" as a myth (pp. 63 ff.) because of the Kantian theories associated with it; and it is both historically and logically untrue that the problem of free-will arises wholly or mainly from Mechanism. Briefly, we are not prepared to say "He ought not to have done it" unless we are also prepared to say "He could have avoided doing it if he had tried or if he had made an effort." "He could not have helped doing it, however hard he tried" is usually a conclusive rejection of the moral imputation "He ought not. . . ." Everyone seems to know the difference between making an effort to stifle (physical metaphor) an impulse and not making an effort, and we sometimes even attach meaning to degrees of effort. The dipsomaniac may be held to be blameless because helpless, where "helpless" means "no effort of will would make any difference," while the culpable drunkard is culpable because he fails to make the effort of will which would make the difference. It is therefore not true that the perplexity arises solely, or even mainly, from asking whether volitions are the effects of mechanical causes, although it is true that "He could have avoided it if he had tried" has often been confused by philosophers with "There is no causal explanation of his action," particularly in the traditional formula "Ought implies can" (= "In his power"). The perplexity arises rather from the effects of increasing scientific (and particularly physiological) knowledge on our readiness (reasonably or unreasonably) to say "He could have avoided it if he had tried." What Professor Ryle with the aid of parody dismisses as the "silly view" of moral philosophers—that increasing scientific knowledge diminishes the field within which moral terms are applicable—so far from being a silly philosophical theory, is a plainly observable fact about common usage. As knowledge advances, sin, crime and wickedness become maladjustment, delinquency and disease ("You cannot blame them: they cannot help it: it is a matter of glands, alterable states of the brain, complexes and neuroses, conditions producing juvenile delinquency," etc.). It was just this revolution of thought and language, this gradual restriction in the use of moral terms as scientific knowledge advances, which Kant anxiously, and Spinoza calmly, anticipated.

(b) *Sensations.* The same ambiguity of purpose, the conflict between general thesis and particular instance produces contradictions. "An oculist who cannot speak my language is without the best source of information about my visual sensations" (p. 209). This is plainly true, but it seems incompatible with "Secondary quality adjectives are used and used only for the reporting of publicly ascertainable facts about common objects" (p. 220). It is also incompatible with questioning the propriety of this non-technical, centuries-old use of the word "sensation" (pp. 200 and 243). Again, " 'He espied the thimble' has a considerable logical complexity but does not therefore report a considerable complication of processes" (p. 230), " 'The field is green' entails (hypothetical) propositions about observers" (p. 200) —these two propositions (which I consider false) might be taken to define Phenomenalism, the theory which Professor Ryle thinks he has refuted. His two main reasons for rejecting the theory are (a) that there are no such things or *objects* as sensations (p. 214, p. 236), the implication being that nouns ought to stand for things or objects, as verbs for processes; (b) that "in its dominant sense" (p. 238), "see" is an achievement word like "solve" and so can only be used "in its primary sense" of perception of physical objects which actually exist (p. 238). The justification given for this revision of ordinary usage is that we cannot be said to "see incorrectly." The confusion in this argument is between seeing and *describing* what we see; of course we cannot see either correctly or incorrectly; we can only *describe* what we see correctly or incorrectly; and of course we withdraw a claim to have seen a linnet when we have been convinced that in fact there was no linnet (p. 238). But this does not necessarily involve us in admitting that we did not see anything, or that it was not a case of seeing, but only that it was not a linnet which we saw. We may see spots in front of the eyes, reflections in the water, rainbows, houses in the distance in a picture—there are hundreds of (for some purposes usefully) distinguishable contexts in which "see" is

111

used, but there is no one achievement or performance which the verb "denotes." "Gate-posts" is a specimen of the sorts of complements which alone can be significantly given to such expressions as "John Doe is looking at a so and so" (p. 238); but when he looks at the gate-post in a picture, or at the sky, or at his own reflection, are these the same sorts of complements?

(c) *Images*—the same ambiguity. First, the sweeping general thesis "There are just things and events, people witnessing some of these things and events, and people fancying themselves witnessing things and events that they are not witnessing" (p. 249). But Professor Ryle does not really cling to this programme: it is plainly false, since we may imagine things without fancying ourselves witnessing them. The lesser thesis is—"Roughly, imaging occurs, but images are not seen" (p. 247). The arguments are the same: restriction of "seeing" to "literally seeing" with "the eyes open," and under conditions in which other people could also see what the subject claims to be seeing; so the drunkard does not literally see snakes, nor do we literally see (presumably) mirror-images, after-images and eidetic images, nor do we literally smell obsessional smells. And this is to prove that "There are no such *objects** as mental pictures" —as though it were wrong to use the noun unless there are solid objects (gate-posts and grit) to correspond to it. To enforce this principle would be allowing the fear of ghosts to drive us into pidgin English—which might be the ultimately literal language.

CONCLUSION

Professor Ryle writes with Aristotelian pregnancy, and almost every paragraph contains observations which require, and will certainly be given, many thousands of words of discussion; for example, the section on "The Systematic

Elusiveness of 'I'" would alone require almost as much space for adequate discussion as is available for this review, and a sentence on p. 189 on the conception of a person as body and non-body in itself provides the clue to the Cartesian myth. It is the mark of enduring philosophical works that by their force and originality they both provoke and endlessly sustain such piecemeal nibbling as this, without their content being within sight of exhaustion; and, like most permanently interesting philosophies, together with a peculiar theory of language *The Concept of Mind* conveys a sharply personal and definite view of the world: a world of solid and manageable objects, without hidden recesses, each visibly functioning in its own appropriate pattern.

The Analogy of Feeling

I am concerned in this paper with only one source of one of the many puzzles associated with our knowledge of other minds. It is often said that statements about other people's feelings and sensations cannot be justified as being based upon inductive arguments of any ordinary pattern, that is, as being inferences from the observed to the unobserved of a familiar and accepted form. I shall argue that they can be so justified. I will not deny that such inferences are difficult; everyone has always known, apart altogether from philosophical theory, that they are difficult; but I will deny that they are *logically* peculiar or invalid, when considered simply as inductive arguments. I believe that modern philosophers have found something logically peculiar and problematical about our inferences to other minds, and have even denied the possibility of such inferences, at least in part because of an incomplete understanding of the functions of pronouns and of other contextual expressions in our language; in particular they have misunderstood the proper use of these expressions in combination with words like "know," "certain," "verify," "evidence." If I am right, it becomes easier to explain why what the solipsist wants to say cannot properly be said, why solipsism is a *linguistically* absurd thesis, and at the same time to explain why it is a thesis which tempts those who confuse epistemological distinctions with logical distinctions.

For reasons that will become clear later, I shall introduce two quasi-technical terms. As specimens of the type of sentence, the status of which, as normally used, is in dispute, I shall take the sentences, "I feel giddy," "you feel giddy," "he feels giddy," and so on through the other cases of the verb "feel." Any normal use of the sentence "I feel giddy"

will be, in my invented terminology, a specimen of an autobiographical statement, where this phrase is simply short-
hand for "a statement describing somebody's momentary
feelings or sensations which is expressed in the first person
singular." Any normal use of the sentences "he feels giddy,"
"you feel giddy," or "they feel giddy," will be specimens of
heterobiographical statements—that is, statements describing somebody's feelings which are not expressed in the first
person singular. "We feel giddy," as normally used, would
be a statement which is partly autobiographical and partly
heterobiographical in my sense. It may sometimes happen
that someone chooses to tell the story of his own inner life,
using not the first person singular, but the third person, or
some fictitious or other name. It is actually possible to write
one's own obituary notice, using the third person and including within it descriptions which are intended as descriptions of one's own feelings and sensations. But on such
occasions the pronouns (or verb-cases for an inflected language) are misleadingly used, and deliberately so. The
ordinary function of the word "I" (or of the corresponding
verb-case in inflected languages) is to indicate explicitly
that the author of the statement is also the designated subject of the statement. The exceptional, deliberately misleading uses mentioned above consciously take advantage of
this fact. By "an autobiographical statement" I shall mean
a statement describing someone's feelings or sensations
which explicitly shows, in the actual form of its expression,
that the author of the statement is also its designated subject. A statement, e.g. in a novel, about which we can argue,
by reference to evidence external to the verbal form of the
statement itself, whether it is, as a matter of fact, an autobiographical statement, will not therefore be an autobiographical statement in my artificial and restricted sense.

It has often been noticed that there are certain peculiarities about these first person singular statements about feel-

ings and sensations, particularly when the main verb is in the present tense. These peculiarities have led some philosophers to characterise them as incorrigible statements and have led others to deny them the title of "statement" altogether. The peculiarities emerge in the use of words like "know," "believe," and "certain" in combination with these sentences. In respect of most statements, "I think that P is true but I may be mistaken" and "I have established that P is true beyond all reasonable doubt" are sentences having a normal use, whatever P may be. But there are no normal circumstances in which one would say "I think that I feel giddy but I may be mistaken" or "I have established beyond reasonable doubt that I feel giddy," and consequently there are no normal circumstances in which it would be in place to say "I am absolutely certain that I feel giddy." By contrast the sentences "you feel giddy" or "he feels giddy" do normally occur in statements of the form "I believe that he feels giddy but I am not certain" or "it is known that he feels giddy," and so on; but again, "he believes that he feels giddy" or "he is certain that he feels giddy" have no normal use. It is the corollary of this that the questions "how do you know?" or "what is your evidence?" are out of place in respect of statements about momentary feelings and sensations, when addressed to the author of the statement, if he is also explicitly shown to be the designated subject of it.

One inference which might be drawn from these facts is that heterobiographical statements about feelings can never be known to be true directly, where "known directly" means that no question arises of how the statement is known to be true and no question arises of any evidence being required to support the statement. But this, as it stands, would be a plainly false conclusion, since the person who is the designated subject of such a heterobiographical statement does generally know directly, without need of evidence, whether the statement made about him is true or false. The proper conclusion is only that the *author* of a heterobiographical statement of this kind can never know directly, in the sense indicated, whether the statement he has made is true or false; the author can always properly be asked how he knows, or on what grounds he believes, his heterobiographical statement to be true; he is required to produce his evidence. So the so-called asymmetry is not a matter of statements expressed in the first person singular, *as such*, being different in respect of the evidence which they require from statements expressed in the second or third person singular. Both descriptions of feelings in the first person singular, and those in the second and third person, may be challenged either by reference to indirect evidence (e.g. "I am sure you are lying; you have obvious motives for lying, and you show none of the symptoms which usually go with feeling giddy") or by a proper claim to direct knowledge (e.g. "I can tell you quite definitely that I do feel giddy, in spite of the evidence to the contrary").

This point is obvious, but it is apt to be dangerously slurred over when philosophers talk in general of "statements about other minds," and then go on to enquire into *the* methods appropriate to confirming or confuting such statements. They may be thought to mean by "statements about other minds" what I have called heterobiographical statements—that is, statements describing feelings and sensations which are not expressed in the first person singular; but the so-called problems of other minds, which is sometimes presented as a problem of how a *certain kind of statement* can be tested, does not attach to *a class of statements of any one particular form*; it arises equally for first person singular statements, if in this case the position of the audience is considered instead of that of the author. The problem of other minds is properly the problem of what tests and verifications are ever possible for anyone who is not in fact the designated subject of a statement about thoughts and feelings; it arises equally for any statement about feelings, whether the statement begins with the word "I" or with the word "you" or "we" or "they."

The commonsense answer to the question, so reformulated, seems obvious—indeed so obvious that simply to give it cannot possibly satisfy philosophers; something more is required to explain why it has been thought inadequate. The commonsense answer is: each one of us is sometimes the designated subject of an autobiographical statement and sometimes the subject of heterobiographical statements; each one of us sometimes makes, or is in a position to make, statements about feelings which are not inferential and do not require supporting evidence, and also makes, or is in a position to make, statements about feelings which are inferential and do require supporting evidence. All that is required for testing the validity of any method of factual inference is that each one of us should sometimes be in a position to confront the conclusions of the doubtful method of inference with what is known by him to be true independently of the method of inference in question. Each one of us is certainly in this position in respect of our common methods of inference about the feelings of persons other than ourselves, in virtue of the fact that each one of us is constantly able to compare the results of this type of inference with what he knows to be true directly and non-inferentially; each one of us is in the position to make this testing comparison, whenever he is the designated subject of a statement about feelings and sensations. I, Hampshire, know by what sort of signs I may be misled in inferring Jones's and Smith's feelings, because I have implicitly noticed (though probably not formulated) where Jones, Smith, and others generally go wrong in inferring my feelings. We all as children learn by experiment how to conceal and deceive, to pose and suppress; concurrently we are learning in this very process how to detect the poses and suppressions of others; we learn the signs and occasions of concealment at first-hand, and we are constantly revising our canons of duplicity as our own direct experience of its forms and occasions widens.

These are the commonsense considerations which seem at first glance to allow us to regard any heterobiographical statement, made by any one of us, as the conclusion of a valid inductive inference, the reliability of the method of inference used in any particular case being in principle testable by each one of us in confrontation with direct experience, that is, with non-inferential knowledge about the successes and failures of this particular method; and I think that, as is usual in these questions, the third glance will confirm the first. But before going further, it is worth noticing how the argument from analogy, as stated by philosophers, approaches what I have called the commonsense position, but also misrepresents and oversimplifies it. There is a sense of "analogy" in which it is true that I could justify my inference that Smith is now feeling giddy by an analogy between the particular method of inference which I am now using and other uses of the same methods of inference by other people in discussing my feelings and sensations. I know by direct experience how such feelings as giddiness are concealed and revealed; both I and Smith have been in a position to test the reliability of those methods of indirect inference about giddiness and cognate sensations which we from time to time use in talking about other people. The argument from analogy, as commonly stated by philosophers, only fails because the analogy has been looked for in the wrong place. What is required is not some simple analogy between my feelings and my external symptoms on the one hand and someone else's external symptoms, and so someone else's giddiness-feeling, on the other; what is needed, and is also available, is an *analogy between different uses of the same methods of argument by different people on different occasions.* The inductive argument, the reliability of which is to be tested by each one of us, attaches both to the sentence "I feel giddy" and to the sentences "you feel giddy," "he feels giddy," etc.; it attaches to any sentence of the form "X feels giddy." Anyone hearing or using any sentence of this form, and anyone needing to test the statement conveyed on a particular occasion, can find such confirmation by looking for an analogy with occasions of its use when he was not in need of such inductive confirmation. To anyone entertaining a doubt about the justification of a particular method of inference about feelings and sensations, the reassuring analogy is between the different occasions of use of the sentence in question; for on some of these occasions the doubter, whoever he may be, was in a position to know non-inferentially that the method of inference now in question led to a correct or incorrect conclusion. Each of us is in a position to learn from his own experience that certain methods of inference to conclusions of the kind "X feels giddy" are generally successful. Of course, if I, Hampshire, have never felt giddy myself, or had any sensation which is even remotely like this one, I would to that extent be at a loss to know whether other people are speaking the truth when they describe autobiographically this utterly unknown kind of sensation. In certain extreme cases this total failure of testability, and therefore failure of communications, does in fact happen. In such cases I am in fact content to admit that I personally have no means of knowing whether what is said by others is pure invention or not; I simply do not know what they are talking about. But over the normal range of statements about feelings and sensations of which I am either the author or audience, I can generally point to occasions on which I was the subject of the particular statement in question and other people had to use the now questionable method of inference.

120

Suppose that Smith and I each suspect the other of deceiving and of encouraging the other to use unreliable methods of inference. This again is a testable and empirical doubt, because we each of us know how we ourselves proceed when we are trying to deceive in this particular manner. We each base our devices of deception on our observations of other people's methods of inference about us. We each know that there is something in common to our different methods of deception, since we each sometimes know that we have failed to deceive and so we each know from our own experience how such deception may be detected. But no common psychological language could be established with beings, outwardly human and sensitive, who never tried openly and in words to infer our feelings and who never acknowledged in words our success in inferring theirs, using the one to guide them in the other in a circle of mutual correction. We would have no good inductive grounds for speculating about the feelings of utterly silent people, or of people who did not betray themselves in speculating about us. It is merely a matter of natural history, and not of logic, that total failures of communication and understanding do not occur more frequently, and that in fact we are each generally in a position to reassure ourselves about our methods of inference to the feelings of others by confrontation with the successes and failures of others in talking about us.

It has been necessary first to insist on the truism that all statements about feelings and sensations, including such statements expressed in the first person singular, are "statements about other minds" for some people, but not "statements about other minds" for other people; for it is precisely this feature of them which allows any one of us to test in direct experience the reliability of the numerous specific methods of inference that he uses when talking about the feelings of others. The importance of the truism can be brought out in the analogous case of "statements about the past"; philosophers have sometimes invented perplexities by writing as if we could pick out a class of statements as "statements about the past" and could then enquire how such statements can possibly be established as true by inductive argument; for how—it is asked—can we ever in principle confirm the validity of our inferences about the past? The mistakes which lead to this question are the same as in the "other minds" case. We cannot pick out a class of statements as statements about the past, unless we mean merely statements expressed in the past tenses. But the tenses, like the pronouns and cases of verbs, serve (among other functions) to relate a statement to the particular context or occasion of its utterance or of its consideration. Clearly the *same* statement may be a statement about past, present or future, when considered, accepted or rejected by different people in different contexts. Similarly, the *same* statement may be made either heterobiographically or autobiographically. A statement in the present tense, which is in this artificial sense a statement about the present, when verified and reaffirmed, may be reaffirmed as a statement about the past, and equally a statement about the future, when finally confirmed, may be reaffirmed as a statement about the present. *The very notion of confirmation involves this possibility of comparing the different contexts of utterance of the same statement.* It does not in general lie *within* the statement itself, or in its grammatical form of expression, that it is a statement about the mind of another, or that it is a statement about the past; these are features of the circumstances of the utterance or consideration of the statement, features that are partially indicated (but not stated) by pronouns, by tenses, and by other contextual expressions, whenever and by whomever the statement is asserted, re-asserted or denied. Strictly speaking, there can be no class of statements about the past, standing in hopeless need of confirmation, any more than there can be a class of past events. Similarly there can be no class of minds which are other minds, or class of statements about them. This confusion of contextual idioms such as "other," "past," with class-terms has its roots in an unnoticed double use of the idioms, which must now be explained.

It is often suggested that the function of pronouns and other contextual expressions ("this," "that," "here," "now," etc.) is to designate or to refer uniquely to some person, thing, time, place, event, etc. Mr. Strawson (*Mind*, October 1950) has suggested the appropriate label, "uniquely referring expressions"; certainly one of the ways in which pronouns and these other contextual expressions are used is in this uniquely referring way—that is, to indicate, in a particular context of utterance, a particular person, thing, event. But it is characteristic of the contextual expressions that they are not always or solely used to refer uniquely or to designate a particular person, thing, event. They also have an important *generalised* use, in which they make no reference to a particular individual and in which they can be interpreted without any reference whatever to any particular context of utterance. Consider the slogan, "do it *now*"; or "never put off till *tomorrow* what you can do *today*." In this use "now," "today," "tomorrow" do not refer uniquely, but have a force in some (but not all) ways like that of a variable, and might be expanded into "now, to whatever moment 'now' may refer," or "today, whatever day 'today' may refer to." Another example: "the future is quite uncertain": as it stands, and, without a context, this sentence is ambiguous, and might be used to make two quite different statements, or even two different kinds of statement; "the future" might be used in the uniquely referring way, so that we require to know the context of utterance in order to know what particular stretch of history is being referred to and described as uncertain; or "the future" might be used in the purely generalised way—"the future, at whatever point in history, is always uncertain." This familiar generalised, or quasi-variable, use is transferred to philosophy when we talk of "statements about *the past*," "statements about the *other* side of the moon," and "statements about *other* minds." Confusion between the two kinds of use arises when a transition is made within a single argument from the generalised to the uniquely referring use, or vice versa, without this transition being noticed; and just this is what generally happens in arguments about our knowledge of "other minds" and in formulations of the so-called *ego*centric predicament. The solipsistic doubter will probably not put his question in the explicitly generalised form, but will ask: "How can *I* ever justify my inferences about what is going on in *your* mind, since I can have no independent means of checking *my* inferences about *your* feelings?" There may be a muddle in this: Does the "I" here mean "I, Hampshire"? Is it a lament about my, Hampshire's, peculiar isolation and the peculiar inscrutability of you, Smith? Or does the "I" mean "whoever 'I' refers to?" and the "you" "you, whoever 'you' may be?" If the latter is intended, and the pronoun is being used in the generalised way, the question becomes: "How can any one of us ever justify any inference to the feelings of someone other than himself, since no one of us, whoever he may be, has any means of checking any inference to the feelings of anyone other than himself?" And to this generalised form of the question the commonsense answer again suggests itself: each and every one of us, whoever he may be, has the means of independently checking the reliability of the methods of inference which he uses, although, naturally, on those occasions when he needs to use any particular method of inference, he cannot be independently checking the inference on the same occasion.

When I, Hampshire, check in my own experience the reliability of the various particular methods of inference which I use when talking about the feelings of others, the statements which I make at the conclusion of these checks are *ex-hypothesi* not themselves the conclusions of an inference; but they are none the less efficient as checks to my methods of inference. The solipsistic problem, cleared of these confusions, can now be re-stated: whenever anyone uses the sentence "I feel giddy," one person and one person only is in a position to know directly, and without need of inference, whether the statement conveyed is true; whenever anyone says "you feel giddy," or "he feels giddy," or "Smith feels giddy," one person and one person only is in a position to know without need of inference whether the statement is true; whenever anyone says, "we both feel giddy," or "they feel giddy," no one can ever know directly, and without need of inference, whether the conjoint statements conveyed are true. So the solipsist may correctly say that it is a distinguishing characteristic of statements about feelings, as opposed to statements about physical things, that at most one person can ever properly claim to know directly, and without needing to give evidence or justification, whether such statements are true. But the solipsist originally wanted to separate, within the class of statement about minds, a class of statements about *other* minds, as being dubious and problematical, from autobiographical statements, which were held to be privileged and not dubious. It is this distinction which is untenable.

Suppose that, in talking about our feelings, we each solipsistically confined ourselves to statements which we may properly claim to know to be true directly and without appeal to evidence or to methods of inference; I, Hampshire, would be allowed to say "I feel giddy," and you, Smith, would be allowed to say "I feel giddy"; but, since all uses of other cases of the verb require problematical inference, we would never be allowed to assent to or dissent from each other's statements, or to place ourselves in the position of an audience discussing them. Under such conditions the pronouns and cases of the verb would have no further function, and all argument and the detection of lies would be excluded: our psychological language would simply serve to convey a set of undiscussable announcements. Communication in the ordinary sense upon such topics would have ceased; for communication essentially involves the use of sentences to convey statements by an author to an actual or potential audience, in such a way that all users of the language, in denying and confirming, may change from the position of audience to author in respect of any statement made. To compare the use of personal pronouns with the uses of tenses again: because those statements that refer to events long prior or subsequent to the moment of utterance are *pro tanto* relatively uncertain at the time they are made, it might be suggested that only statements in the present tense should be accepted as completely reliable. But unless we recognise the sense of "same statement" as something to be re-affirmed in different contexts, we remove the last possibility of correcting and denying statements, and with this we remove the possibility of all argument about them and testing of them, and also the possibility of expressing belief or disbelief; we therefore remove the essential conditions or point of statement-making; and this we would have done by failing to recognise the function of those devices which relate the same statement to the changing circumstances of its assertion. The formula often used, "I am in a position to judge of the truth of statements about my own feeling, but not about the feeling of others," has only succeeded in misleading, because of the two ways in which the expression "I" and "other" may be used, and the often unnoticed shift from one use to the other. It is this shift that suggests a solipsistic conclusion —e.g. that one mind only can be known with certainty to exist and one set of feelings and sensations known with certainty to have occurred. But of course no such conclusion about *one* mind follows from the argument when correctly stated. The proper truism is, "No one of us, whoever he may be, is in need of inference to assure himself of the truth of statements about his own feelings, but he can never assure himself directly, and without needing to appeal to evidence, of the truth of statements about the feelings of others"; stated in this form, with a quasi-variable expression as the subject term, the truism cannot serve as a premise to any *solipsistic* conclusion.

The peculiarity of the word "know" and of its cognates—that the conditions of their proper use in combination with any type of statement vary with the indicated context of utterance—is not confined to discourse about minds and feelings; it applies over the whole range of application of words like "know," "certain," "verify," with whatever kind of statement they are combined. Whatever may be the topic under discussion, whether a claim to knowledge or certainty is or is not in place must always depend upon who makes the claim, when, and under what conditions; it can never be solely a matter of the form of the statement itself or of its topic. Any empirical statement whatever is a matter of uncertain inference under some conditions of its use or consideration. There is no mystery in the fact that a statement which may be a matter of direct and certain knowledge for one person will always be a matter of uncertain inference for another, any more than there is mystery in the fact that the same statement which may be known with certainty to be true at one time must be a matter of uncertain inference at other times. Philosophers (Plato, Descartes, Russell) have invented the mystery by writing as if being known to be true and being uncertain were intrinsic properties of statements, properties somehow adhering to them independently of the particular circumstances

127

in which they were made or considered. It is proper and necessary that formal logicians, who study patterns of transformations of sentence-forms, should disregard those features of statements which relate them to a context of utterance; but philosophers' questions about use and meaning hinge on the different contexts in which words like "know" and "certain" may occur in combination with sentences of different forms and different topics.

CONCLUSION

"Past," "Present," "Other," are not class terms but contextual terms, and there can be no class of events which are past events, and no class of minds which are other minds, and no class of statements which are statements about either of these. "Statements about other minds" is either an incomplete expression, requiring knowledge of the particular circumstance of its use in order that it should be intelligible— e.g. "minds other than mine, Hampshire's"; or the contextual expression may be used in the generalised sense and mean "statements about minds other than the author's, whoever the author may be." If the latter is intended, then in raising the problem of other minds we are enquiring into the analogy which enables anyone to compare the situation in which he knows a statement about feelings to be true, independently of inference, with the situation in which he does not; and it is to this comparison that we refer when we talk of checking the reliability of any method of factual inference.

On Referring and Intending

The relation of thought to action, as compared with the relation of thought to statement—this is one of the oldest issues of philosophy. What is the relation of what we mean to what we actually say? And how does it differ from the relation of what we mean to do to what we actually do?

(1) "I intended to speak next, but then we were interrupted." (2) "When I made that statement, I was not referring to you but to that man in the corner." It is now often said that the words "intend" and "refer," as they occur in these two sentences, do not stand for anything that was going on in the mind of the speaker, or for any characteristic and recurrent experience of the speaker's; secondly, it is often said to be untrue that the correctness of their application on any particular occasion can only be finally and conclusively established by the subject's own introspection or reflection. These two negative theses about the verbs "intend" and "refer" seem to be interconnected, in that anyone who commits himself to one would also commit himself to the other. But the second is much clearer than the first; it is not at all clear to me what is meant by asserting or by denying that a verb stands for some characteristic and recurrent experience, unless this is taken as a remark about the method of confirmation appropriate to the statements in which these verbs occur. I shall review some arguments that are now widely used to support these two theses and will try to show where they are inadequate.

(1) In order to show that a particular verb does not stand for something introspectable, it is not enough to show that one often, or even generally, refers to the environment or to the external situation in supporting or disputing the statements in which it occurs. If we take my expression

from the vocabulary, whether psychological or not, the truth of the statements into which it enters will often have to be established by inference and indirect evidence. To show that a verb does not stand for something introspectable, one would need to show that, when it is applied in conditions that make inference and indirect evidence unnecessary, the truth of any categorical statement into which it enters is not established beyond doubt by the subject's own introspection or reflection. One would need to show that the subject's own reflection is not necessary in justifying a claim that a particular statement, involving this verb, is as certain as any such statement could be.

(2) In order to show that a psychological verb does not stand for something introspectable, it is not enough to show that, on some occasions of the use of the first person singular present tense form of the verb, the utterance is generally taken as some form of performatory utterance and not as a statement, to which an appropriate reaction would be "That's not true." Even if one could show that the verb was *never* used in the first person singular of the present tense in such a way that the reaction "That's not true" would be an appropriate reaction, the conclusion would still not follow. For it may be that in reporting the results of introspection one needs always to use the past tense, even when one is reporting contemporaneously, in order to avoid confusion with another, non-statement-making kind of utterance. Change of tense very commonly has other purposes than a mere change of time-reference. If I am asked what I am doing at some particular moment, I may answer: "I was promising to come tomorrow." It does not follow from the fact that "I promise to come tomorrow" is not taken as a true or false statement that we cannot ask how the statement "I was promising to come tomorrow" might be confirmed or falsified, and so determine what the word "prom-

ise" stands for, or what a promise is—namely, a particular kind of transaction between persons.

(3) In order to show that a verb does not stand for something introspectable, it is not enough to show that it does not stand for what would naturally be called "an act," "an action," or "an occurrence," or that it would not naturally be used in answer to the questions "What did you do next?" or "What happened to you next?" This would not be sufficient, because there is no a priori principle by which we can affirm that all introspectable phenomena which can be referred to by verbs must also be naturally describable as "acts," "actions," or "occurrences." We cannot begin by using these category expressions as the basis of our argument; for, as category expressions, they have no independently established use. We must first give them a sense in terms of our actual idioms and of our actual procedures of confirmation.

(4) Lastly, it is not enough to show that among the necessary conditions for the correct application of the verb there are included certain features both of the linguistic context and of the external situation, such that, if it is admitted that the linguistic context and the external situation were utterly remote from the required kind, it follows that the verb cannot have been correctly used. This is not a sufficient argument, for it would still be possible to maintain that the verb does stand for something introspectable, *but only for something introspectable in a standard kind of situation.* And I think that most philosophers who have wished to maintain, or have assumed, that a particular psychological verb could be said to stand for something introspectable would have agreed that careful introspection was a necessary, but not entirely sufficient, condition for the particular verb's being applied correctly and with the greatest possible confidence. For instance, they would have assumed, perhaps naïvely,

that "I feel frightened" stands for a characteristic experience, in a perfectly ordinary, and indeed standard, use of the word "experience"; but they would have admitted, as a matter of course, that there are certain conditions of the external situation in which it would be more natural or correct to use another closely related form of expression—perhaps "I feel anxious" rather than "I feel frightened," e.g., in situations where there is absolutely nothing to be frightened of. For it may be that there is a group of psychological expressions in the vocabulary, each of which may be used to report something introspectable, say phenomenon E, and such that no one of them is properly and truly applied unless E occurs, but also such that the choice among these expressions is determined, at least in part, by features of the external situation. But one could maintain this thesis about a group of expressions only if one could point to some expression of the group which was used solely to refer to the introspectable phenomenon E, and the use of which was not restricted by any features of the external situation; unless one could point to some independent means of referring to the introspectable experience E, as it were, in isolation, the thesis about the group would become untestable and therefore uninformative.

I think there is in fact a verb which might be said to have this central place within that group of words to which "intend" and "refer" belong: namely, the verb "to mean" as it might be used in each of the following sentences: (1) "I meant that book, not this one." (2) "That was a slip of the tongue. I meant the seventeenth century, not the sixteenth." (3) "That is what I meant to say next." (4) "I did not mean to insult him."

But I will admit that it would be very odd to talk of the verb "to mean" in this, as in any other of its uses, as standing for an experience, or some similar experiences, of which we are aware when we introspect; the principal oddity would be in the use of the word "experience." While one might mention having felt frightened, or having experienced fear, in the list of one's experiences, one could scarcely mention having meant one thing rather than another in the list of one's experiences, even though one might ask "Have you ever had the experience of meaning to write one thing and in fact writing another?"

The reason is, I think, that the word "experience" in its ordinary use, and even more in its philosophical use, is generally connected, in some loose way, with the word "feeling." One might easily ask "Have you never had the experience of wanting something very strongly?" just because one might here substitute for "experience," the word "feeling." And yet a philosopher might deny that whenever I say truly that I want to do something very strongly, I am referring to the same recurrent experience. His reason might be that the feeling that goes with wanting to sleep is very unlike the feeling that is associated with wanting to eat, and therefore that there is no characteristic similar feeling which is a condition of the correct application of the word "want." But even this argument has to be regarded with caution; for it seems to hinge on the assumption that there is, or could be, some single and independently established criterion attached to the phrases "same feeling" and "similar feeling," and this assumption is mistaken. Even when I have reported correctly on two different occasions that I felt frightened, there is a sense of "same feeling" in which it may be true that my feelings were very different on the two occasions, that is, that the fear affected me quite differently on these two occasions. But there is inevitably also the sense of "same feeling" in which I did experience the same feeling on these two occasions, namely, the feeling of fear. The fact is that the expression "same or similar feelings"—like "same or similar thing," "same or similar experience," "same or similar action," etc.—is applied relatively to the descriptions that might be given of what I felt, and cannot be given an absolute sense independent of these possible alternative descriptions. I may ask the question "Is this a case of fear or is it excitement?" just as I may ask "Is that a dagger or is it a figment of my imagination?" In both these cases I am using the indicator words "this" and "it" to refer to some present phenomenon, and in the case of fear, probably, to some perturbation going on within me. In both cases I am trying to identify the phenomenon before me as falling under one concept or another, and in both cases the correct identification must necessarily be determined in part by considerations other than the quality of that particular experience at that particular moment. Therefore, if I speak of "having the same feeling today as I had yesterday," I may mean that exactly the same description could truthfully be given of the internal perturbation, as I felt it on the two occasions; or I may mean that the same diagnosis of what the perturbation was applies to the two occasions, e.g., that they were both cases of fear. For this reason it is misleading to speak of the word "fear" as *standing for* some characteristic introspectable phenomenon and misleading to speak of the word "dagger" as "standing for" some characteristic set of appearances. But it is equally misleading to deny that a feeling of fear is an introspectable phenomenon, if this is taken as a denial that introspection is required in any final confirmation of a categorical statement about the presence of a feeling of fear, just as perception is required in any final confirmation of a categorical statement about the presence of daggers.

But it remains true that, given any psychological verb which requires completion by a "that" clause or an infinitive, and which cannot stand in a complete utterance alone, one would not naturally say that the verb stands for a characteristic *feeling*; and for this reason one would also be inclined to say that it cannot stand for a characteristic experience. Empiricist philosophers have often assumed that there is a simple dichotomy: either an expression can be said to stand for or describe some inner experience or feeling, or it must be taken to refer to, and to depend for its correct use upon, some features of the external situation. The effect of this dichotomy, taken together with the use of the unfortunate expression "stand for," is to suggest that the so-called data of introspection must be of the type of feelings or sensations distinguished by simple sensory predicates, much as colors are distinguished by color adjectives. It is therefore natural that those who are arguing against the view of the mind as an inner forum should assume it to be sufficient to show, of any particular psychological verb, that there is no characteristic feeling which must always be present whenever it is correctly applied and that the verb does not have all the features characteristic of expressions that describe feelings. For instance, they will ask whether knowing what we intend is like knowing what we feel frightened of. With a rhetorical question such as this, they will seem to themselves to have shown that to confirm beyond further doubt whether a verb of thinking, as opposed to a verb of feeling, is applicable on a given occasion does not necessarily involve the subject's own introspection or reflection. But this argument, being based on a false dichotomy, seems to me unconvincing; and I still think that in reporting what our intentions were on a particular occasion, and also in stating which of two objects we were referring to when we made a particular statement, we can in the last resort confirm our statements only by our own introspection and reflection.

I suggest that there is a general overriding distinction between those expressions which are so used that any affirmative categorical statement in which they occur can only be finally and conclusively confirmed, on any occasion of doubt, by the designated subject of the statement, and must always be a matter of indirect inference for anyone else, and those expressions of which this is not true. To state the conditions in which a speaker can claim final certainty beyond the possibility of doubt, in the application of expressions of the first type, is simply to point to the occasions when the speaker is also the designated subject of the statement; for one can only be certain beyond the possibility of doubt, or beyond further question, when one speaks of one's own thoughts. It follows, I think, that nothing that can be properly called a general criterion or set of decisive tests, governing the use of such expressions, can be stated. For to state such a criterion or set of tests would be to state how *anyone*, whether he is the designated subject of the statement or not, can make sure that the expression has been correctly applied on a given occasion by making certain tests and by finding whether certain other expressions are applicable; and *ex hypothesi* the "anyone" would be out of place here. The most that one could do, in teaching or clarifying the use of the word, would be to explain how anyone, whoever he may be, may determine that he is not misusing the expression when he applies it to himself. So, explaining the use of the word "intend," one might say: "You cannot properly say that you intended to do so-and-so unless you had to some extent at some time thought of doing so, however provisionally and inexplicitly." But such an explanation of the logical connection of the word within the psychological vocabulary is not the provision of a test, in that sense in which I may specify the tests which determine, for example, whether someone understands some particular subject matter; not does it provide a criterion, in that sense in which I may provide the criterion that determines whether one individual understands some particular subject matter better than another. And these typical cases seem to me to provide the standard and normal senses of "test" and "criterion." It seems to me that we blur an essential distinction between different types of expression if we extend the use of the words "test" and "criterion" so widely that, for any descriptive expression whatever, there must be some test or a criterion by which we can determine whether it has been correctly applied on a given occasion. From the fact that the question "How do you know?" cannot arise with statements of the form "I intend to do so-and-so," it follows that no criterion or test can be stated which governs the correct application of the word "intend"; to state such a criterion or test would be precisely to state what would constitute a sufficient answer to the question "How do you know?"

But I have so far neglected one very important difference between "intend" (in the sense of "What do you intend to do next?") and "refer," as this verb occurs in the question "Which of these two are you referring to?" When I state in the present tense my intention to do something, my statement may be a lie, a deliberate concealment of what I actually mean to do. But when I state in *the present tense*, and only in the present tense, which of two things I am referring to, my announcement cannot (logically cannot) be a lie. For, if I use the present tense, I am taken to be completing and amplifying the statement which I have already made; and if this is what I now say that I mean in the statement, this becomes part of the statement itself, unless and until I make some further correction of it; I am simply giving a sense to my words. But if, as a matter of history, I am stating which of two things I meant, or was referring to, in some statement, I may lie or my memory may deceive me, and my statement may be disputed as historically incorrect. If I use the past tense, I show that I am not completing my original statement, but that I am making another statement, a statement of historical fact. I am not then giving a sense to my words, but reporting what sense I actually gave. I am reporting what went on in my mind at the time, even if it was only a few seconds ago. Someone who had said, "That man over there is an enemy," might immediately afterwards be asked, "Which man were you referring to when you said that?" Suddenly seeing a danger, he might indicate someone other than the person to whom he was in fact referring when he spoke. Similarly, when I am presented in a philosophical argument with two different interpretations of some statement that I have made, it is possible for me to tell an untruth, saying that I meant or intended the first, when in fact I meant or intended the second. I may suddenly see a possibility of refutation and suddenly switch and misrepresent what I meant. In neither of these cases is there any general criterion or decisive test by which an observer can determine whether I am reporting honestly; he must take my word for it or judge by the probabilities. And I myself can only answer by reflecting upon what was going on in my mind at the time, or, more naturally put, by considering what I had in mind at the time.

This difference between "intend" and "refer" may help to illustrate the general difference between the relation of thinking to acting and relation of thinking to doing. The thought lies behind the actions; but it need not in the same sense lie behind the words. I may *give* you my thoughts in my statements and questions; but I cannot give you my thoughts in action, not even in the act of speaking. If I do in the same sense give you my thoughts in action, then I am miming or acting, using the language of gesture. It is a corollary of this difference that I may mean to do something, in the sense of intend to do it, without ever doing anything of the kind; the intention may exist quite independently of any action. But I cannot mean, in the sense of refer to, something without having made some explicit use of words or symbols; I cannot have meant anything or anybody without having mentioned something or somebody, either in speech or in writing.

138

But still it may be objected that it is incorrect to say that, in stating what I was referring to or what I was intending to do, I must always consider what was "going on in my mind" at the time. For, it is argued, not only might a vast variety of quite different things have been going on in my mind at the time compatible with my having meant or intended one thing rather than another; more than this, nothing at all might have been going on in my mind during the time when I intended, or was intending, to do so-and-so. The argument again takes the familiar form of a rhetorical question: if it is true that I intended to come home early on Monday, does that mean that throughout the day there was an introspectable process "going on in my mind" which was my intention to go home early? Triumphantly the answer comes: of course not. And the conclusion is drawn: when someone says that he intended to do something, he cannot be said to be reporting what was going on in his mind at the time.

But this rhetorical question only seems to have force because of a simple mistake. The simple mistake is the assumption that a report of what was going on at the time in the house, in the city, in the country, in my mind, must be a report either of a continuous, uninterrupted process or of an instantaneous event. "What was going on in England while I was away?" "Prices fell and real wages rose." There is no implication that this falling and rising was going on uninterruptedly in this period and that every moment was filled by some phase of a continuous process. Similarly I may be summarizing what was going on in my mind, or reporting the upshot of many otherwise distinguishable processes, when I say what I intended to do; and I may mention a greater or lesser period of time as the period during which the intention lasted. "Ever since I was young, I had intended to go to Athens." Or "I intended to speak, but almost as soon as I had formed this intention the opportunity was gone." However different the phenomena with which these intentions were associated, both statements are reports of what was going on in my mind at the time, in the sense that in both cases I need to recall what I thought and what I did not think, what I decided and did not decide, at various moments during the period referred to, in order to be assured that the statements are true. Anyone other than me, any friends and observers, will be left to infer, with greater or lesser certainty, what was going on in my mind at the time and therefore whether, among a myriad other things that might truly be said in summarising what was in my mind at that time, it can also be said that I intended to go to Athens and intended to speak. Similarly, when I am asked, "Were you referring to Jones or Smith when you wrote that?" I stop to recall, if I am in doubt, what was going on in my mind at the time when I wrote the phrase in question. Perhaps I wrote without having anyone in particular in mind; perhaps my mind was in this sense blank, in which case the correct answer would be "Neither." Perhaps I can recall the scene as I wrote the words, but still cannot recall what I meant by them, or to whom I was referring, and then suddenly my train of thought, what was going on in my mind at the time, comes back to me, and with this I remember whom I meant. This is a story often told in this form of words, and there is no reason, for the sake of a theory, to deny their inevitable appropriateness.

One need only discard the primitive prejudice that all mental verbs must either stand for an instantaneous event or for a continuous process which is always the same whenever it occurs, in the sense that it always admits of one and only one description; or, failing this, that the criterion of application for the verb must be found in overt behavior and the external situation. When we see through this dichotomy, we are free to consider what does count as having established, beyond further question or doubt, that a statement about someone's meaning or intention is true. Where these verbs are involved in some statement about the present or the immediate past, the strongest of all claims to certainty and authority appears in the words: "Of course that is what I meant when I said that just now and that is what I intend to do; or are you accusing me of lying?" And where these verbs occur in some statement about the more distant past, the strongest of all claims to certainty and authority appears in the words: "Of course that is what I meant and that is what I intended to do; I remember quite clearly what was going on in my mind (or what I had in mind) at the time."

But there is a last objection. It might seem that I am representing first-person-singular statements about referring and intending, when they refer to the present or to the immediate past, as incorrigible statements, as if either they must be true or must be lies; as if they are immune from error. I have not so represented them and they are not immune from error. I may fall into error in reporting that I was referring to a certain person by using a name or title which is not in fact the name or title of the person to whom I was actually referring, or by using a definite description which does not in fact apply to that person. Similarly, I may fall into error in announcing what I intend to do by describing wrongly the action which I have in mind. I may say, for instance, that I intend to buy the woodcut when in fact the picture that I have in mind is not a woodcut at all. An observer, judging by the probabilities, may infer with reasonable certainty that I have made a mistake in reporting whom I meant or what I intend. My point has only been that for the observer it remains always an inference that I have made such a mistake, however certain he may reasonably claim to be. I may myself be in doubt whether the man I meant is called Smith or Jones, or whether the picture I intend to buy is a woodcut; I may have to infer what is the correct description of the person or thing I am referring to or the correct description of the action I intend to perform. "I think the man I am referring to is called Jones, and is the president of the bank, but I am not sure"; this is the clearer way of expressing what is meant by "I think I am referring to Jones, the president of the bank, but I am not sure." If I admit that I do not know whom I mean or I am referring to, then I admit that I do not mean, and am not referring to, anything. And if I do know whom I am referring to, it must be true either that I am able to pick out the person referred to when he appears or that I am able to furnish some true description of him; and if I could pick him out, I could also furnish at least one true description of him, however unspecific the description may be. Even in reporting my hopes, fears, desires, attitudes, and feelings, when my feelings are directed towards objects in the external world, a form of doubt may be raised; I may always misdescribe the object that I want, dislike, or fear. But this possibility of doubt gives no reason to deny that only the subject's own reflection can justify a claim that a particular statement about what he wants, dislikes, or fears is as certainly true as any such statement can be. For the same reasons only the subject's own reflection can justify a claim that a particular statement of meaning or intention is as certain as any such statement can be.

Feeling and Expression

I shall argue that, in the particular case of feeling, the inner life of the mind is to be understood as a development from something more primitive in every man's behaviour, of which it is the residue and the shadow. Secondly, that the primitive faculty of imitation, and of imitative play and fiction, are a necessary background to the communication of feeling.

The first problem is: how do we identify a mere something that we feel as anger or as amusement? There is at least one necessary connection that is clear in the normal use of language. If I am amused, I am inclined, or disposed, or have a tendency, to laugh or to smile. If I am angry, I am inclined, or disposed, or have a tendency, to attack or to behave aggressively. Wherever there is this necessary connection between an identifiable feeling or emotion, and the inclination to behave in an identifiable way, the pattern of behaviour may be called the natural expression of the feeling. A certain pattern of behaviour is a natural expression of a certain feeling, if, in distinguishing this feeling from other feelings with which it might be confused, we would specify an inclination towards this particular pattern of behaviour, together with some standard circumstances, actually existing or believed to exist, which provoke the inclination. So in explaining what anger is, as opposed to some other emotion, I would refer to a disposition to attack when the subject has been, or believes that he has been, in some way harmed or hurt.

Human beings are from the beginning recognised as potential language-users, and as potential observers of social conventions which they will later learn to formulate. The conditions of application of the vocabulary of feelings to human beings are determined by the fact that two capacities—the capacity to control their inclinations, and the capacity to identify their inclinations, and their circumstances, in words—are gradually developed together. I know that I am angry, and I am able authoritatively to disclose that I am, because I know what I am inclined to do, which is to attack; and I can identify the external situation that is associated in my mind with this inclination. If I do not try to attack, I must have inhibited the natural expression of my anger, which remains as a merely felt inclination. If I have deliberately cut off the natural expression of the anger, then I will certainly know what the residual feeling is, in at least one sense of this deceiving phrase. The subject's own identification of the inner perturbation as a case of anger rather than of some other emotion, such as fear, would not be intelligible, if it were not for the inclination that remains as the shadow of the natural behaviour. About the contained excitement that he feels, the angry man may ask "What is this feeling that I have?" He identifies it as a feeling or sentiment of a certain kind in virtue of his inclination to act in a certain way, taken together with those features of the situation with which he associates his action or inclination. The vocabulary of feeling and sentiment with which we communicate, each sometimes subjects, sometimes observers, could never be established if this primary identification of an inclination to behave in a certain way could not be made prior to the classification of inner and contained feeling.

The contrast between that which a man feels inclined to do, and that which he is by social convention required to do, runs all through his experience. He therefore easily learns to abstract his inner perturbations, and the controlled inclinations associated with them, from the behaviour that was their original context, and to attend to these perturbations, and the associated inclinations, as separate subjects of interest. If he restrains himself from doing something that he is inclined to do, he must at least know, through the exercise of this restraint, what it is that he is inclined to do. He can identify his own state of mind from his own incipient behaviour, taken together with the external situation. He is at the same time learning to read these signs in the incipient behaviour of others.

At this point we come to the central distinction between natural and conventional signs of feeling. If one could state this distinction exactly, many problems both of the philosophy of mind, and also of aesthetics, would lie open to clarification. At least it is evident that any surviving residue of the distinctive behaviour of an angry man is by itself to be counted as a natural sign of anger. In order to recognise some residual behaviour as a sign of anger, it is not necessary that one should have learnt a general rule of significance, as the rule of use of a conventional sign has to be independently learnt. The residue is taken as a sign, because it is immediately recognisable as a part subtracted from a whole. For this reason no general rule of correlation needs to be learnt between sign and thing signified. Suppose that I see half the surface of a familiar kind of physical object: no learnt general rule of correlation is required to explain the sense in which I immediately take this visible half-surface as the sign of the presence of the whole.

The medium of behaviour is the body. Bodily expression may take many distinguishable and subtle forms. The more obvious sub-headings are posture, gesture, facial expression. Posture, gesture, facial expression are often immediately legible by others, as signs of an inclination to behave in a specific way, when they are the last vanishing vestige of a familiar and classifiable pattern of behaviour. So the man who looks daggers at his neighbour has cut off the action of aggression, and the vestige of it remains in his glance, voluntarily or involuntarily directed. The man who

145

cowers or shrinks, only sketching the action of flight, makes a gesture, or assumes a posture, that is the suggestion of the action, with the effective remainder of it removed. The inclination has shown itself, and, because it is less than quarter realised, the truncated action is legible as a sign of the contained, and therefore felt and inner, inclination.

But we cannot continue any further along this path, following the notion of expression, without noticing that we have from the beginning left out of account one of the most fundamental of the facts of human nature. Fundamental as it is, it is nonetheless a fact omitted from many contemporary philosophies of mind, which are in consequence misshapen. There is a primitive activity, or rather, a set of primitive activities, which involve the use of natural signs, in childhood and throughout life: that set of activities which can be very roughly grouped together under the heading of imitation. From the beginning of their development, men not only learn not to behave as they feel inclined to behave, and learn to cut off the natural expression of their feelings. They also concurrently have the instinct to mimic, and the institution of mimicking, the forms of behaviour which they observe in others. In imitative play they go through the motions of doing things without believing that the conditions for effectively doing them are present and therefore without the intention of actually doing them.

Imitation is one primitive and natural way of learning routines and customs and the use of language itself, and it is the child's first way of entry into social life. That it must be counted as an original disposition of men seems certain. The overt behaviour, and the visible expression, of a man who is angry or amused are in imitation adopted gratuitously, in the absence both of the type of external occasion, actual or believed to be actual, and of the ensuing inclinations, that are essential to real anger or real amusement. We have here the converse of an inclination to behave in a certain way, of which the manifestation is inhibited; there is the behaviour alone, without the original inclination to effective action behind it. The power to conceal a present inclination, and the power to simulate a nonexistent one, come into existence together. It is difficult, and perhaps impossible, to suppose creatures, capable of full communication in a language, who possessed the one power without also possessing the other. No one who has been angry has, in addition, to learn the rules for expressing anger, as he has to learn how to *say* that he is angry in the course of learning a language. He does not normally need to look in a mirror to see that his physiognomy is correct, and that his posture and facial expression are the right signs to convey that which he wants them to convey. When he sees in another the facial expression and posture of an angry man, and sees them as such, he would know what to imitate, if he was imitating the expression *as* an expression of anger. This is part of his ability to place himself in the position of another, where this involves reconstructing in himself the dispositions of another man through their natural expression. So the operation of sympathy, which was mysterious in Hume's immaterialist philosophy, may pass through this primitive tendency to imitate an expression, which may bring into existence the whole of which it is naturally a part. But if a man was imitating the face and posture of another, as he sees them in front of him, without any thought of them as natural signs, he would so far have no ground to distinguish the relevant and expressive, from the irrelevant and inexpressive, features of the physical object which he sees before him. He would then be aiming at a photographic likeness, or at a copy, of the face; and for this he might indeed need a mirror.

Imitative play takes many forms. It is commonly a form of fiction. That kind of fiction which is imitative play may begin at an age when the idea of a true statement, and of the use of conventional signs to convey information, has not yet occurred to a child as a distinct possibility. The child may merely imitate for the original pleasure of creating a likeness, and under these conditions we would normally speak of his imitation as mere play. Imitation and play are the two related concepts that in general aesthetics have to be explored in great detail; imitative play enters into the present inquiry only as a form of human communication that has to be considered alongside the use of conventional signs, and alongside the use of language. When a child has learnt to use conventional signs according to rules, and then learnt how to convey information and to make statements, and thereby to distinguish truth from fiction, playing at doing things, and imitating others for the sake of imitation, become for him autonomous activities, distinguishable from all others, and requiring their own particular skill. Then he may engage in imitative play, deliberately and at will, and knowing what he is doing. He assumes the expression and posture of an angry father, or of a frightened child, distinguishing this fiction from fact. The success of the imitation, as imitation, carries its own satisfaction with it, as truth-telling carries its own satisfaction with it. They are both cases of making or doing something which matches, and which is in its own medium an equivalent of, an independent reality. The making, or discovery for oneself, of such an equivalence is at once the source and the evidence of an adequate grasp of the reality. The making of an equivalence may be taken as a kind of mastery of the independent reality, a reduction of it to our own terms, and its independence may no longer be felt as threatening. The ancient problem is to find the points at which imitation, as the making of a match that is a likeness, supplements, or replaces, the kind of matching that, as an arrangement of conventional signs according to learnt general rules, can for this reason constitute knowledge. We do not here have simple and unmixed opposites, but rather a continuous scale from natural to conventional sign, from likeness to statement, and complicated intertwinings of the two. We are more ready to speak of *knowledge* of reality in proportion as the medium, in which the match or equivalence is found, consists of conventional signs arranged in accordance with a system of rules, which are learnt as general rules of interpretation and of syntax. A good map of the countryside by itself conveys knowledge of the countryside, but is scarcely a likeness. A good free sketch of the countryside may constitute a kind of likeness; in virtue of its comparative freedom, where freedom is opposed to rule, it is less readily considered as by itself conveying knowledge of the countryside.

The sense in which we may come to discriminate more exactly the various emotions and sentiments through an imitation of their natural expression may be approached through an analogy. Suppose that I am asked what a particular person is like: it might be difficult to find the exactly fitting words to describe that which is peculiar to this man. I might then turn to parody, and in imitation of him reproduce some of the idioms, turns of phrase, tones of voice, that are typical of him, isolating them from their more commonplace accompaniments. If it is admitted that I have in fact succeeded in my imitation in isolating that which is peculiar to him, it will be admitted that I have in a sense answered the inquiry. But the answer was in sensory terms and not in a conceptual or discursive form. Suppose similarly I am asked, not about an individual, or group of individuals, but rather about a general and abstract thing— "What is it like to be jealous?" or, a rather different question, "What is it for a man to be jealous (e.g. rather than envious)?"—I might similarly convey that which is peculiar to this emotion by isolating in an imitation the typical features of its natural expression. In the literature of aesthetics one will meet the portentous phrase—"Seeing the universal in a concrete and sensory embodiment." One can, I think, forget this phrase with its pseudo-logical air and try to be a little more precise.

There is a rough general law of revealing imitation that is most clearly illustrated in the fundamental arts of mimicry and parody. He who mimics the speech and expression of another communicates more effectively the personal peculiarities of his victim in so far as the likeness in speech and expression shows through an unlikeness, with the imitation superimposed on an alien and contrasting personality. The essential qualities of the thing imitated are then filtered through the resisting medium. A totally faithful reproduction of the voice by a reproducing machine would not serve the same cognitive purposes as a revealing imitation. There would not be that primary abstraction that is involved in any contrivance of a likeness in a naturally resisting medium. In the representative arts the medium, and the conventions governing the use of the medium, produce this tension between likeness and unlikeness in the imitation, which makes the imitation revealing. The solidity of material objects is most strongly felt, as a visual experience enjoyed for its own sake, when a likeness is contrived on a flat surface. The recessions of space can also be vividly revealed and enjoyed through a contrived equivalence in this resisting medium. So also the making of an equivalence of the natural expression of an emotion in a resisting medium seems to give some insight into the general nature of the emotion itself. Because we are faced with an imitation, we respond to it, not with an immediate inclination to action, as with any direct expression of emotion in an individual suffering man, but rather in a contemplative way. Any too complete copying and reproduction of a natural expression of feeling tends to excite in us a disposition towards appropriate action. This will destroy a purely contemplative and

150

inquiring attitude. For this reason the representation of feeling in any of the arts must always be in some way distanced and filtered by the artificialities of the art: for instance, by the mere existence of a stage in a theatre, which still may be not enough to prevent a too immediate, or a confused, response in the audience. A representation is felt to be obscene, when there is a felt conflict in the audience between the contemplative and inquiring attitude, the attitude of the perceiver, and the controlled disposition to act. Then the conditions of a revealing fiction have been destroyed, as they are destroyed by a successful *trompe l'œil* painting, which is designed to excite a disposition to respond as we would respond to the material thing represented.

In any representation of persons in any medium, and particularly of a face, we naturally look for physiognomic features within the representation. We try inquiringly to read through the conventions of representation some expression in the face. In direct dealings with men, and outside the context of fiction, we perceive, and react to, the physiognomy of persons almost as immediately as to the full behaviour of which the facial expression is the residue. The expression, considered by itself, is as much a sign, or even a part, of incipient behaviour as it is a sign of inner feeling. Expression can therefore be considered as the connecting arch between a person's disposition to behave in a certain way, which, if it is inhibited, may remain as an invisible affect, and his perceptible behaviour.

Because of the connecting arch of expression, we cannot truthfully say, as many philosophers have implied, that we perceive only the behaviour of others, if behaviour is interpreted as that which is described in terms of effective actions performed and in socially recognised routines. We perceive also that kind of residual, shadow behaviour which constitutes an expression. And we can show that we have perceived it by adopting the same expression in imitation, without trying to reproduce, item by item, the physical features of the face or posture of another. The criterion of identity, which here justifies the phrase "same expression," is to be found partly in the common behaviour of which the expression, in each case, is taken to be the residue, and in part also in certain common physical changes. The phrase "same expression," in virtue of its connecting role, cannot derive its sense exclusively from one side or the other. If therefore I am to imitate successfully your angry expression, it seems that I must pass an exacting double test. I must make, within the medium of my own face, an equivalent of the deviations from the peaceful norm in your face; and at the same time the whole, or gestalt, must be convincing as a sketch of aggressive behaviour by me.

Consider now the link between feelings as dispositions to behave in certain ways and the full corresponding behaviour. I have suggested successive stages of the interiorisation of feeling. First, there is the angry man who, being provoked, immediately attacks. If, in answer to the question "Why did he attack?" we were to answer merely "Because he was angry," the explanation would be, on its own level, complete. Compare with this "Why did he laugh?"—"Because he was amused." There is no unexplained gap between the disposition attributed to him and the behaviour to be explained. To ask the further question "Why does his amusement lead to laughter?" would be like questioning a tautology. The question would suggest that the questioner did not know what is meant by "amusement" or by "laughter." If we have said that he was angry, we have already said that, considering himself to have been provoked, he was inclined to attack. The connecting "because," in giving the reasons for action, has here its minimum force; it makes no allusion to any implied general proposition correlating his behaviour with any independently identifiable event, or with any ulterior calculation. The inquiry into the reasons for his behaviour could only be pressed further by asking why he was angry. This line of inquiry will only terminate when it leads to those fundamental dispositions that constitute a standard of normal response. At the second stage, there is the angry man who, being angry, is inclined to behave aggressively, but for some reason controls his inclination. Suppose that we identify the contortion of his face as a scowl: we imply that he is behaving as an angry man behaves in at least one respect. "Scowl" is a physiognomic predicate, as opposed to a physical state description. A scowl, or an angry glance, are allowed to survive, when the rest of the behaviour is inhibited, partly because they are largely ineffective as action. Generally speaking, we effectively do things, and make changes in the world, in the primary sense of these words, that is, in the sense that is associated with physical change, with our hands and with other limbs rather than with our face. This is a contingent matter of fact, a fact of natural history. When a disposition to behave in a certain way is controlled, the last vestige of the behaviour is apt to survive in facial expression, and particularly in the eyes, as being the ineffective part of the behaviour, the most subtle and insubstantial, and therefore the most immediately expressive of the inner movement of the mind. If the angry man had shaken his clenched fists at his adversary, he would have gone through motions that show only too coarsely his inclination to attack. This gesture is the full action that flows from the inclination without its proper climax, and rendered ineffective; and therefore it is an unmistakable natural sign. If a movement is seen effectively to serve some evident and familiar human need or purpose, its significance as gesture is lost. The behaviour generally needs to be uneconomic and useless, as action, in

153

order to be taken as a sign. Again the imitation is effective as imitation, just because it is in this respect also strikingly unlike that which is imitated.

If a feeling or sentiment necessarily includes a disposition to a certain pattern of behaviour, and if every feeling therefore has its appropriate physiognomy, it follows that every feeling can be portrayed in some perceptible imitation, and that its occurrence on any occasion can be communicated by some perceptible natural sign. As it is of the nature of feelings or sentiments that they can be expressed by natural signs, so it is of the nature of a thought, and of a process of thought, that any perceptible expression of it is a conventional sign, the significance of which is determined by learnt rules of use and of syntax. My facial expression and gestures may express my expectancy and excitement. But I cannot (logically cannot) express my thought that my prodigal son will return without converting my gestures into separate signals which require rules of interpretation and of syntax. When Wittgenstein suggested that the words "I am in pain" can be said to replace a cry of pain, he concentrated an immense transition, a whole natural history, into this single word "replace."

It will be evident that, in dwelling on the notion of expression, I am hoping to correct a particular philosophical view of the relation of feeling to behaviour, and therefore of the relation of mind to body: namely, that prevailing, semi-Cartesian view which leaves us with the difficult problem: Can the existence of a feeling or sentiment, independently identified, ever be validly inferred from the behaviour with which it happens to be correlated? And if this cannot be a valid inductive inference, can there be any test that guarantees that the terms of our common psychological vocabulary are applied with a common significance? If not, how is rational communication about our inner feelings ever possible at all?

154

The picture from which this problem arises is of feelings and states of mind, which are *first* distinguished and identified by the subject as feelings of certain kinds, and which are then *independently* found to have typical manifestations in behaviour. The manifestations in behaviour are conceived as something altogether independent which is added to the states of mind. We move, as it were, outwards from the identification of a specific feeling to the recognition that certain patterns of behaviour are contingently connected with it. I have been suggesting an order of dependence in classification that is the very reverse: that we must first have distinguished certain patterns of behaviour in certain standard circumstances, actual or notional; and then, on the basis of this kind of classification, we can distinguish the various inner sentiments as controlled inclinations to behave in these ways in these standard circumstances. We arrive at the distinctions between the different feelings and sentiments by abstracting from the manifesting behaviour. In our classifications we move, as it were, inwards from expressive behaviour to inner feeling.

Between these two philosophies of mind there are two principal dividing lines. The first raises one of the most general of all philosophical issues, and one that has been at the centre of recent discussion. What conditions are necessary for the establishment of a common vocabulary? Must the common vocabulary, including the vocabulary of states of mind, be established on a common basis of reference to publicly observable things? Must any classification of a state of mind be in principle testable by reference to something other than the felt quality of the experience? Or can I identify my feeling immediately as a feeling of a certain kind, irrespective of anything else, as it seems that I may recognise and name a shade of colour that appears in my visual field? This problem of the conditions of classification leads to the second issue between the philosophies. Does the order in which every man learns to apply mental concepts of certain types in common language determine the conditions of application attached to these concepts? I believe that the answer to this second question must be "Yes," and that this answer already settles the issue of classification, as it applies to the more refined distinctions within the vocabulary of sentiment and emotion. Entry into a certain "form of life" is a necessary background to using and attaching a sense to these concepts: namely, entry into that adult human form of life which includes, among other things, the habit of deliberately controlling the natural expression of inclination, and includes also a growing knowledge of restraining conventions of speech and of behaviour. It is characteristic of the more refined concepts, which we use to distinguish between one sentiment and another, that the subject's own avowals are a necessary part of the conditions of their application. A person gradually acquires the power to apply these distinctions, both to himself and to others, in conjunction with his power to dissociate his inclinations from their immediate natural expression. When I speak of *deriving* the concept of feeling and sentiment from the concept of inhibited behaviour, the order implied is both the order in which a person learns the use of two classes of expression, and also the order in which he himself acquires the faculties of mind to which these expressions refer. Whenever these two orders coincide, the method of derivation will be appropriate to fixing the sense of the concepts in question; and they will coincide, whenever the subject's own avowals play a necessary part in the application of the concept.

Consider a concept of a contrasting kind: that of intelligence, which is a power or capacity, and therefore not a disposition, in the sense in which an inclination is a disposition. A person's avowal that he is intelligent has no special authority in determining whether in fact he is. We have no difficulty in determining that a child is in fact an intelligent child, when he is still too young to be a judge of intelligence either in himself or in others. There is therefore no reason to demand that the conditions of application of this concept should be explained genetically, that is, by reference to the order of a human being's development. Similarly, of a creature, infant or animal, which is incapable of confessing to anger or fear, we can evidently say that it is angry or frightened. The standard behaviour in standard circumstances, notional or actual, is sufficient to give this kind of application of these elementary concepts a definite sense. But as soon as more finely marked distinctions between dispositions and sentiments are drawn—for example, between anger and indignation, between fear and embarrassment— and as soon as we begin to apply a full vocabulary of intentional states, the testimony of the subject, and therefore his developed capacity to make these distinctions for himself, are indispensable in giving the distinctions a sense. Manifestations in behaviour become in these cases correspondingly less decisive in determining whether the concepts have been correctly applied in any particular case.

The derivation of the concept of inner feeling and sentiment from that of inhibited dispositions still leaves a final problem, and one that has been abundantly discussed among philosophers in recent years: What is a disposition? When we say of a man that he is disposed, or inclines, or wants, to do something, which he is not actually doing, what kind of potential behaviour is this? Until we have answered this question, we have still said little that is definite and clear about the relation of the inner life of feeling to perceptible behaviour. I have time only to say something negative in order to prevent misunderstanding: that to attribute a disposition to someone, in the sense of "disposition" that enters into the analysis of the concepts of feeling and sentiment, is not to make a hypothetical statement

157

about him, to the effect that he would behave in certain ways if certain conditions were satisfied. The word "disposition" has sometimes been used in such a way that a capacity or power, such as intelligence, is to be counted as a disposition. It is at least plausible to interpret statements about capacities and powers as implicit hypothetical statements about possible performances. The kind of disposition that is an inclination to behave in a certain way is something that may occur at a certain moment, and may then immediately disappear, although it may also continue over a certain period of time. Both the statement that it occurred at a certain moment, and the statement that it lasted for a certain period, are irreducibly categorical statements about that person at that time or during that period. As statements, they are no less categorical than the statement that a man had at a certain time a certain facial expression.

The analysis of inclinations to action in terms of hypotheticals might be defended, on the ground that a statement that someone was inclined to do something entails the statement that he would have done it, or tried to do it, if he had not restrained himself, or, alternatively, if another inclination had not supervened. But I think that it could be shown that the hypothetical statement allegedly entailed here is vacuous (cf. "If nothing occurs to prevent it, it will rain tomorrow.") The conditions specified in the words "If another inclination had not supervened" and "If he had not restrained himself" are too utterly unrestricted and general to allow the hypothetical statement a sufficiently definite sense. There would be no acceptable method of establishing the truth or falsity of the hypothetical statement except by a reference to the original inclination. The alleged analysis would therefore be circular.

I make this point, briefly and dogmatically, in order to dissociate myself from that philosophy which might be called logical behaviourism: the philosophy that claims that

statements about the inner world of feeling and of sentiment are all in principle reducible to complicated statements about overt behaviour. My motive in dwelling on the
concepts of expression and imitation, and on the derivation
of inner feeling from inhibited behaviour, is precisely to
point to a possible middle way, which is neither a Cartesian
dualism on the one hand, nor on the other hand a reduction
of that which is distinctively mental to its overt behavioural
expression.

Disposition and Memory

One may argue that, for every distinct state of mind and private sentiment there must exist a distinct expression of this state in a perceptible pattern of behaviour; for it seems that the perceptible patterns of behaviour must be the original endowment from which the purely mental states or activities developed, as a kind of shadow of the original, or as a residue from it. Various metaphors might be suggested here, but I think this metaphor of the "shadow" is peculiarly appropriate to the relation of inner feeling to behaviour. When I speak of "original endowment" and of "development," I might be taken to be speaking of the natural process of evolution, the evolution of the human species from the other animals, or, alternatively, of the development of man in history. This is not my meaning. I am referring to the development of any single individual of the species, from infancy onwards.

It is natural to begin with the assumption that infants, like the higher animals, exhibit for our inspection definitely discriminable patterns of behaviour and that at the very beginning they exhibit no powers that are distinctively mental for our easy discrimination, beyond and behind these patterns of behaviour. As young children learn to communicate, and learn routines of demand and response, and as they finally learn to communicate freely in a language, the notion of the mental states that lie behind their behaviour and expression, as something distinguishable from them, becomes more and more definitely applicable to them. Part of the process of becoming more and more adult, and of mental development itself, is the process of learning to inhibit and to control inclinations. There is a primary sense of disposition, disposition in the sense of inclination, typically applied to persons rather than to physical objects: the sense in which I may report that I was at a certain moment disposed or inclined to laugh or to cry. A disposition in this sense is something that may occur at a particular moment, may be felt, may be disclosed, and may be inhibited or indulged. When children learn in relations with others to control their own behaviour at will, they will sometimes be in the position of being inclined to do something and yet will intentionally refrain from doing it. Concurrently, or a little later, they are also learning to express their inclinations in words, and are learning to identify things and persons and actions as having certain names, or as satisfying certain descriptions. They thereby arrive at the position of often knowing what it is they want, or are inclined, to do, in the sense of being able to say and to think what it is that they want or are inclined to do. They are able to identify their wants and inclinations as directed towards this or that object, or kind of object. The power to identify and declare one's wants and inclinations necessarily brings with it an extention of the range of these wants. Not only is the subject able to discriminate specifically the objects of his inclinations, but also his inclinations can be directed towards objects that are not immediately present to him, and that are not even causally connected with anything present to him. Finally, he acquires, together with the power to name and to describe, the power to place the objects of his inclinations in a clearly identified future, and of his wishes also in a clearly identified past. To learn the use of concepts is, among other things, to be able to give a definite ordering to one's experiences in time. A creature who uses language is no longer confined to an undiscriminated present in the direction of his inclinations and in the objects of his desires.

All this happens to a child in a social context, in primitive dealings within a family. From the beginning he is responding to the expected gestures of others. He very soon finds himself in a social world: that is to say, he finds himself learning to observe conventions and rules that conflict with his instinctual needs, and to observe the rules *as* rules. He gradually learns, largely by imitation, routines of behaviour, and he learns also the names and proper descriptions of these routines. Thereafter his inhibition of his inclinations is to be distinguished from the inhibition of a trained animal: for example, of a dog trained to restrain its natural inclination to bite something. Because the child may know what it is that he is inclined to do, the question of whether he will do it comes up as a question for him to decide. He may *decide* to restrain his inclination to do something, in a sense of "decide" that is not applicable to an animal, which is not a potential language-user. Whether we say that the deliberate and self-conscious inhibition of an inclination by a human being is an inhibition in a different sense, a sense not applicable to animals, is a philosophical issue that need not detain us here. Must we recognize a difference of sense when there is a difference in the method of verification attached to a context transferred from its original context? I think not. But whatever answer philosophers may give to this question, it is obvious that we can give a clear sense to the inclinations that lie *behind* a creature's behaviour, when that creature can report that it is, or was, inclined to do something and that it restrained its inclination. An animal that cannot use a language may be trained not to do that which it would naturally do. But that it was on a particular occasion inclined to bark or to bite, although owing to its training it did not in fact do so, must be shown in its behaviour, if it is to have sense at all. One must see it behaving in a constrained way, just as when it is frightened one must see it behaving in a frightened way. The inclinations that lie behind the behaviour, the extra dimension that is gradually added to a human being as he grows up to be a language-user, depend for the possibility of their existence on his ability to recognize them as being what they are. This is not only because his disclosures are in the last resort necessary to the confirmation of the existence of the inclination; but also because the action of inhibiting, as an action of his, requires that he recognize his inclination as an inclination of a certain kind.

It will be evident that I am representing a human being's learning of a language as at the same time the acquisition of inclinations which he may on any occasion choose to realize or to inhibit. His full inner life begins with, and is constituted by, this power of intentional inhibition. To describe the development of conscious emotion in a very simplified form: a creature attacked becomes frightened or angry in the sense that it perceptibly behaves in the way that we would specify if we were asked for the natural response to attack—that is, by flight or counter-attack. At the next stage of mental development away from the primitive reaction, the behaviour typical of anger—i.e. aggression—may be inhibited, and only the physiognomy, or expression, that normally accompanies the behaviour may remain. The important point is that we know that his expression is an expression of anger because we recognize it as the abstracted residue of aggressive behaviour; it is this aggressive behaviour at its vanishing-point. At the third stage of inhibition, even this remaining natural expression of anger may be intentionally controlled; perhaps because it is recognized to be a sign of anger that others can dangerously interpret as such. When this stage of interiorization is reached, the natural expression of anger may be used intentionally as a sign in letting others know that one is angry. If there is the power deliberately to inhibit the expression, there is also the power to assume the expression, as a gesture, as a means of communication, and in deceit, mimicry, and play; or at least the idea of assuming the expression must be present to a man's mind as a possibility, if the habit of concealing has once been acquired.

That which remains as a residue, when both the behaviour and the physiognomy primitively associated with anger are controlled, is the mere feeling as a state of consciousness, the inner perturbation, the effect by itself. It is "inner" in the sense that nothing of the anger remains to be perceived by an observer. If an observer is ever to know that the subject is angry, he must primarily rely on the subject's avowal of those inclinations, or upon some inference from the situation and from its correlation with these commonly disclosed inclinations. Plainly there will still be many occasions when the inhibition of the natural expression of the anger is incomplete and only partially successful, and when sufficient signs remain as the basis for an inference, or as confirmation of the sincerity of an avowal. On the borderline of these two stages of inhibition there will be many impure cases—of angry behaviour half controlled, or of the physiognomy of anger just showing through, in spite of an effort to suppress it. The pure case of mere inclination, as a state of consciousness, with every natural expression of it suppressed, certainly exists; and it is the interesting case, as being part of the pattern of inner, unseen mental states, and of the difficulty, or, as some philosophers have thought, impossibility, of inter-subjective descriptions of them.

A man who feels angry, while concealing every overt sign of his inner perturbation, may not need to exercise his will in the act of concealment. The restraint may already be a habit, natural to him as a civilized man. But the habit of intentional inhibition has been acquired during his lifetime, and acquired gradually as part of the observation of social convention. If he is perturbed in the presence of an attacker, he knows, in a simple case, whether he has the disposition to counter-attack or to escape or both. Therefore he knows, in very simple cases and at a superficial level, whether his excitement is anger or fear, or a mixture of both. He does not have to learn to distinguish anger from fear, as a mere quality of feeling, in the way that he distinguishes one colour from another. He is aware of his own controlled inclination in the situation that confronts him. He feels at once the inclination to flight or to counter-attack and he makes the counter movement of restraint. If his feelings are complex, in the sense that he is, in the normal sense of these words, both frightened and angry at the same time, he has opposing inclinations towards flight and counter-attack; and these inclinations may again not be translated into spasmodic and interrupted actions, but rather remain as mere inclinations. I am not of course denying that a man may experience confused and conflicting inclinations, which he may be unable clearly to distinguish and to describe. Nor am I denying that by some methods of analysis, anger and fear may perhaps be shown to be similar and related strategies in the defence of an organism against danger, the one a variant of the other. But it is enough that the simple case of identification of states of consciousness do occur: for it is on these that the whole psychological vocabulary is ultimately founded. We make a mistake if, as philosophers, we think of the emotions and sentiments as primarily something hidden in a man's consciousness and as linked by a contingent and causal relation to their outcome in behaviour; and this has been at least one prevailing picture in contemporary philosophy. The expression of a sentiment or emotion is not something that is extrinsic to the sentiment or emotion itself, as something that may or may not be added to it. On the contrary, that which we call the natural expression is originally constitutive of the sentiment or emotion itself, and may or may not be subtracted from it. This subtraction is the work of a convention-observing creature who already has an intentional control of his behaviour, and who can recognize his own inclinations while refusing to follow them. So much for the simple concept of primary dispositions, or inclinations, in the conscious mind, as these are identified at the most superficial level.

You will perhaps at this stage want to ask for the justification of this, or for any other, simplified philosophical theory of the emotions in their relation to behaviour: is this a priori psychology, and, if not, what is its scientific basis? What is a philosopher's authority for distinguishing phases of human development beginning with primitive behavioural reactions and ending with inner concealed emotion? What is the purpose, and the criterion of success, in such an inquiry as this? It may seem that any such theory must be tested by the observation of children and by careful experiment; and yet this is not the work of philosophers. The answer is that these considerations about the emotions are part of a more general, and of course disputable, theory of language, a theory of how concepts must be properly introduced and applied in their normal contexts. I am, or I take myself to be, specifying the implications, and the method of confirmation, attached to uncriticized, ordinary statements about human emotions of the most rudimentary kind. And surely this must be the starting-point in prescribing the use of the vastly complex and derivative concepts of psychoanalysis. They also have been developed, through many stages of complication and theory, from a rudimentary base in commonplace usage. We have to retrace the path back to this base if we are to understand how they are made up. We have first to see the rudimentary base clearly before us in some simple form, and then we can make the corrections to the commonplace conceptual scheme which the discoveries of psycho-analysis require.

This is the simplified picture of the concept of disposition, in the sense of inclination, which is, I think, a fundamental mental concept. For the conscious mind has to be

conceived—at least in the present state of our knowledge—
as, at least in part, a vastly complicated set of dispositions
of different orders of complexity. I am speaking only of
those dispositions that are inclinations to behave in certain
more or less determinate ways in certain determinate circumstances. But now doubts arise, doubts that infect the
whole study of the philosophy of mind at this time. Let it
be admitted that it is characteristic of mental, as opposed
to physical, concepts that the conditions of their application
can only be understood if they are analyzed genetically:
that is, we need to trace the order in which their use is
learnt in the history of any individual, beginning with the
primitive concepts of sensation, desire and behaviour, concepts that are applicable also to creatures who are not
potential language-users, and showing the use of the more
distinctively mental concepts as developing from them in
successive stages of interiorization. The use of concepts in
communication is learnt in parallel with the development
of corresponding powers of mind—the power to feel without acting and the power to think without saying. But "in
parallel" is an inadequate phrase here; for the one conditions, and makes possible, the other in a complex interaction. A child can have desires and intentions, fears and
hopes, directed towards future events, only because he has
the means of describing and identifying the remote objects
that he desires, fears, or hopes. And the more finely discriminated states of consciousness—embarrassment rather
than fear, shame rather than guilt, remorse rather than regret—can be attributed to him, only because his thought
about himself in relation to external objects is of a degree
of elaboration that allows him to decide which of these
words accurately represents his state. The refined vocabulary of intentional states requires disclosures, not only of
the inclinations, but also of the beliefs that enter into the
definition of these states. A man whose state of mind is re-

morse must, of logical necessity, believe that he has done wrong, and this belief of his must be in principle expressible. One could summarize this double development—learning the use of mental concepts and simultaneously acquiring the corresponding powers of mind—as the development of intentional states. An intentional state, like an intentional action, is directed towards an object usually identified as the object of the state by the subject's conception of it as having a certain name, or as satisfying a certain description. Neither intentional states, in this sense of the phrase, nor intention in action, can significantly be attributed to creatures that are not language-users or potential language-users. Such creatures may want and fear, pursue and avoid, certain objects, and we may inquire into, and see, the purposes of their behaviour. We may experimentally distinguish the objects of their desires and fears, their rages and their repugnances; and we may also by experiment distinguish those features of the objects that make them objects of desire and fear, of rage and repugnance. But the intentional object is identifiable, apart from the evidence of variations of behaviour, through the subject's expression of his thought of the object as having a certain name or as satisfying a certain description. With imputations and acknowledgements of beliefs and intentions, which are not simple inclinations to behave in certain ways, we therefore enter another phase of the mind's development.

The first difficulty can now be stated. I said earlier that infants are born into a social world, and that they sooner or later learn to inhibit their inclinations in accordance with social conventions. They learn also conventions of communication in responding to, and imitating, the meaningful gestures of adults. They gradually acquire an inner life of unexpressed feeling, which becomes more and more distinct from their overt behaviour; and they acquire intentions that point forward in time, remote from the observed present, and that may be left unrealized. But we must now admit that their earliest behaviour, and particularly their play, already foreshadow the added depth of concealed disposition, and inner emotion, that will come with their own later recognition of this depth. The signs are legible in their play, and in their ordinary behaviour, of that which is beyond and behind them—namely, dispositions and inclinations that are repressed, contained within the child's mind as affects or inner feeling. But the signs of inner feeling can never at this stage be intentional signs, and they still have to be read by someone other than the subjects themselves.

Neither philosophy nor psycho-analysis can be satisfied at this point. How much is included in the child's response to, and imitation of, the meaningful gestures of adults? Is the play of a child revealing of inhibited dispositions, and therefore of a depth of feeling, unrecognizable by the child itself, in a full sense of disposition and of "feeling"? The answer to this last question, on the abundant evidence of psycho-analysis, is certainly "Yes." But how can this be?

One possibility suggests itself. When a man looks back in memory, later intentional expressions of feeling may sometimes be associated with the memories of the earlier play. He finds a continuity from the earlier to the later, the continuity of a familiar pattern repeating itself. The inner inclination, which, as he is now persuaded, was originally expressed in his play, may later, preserved in unconscious memory, be expressed in intentional conduct; or it may at least be recognized as an inclination to behave in a certain way.

The essential problem of the unconscious mind is one of time and of memory. The child's responses to meaningful gestures, and his imitation of them, are the earliest phases of a continuous history, which ends with the use of language, and with those intentions directed towards the future, and those memories of past events, which depend on the use of concepts. The continuity of this history lies in the subject's memory. But the power of memory itself develops from a primitive and pre-conceptual form to an adult's fully articulated dating of his experiences in a definite time-order. We may relapse, in dream and fantasy, into the pre-conceptual, childish world, in which past and present are not discriminated by the recognition of memories as memories. But still the power of conscious memory develops alongside these regressions. The word "development," when we speak of the development of a mind or person, implies an order that is held together by manifold links of conscious, half-conscious and unconscious, memory. Looking back in conscious memory, a person can trace a continuity between that which he may with difficulty remember of his early fantasies and play, and his later self-conscious intentional states; and his earliest surviving conscious memories are still memories of a person already carrying a burden of memories, which are no longer available to him. Then, by analogy, it seems that the actions and experiences that he does still remember were originally desirable or repugnant to him partly at least because of memories of earlier experiences now beyond recall. In investigating the development of a man's body, we take it for granted that its earlier states, taken in conjunction with external factors, determine its later states, and its causal properties, in accordance with a great variety of exact and confirmable natural laws. In investigating the development of a man's inclinations, his emotional development, we cannot always, or even generally, in practice apply such a simple scheme of past states determining future dispositions, although the theoretical possibility is always open. It is a fact that the stored, and potentially available, but still unconscious, memories of the past are influencing present inclinations at any time. But what is contained in the word "influencing" here?

Memory of one's own past may take several very different

forms. In the most simple case, we may be aware of our memories as memories, and a memory of something that happened may be the fully conscious ground or reason for a present feeling, or for the behaviour that is the natural expression of this feeling. I am inclined to behave harshly towards him because I remember him harassing me. The word "because" here introduces my reason for my being inclined to behave in this way. But the memory of this same event in the past may have previously existed below the level of consciousness, ready to be evoked as a conscious memory, when the right questions are asked in the right conditions; but the memory is still unrecognized. As soon as the memory is called into consciousness as a memory, the question arises for me—am I only behaving in this way, and do I only have this inclination, *because of* my memory of this past experience? This might perhaps begin as a causal question, as a matter of objective curiosity about psychology. But it immediately becomes an inquiry into the grounds of my behaviour: are they sufficient grounds or not? I had not realized the fact that I had unconsciously remembered this past experience. This fact—the fact that I had preserved this memory below the level of consciousness—becomes something that I must now take into account in considering my present inclinations. Is it reasonable that this past experience should influence my inclinations and actions in my present situation? Is there a relevant similarity, relevant, that is, to consciously recognized ends, which I can rationally acknowledge, between the past situation and my present situation? Once the question is raised, I may, or may not, consider the past experience relevant to my present situation. This is something that I must now decide for myself.

But at this point any true empiricist will ask—what is the sense of speaking of a memory of a past situation, a memory that exists below the level of consciousness, as a reason for present feeling and behaviour, potentially to be acknowledged as a reason? Is it not clearer, and more economical, in such cases to speak of the past event as the cause of the later feeling or behaviour without the interposition of memory at all? Is it not clearer to speak of memory only as a form of knowledge? And therefore always as conscious memory? I think that the evidence compels us to give the answer "No" to each of these questions. The bringing to the surface of consciousness of an unconscious memory is not to be assimilated to the discovery of a causal connection. These are discoveries of quite different kinds, and they require quite different methods of inquiry. The bringing to the surface of consciousness of a memory that has all the time been concealed, and the recognition of it as a reason, are specific experiences that are not to be confused with that recognition of the truth of a general statement, which is entailed by the recognition of a cause.

The nature of dispositions of the mind, as contrasted with the causal properties of physical things, turns on this problem of how far the concept of memory is to be extended. Suppose we allow ourselves to speak of early satisfactions and frustrations of instinctual needs as stored in unconscious memory, and as constituting the reasons, or the motives, for conduct on many later occasions; then we have already begun to substitute a memory-relationship between past and present, peculiar to mental processes, in the place of the normal causal scheme of the natural scientist. This is exactly what Freud did, from the beginning, in his early studies of hysteria. Had he not taken a leap forward in his discoveries of clinical method, he might simply, as a good empiricist, have correlated early alleged sexual experiences, and then later, the fantasies of such experiences, with subsequent hysterical disorders as causes to effects. He might have adhered to the normal scheme of natural law, without any doctrine of early fantasies remembered, interposed as a middle term. He would thereby have precluded himself from relating his method of treatment to his method of diagnosis within a single theory, each confirming the other. The fantasy elicited from the unconscious memory is the underlying motive of, or reason for, later conduct and inclination; and a motive or reason, unlike a cause, is liable to be immediately acknowledged or repudiated as the real motive, and then judged and criticized by the subject. The connection between the now recalled, unconsciously remembered fantasy and the later behaviour symptom must be such as to make the behaviour intelligible to him. It is intelligible, if it is a variant of behaviour that is normally adapted to the satisfaction of desires, and if this variation is explained as the superimposition of the unconsciously remembered fantasy on the present situation. Then he understands the motive.

There are specifiable differences between the discovery of a correlation between two classes of events in a person's history, the occurrence of one determining, under statable conditions, the occurrence of the other, and the discovery that a memory of something in the past has been continuously the reason for inclination and conduct, unknown to the subject and without his having been aware of the memory as a memory. In the second case the influence of the past is something that may be recognized by the subject as the explanation of his inclination and conduct when he becomes aware of the memory as a memory; and to say that he recognizes the unconscious memory as the *explanation* of his inclination and conduct is not to attribute to him the discovery of a correlation between two classes of events. When the repressed memory is revived, there is an instant recognition of the continuity and unbrokenness of the memory discernible in a consistent misreading of situations confronting him. When the memory is recognized as a memory, he recognizes also the consistent superimposition of the

notional past upon the present. Then he finds that the now
consciously remembered fantasy explains his inclination in
the same way that an observed feature of his present situation might explain his inclination. The only difference is
that, unknown to himself, he has been trying to alter the
notional past instead of acting on the present. It might be
shown that there was no universal correlation between the
unconsciously remembered event and the later behaviour;
and still the subject might be sure that this unconscious
memory contains the reason that explains why he, in this
particular case, felt and acted as he did. And one of his reasons for being so sure might be that, with his now fully conscious memory of the past situation as he conceived it, the
inclination to behave and act in the same way returns to
him with the same force, even though now, recognizing the
past as past and unalterable, he restrains himself. Feeling
himself inclined to respond to the fully conscious memory
in the same way, he is aware, again by memory, that there
is an old cycle repeating itself. Having the memory present
to him as a memory, isolated from present realities, he recalls that, at every stage of the repeating cycle, this remembered situation was superimposed upon the present realities, however different, as he now realizes, they were.

The conclusion that, over almost the whole domain of
conduct, there are unconscious motives of behaviour to be
discovered follows harmlessly from the hypothesis that
there are countless memories below the level of consciousness waiting to be elicited. Where explanations in terms of
instinctual needs and rational calculation are inadequate,
we can look into the past for explanations of any individual's conduct and inclinations, without recourse to general
propositions of natural law, which, in default of experiment,
are not generally available. But motives, which explain behaviour and inclination, are one thing and intention is another. "Intention" is the one concept that ought to be pre-

served free from any taint of the less-than-conscious. Its function, across the whole range of its applications, is to mark that kind of knowledge of what one is doing, and of what one is inclined to do, that is fully conscious and explicit. I have motives for doing things, or for feeling inclined to do things, and I may have purposes in doing things, without recognizing, and without being aware, that these are my motives and my purposes. When I come to recognize what my motives are, or were, or what my purposes are or were, I may certainly be surprised that these were in fact my motives. I may make a discovery. My motives are typically matters for investigation. But I do not investigate, and then discover, my intentions. I may indeed carry out an investigation to see whether my intentions have been consistently related, as they should be, to my actual conduct, externally regarded; and I may then discover, disagreeably, that in fact they have not. And then I need to look for underlying motives and memories, in order to explain this deviation.

If it is once accepted that there are countless unconscious memories of our past satisfactions and frustrations, we see many of our actions and inclinations as, at least in part, directed towards situations in the past, but superimposed on, and confused with, a present situation. When the memory is brought into consciousness, and we retrace the recurring cycle of motive and conduct back to this starting-point, our action may appear as motivated by a desire to alter the past, even though the conscious intention was normally directed to the future. If I am convinced that I would not have formed the intention, had I not had the unconscious memory, I may for some purposes re-describe the conduct by reference to its motive rather than to the conscious intention. Then my conduct can be represented as an attempt to change the past, in defiance of the reality principle. For recognition of reality, as it affects behaviour, is

175

recognition of the *present* situation as present, as opposed to the projection into the present situation of the objects of memory and fantasy. Its opposite, loss of the sense of the present, is a partial regression to the childish, pre-conceptual world in which the objects of conduct and feeling are disconnected from an objectively recognized and definite time-order. The ideally rational man would be constantly aware of all his memories as memories, in so far as they influenced his present conduct and inclinations. Correspondingly, his wishes would be attached to definite possibilities in a definite future, and would not be freely floating fantasies, timeless and without attachments to possible occasions. He would always distinguish his present situation from unconscious memories of the past projected upon, and obliterating, the present, and would find his motives for action, in satisfying his instinctual needs, within the objectively observed features of the situation, as he sees it now. But this is an ideal of rationality that can never be attained —which is perhaps fortunate, since it would leave us without art, without dream or imagination, without likes and dislikes unconnected with instinctual needs, and indeed without any character at all as individuals. It can never be attained, because our secondary dispositions to behave in certain ways in certain situations, assimilated to unconsciously remembered primitive situations, are being formed, and superimposed upon each other, from the beginning of our life. I speak of "secondary dispositions" here to distinguish dispositions, in the sense of character traits, from dispositions in the sense already mentioned—namely, inclinations to behave in a certain way on a specific occasion. The original formation of secondary dispositions can be traced back to unconscious memories of primitive satisfactions and frustrations of instinctual needs, modified by complicated and continuing processes of repression, projection, displacement, transference, and so on. Ideal rationality, defined as motivation by the recognized features of the present situation alone, together with instinctual drives, would impossibly require that no such dispositions should exist. Every memory of past satisfactions and frustrations would be present to my mind as a conscious memory, and therefore the relevance, for the satisfaction of my instinctual needs, of the past experience to the present situation would be objectively assessed. In fact I necessarily approach situations with already formed dispositions to respond in my conduct principally to those features of them which are easily associated with unconsciously remembered primitive situations. These dispositions, resting on the weight of my earliest memories, constitute my character as an individual. This may be strong or pliable, making me more or less impervious to changing external realities in my feeling and conduct.

It is now possible to see why the genetical method of explanation, which is no less essential in individual psychology than in the philosophy of mind, will lead to apparent paradoxes. In any individual mind, past frustrations and satisfactions, particularly in the earliest phases of the mind's continuous history, foreshadow the direction of later behaviour and inclinations. This foreshadowing is the other face of the fact that experiences that have once aroused strong inclinations are, in one way or another, remembered, if not consciously, then unconsciously. If they are repressed and unconsciously remembered, they remain as unrecognized motives, which explain a recurring inclination to behave in a characteristic way, in comparative independence of the unchanging external realities. A paradox arises when the arrow of historical explanation of a man's secondary dispositions, from past to future, is thought of as causal determination. If the determination were causal, it should equally allow prediction. But the determination claimed is only the fact that unconsciously remembered situations in the past supply unconscious motives for present conduct and inclination. This confusion has sometimes led interpreters of Freud to speak of retrospective causal explanation, which is a logical absurdity. Of motives it can indeed be said that they explain retrospectively, and that they do not provide a corresponding basis for prediction of future behaviour. In my stating, that it was so-and-so that moved me to laugh or to protest, I have not so far committed myself to any general proposition which justifies a prediction of my behaviour on future occasions; and, least of all, is there a basis for prediction when the transition may be made from an unconscious motive to the conscious recognition of it. Once the imposition of the unconsciously remembered past on the present is fully recognized, and the realities of the present situation are no longer consistently misperceived, the foundations of the secondary disposition have been loosened, and therefore the former character trait may be controllable. This character trait was after all something that I found myself to possess, and not something that I had chosen for myself. And now I may be for the first time in a position to choose, within the limits of the other secondary dispositions that constitute my character.

Something is always being added to the weight of motivating memories, both conscious and unconscious, and it is in practice, although not in theory, impossible to isolate the initial conditions on which a scientific prediction could be based. If we accept the hypothesis of total memory of past satisfactions and frustrations, it certainly follows that we could only approach complete explanations of inclination and behaviour in any individual case through an interminable analysis. The formation of secondary dispositions is a perpetual process, in which recurrent patterns of inclination and behaviour, originally motivated by memories of some primitive situation, are being at all times complicated by displacements and identifications, and by the stress of further frustrations of the dispositions themselves by external realities. And one of the effects and signs of stress, at primitive stages and later, is to make conscious recall more difficult. In any individual case we may be able, by successfully reviving memories, to travel backwards towards the first member of a series, along a series that recalls the recurring motive of inclination and behaviour at every stage. But we cannot infer from this history, or from any finite set of such histories, exactly how the series will be prolonged into the future, if it is prolonged. The vast and continuing accretions of repressed memory provide too many independent variables for any general law of cause and effect to be formulated and tested. We are left only with the recurring pattern itself as a mere tendency; that is, we are left with the old notion of character, of dispositions in the second sense. In the extreme cases of neurosis, a man's character and secondary disposition, which represent attachment, through repressed memory, to the past, will be so strong that patterns of inclination and behaviour will be almost unvarying in changing situations. Selected features of these situations will be read always as changing symbols of emotionally charged features of his primitive past. Then indeed confident prediction may be possible. The cycle of inclination and overt behaviour will simply repeat itself. But when the second dispositions are only of normal (in the sense of "average") strength, and motives for inclinations and action can still be found in changing situations, the interaction between present and past, between fate and character, in forming feeling and behaviour becomes, on this hypothesis, too complicated for confident prediction.

The second difficulty that we confronted was this: that we should not only attribute motives and purposes that have not been previously recognized by the subject himself, but also that we should attribute them to children at a stage of development when they would have been incapable of formulating them, or of recognizing their existence in any way. Searching under guidance through repressed memories, and meeting resistance to their recall, an individual will find one of these recurring patterns of motive, of inclination, and of behaviour in his history. The recurrence is itself at every stage an instance of unconscious remembering. If the hypothesis of total memory is correct, the earliest memories of the earliest instinctual satisfactions, and of primitive frustrations of instinctual need, must be the terminus of explanation. This is the hard foundation to which we always return in explaining any individual's secondary dispositions. In order to assert the constancy of the motivation from its starting-point in the individual's history, and simultaneously to show the motives for the repression of the relevant memory, the early formation of character-traits is assimilated to the problem-solving of an adult man. It is characteristic of properly causal explanations of mental processes that highly developed and rational processes are assimilated to the more primitive responses to stimulus; for specifically described behaviour has to be regularly correlated with specifically prescribed initial conditions. It is characteristic of an individual psychology based on the memory relationship that the least developed mental processes are assimilated to the rational or problem-solving kind. We look backwards, from the later to the earlier, in order to understand the present as a lightly or heavily disguised re-enacting of the problems of the past. And in extreme cases of neurotic behaviour, the lapse of time, and the development of rational powers of mind, may be virtually eliminated as an irrelevant superstructure.

This substitution of a scheme of explanation depending on an extended concept of memory for explanation by causal laws will not be fully understood and evaluated by philosophers for many years. The implications are too far-reaching, the logical obscurities of explanation by motive, and by the acknowledgement of motive, are too numerous, even in the most simple cases. For centuries the workings of the mind, in forming inclinations and attachments to objects, have been construed by empiricists on a mechanical model, which the causal scheme of explanation seemed to require: the association of ideas. The laws governing the association of ideas were taken to be strictly analogous to the laws governing the movement of bodies. No reference was required to any central, co-ordinating activity of the self, as a self-preserving agency, in forming its inclinations. The separate inclinations formed themselves according to universal causal laws. For the simple machinery of the association of ideas, Freud substitutes complex activities of projection, introjection, and identification in the solution of conflicts. The importance of this substitution, from the philosophical point of view, is just that these activities are represented as activities; and because they are so represented, the underlying motives of them can be investigated. Within this scheme, the question of "Why?," the demand for an explanation in any particular case, does not call for a universally valid psychological law and a statement of initial conditions. Since these processes are represented as activities of mind, the question "Why?" asks for a description of the situation or situations, real or imagined, and therefore of the given problem, to which these continuing activities were the solution adopted. The effect of the substitution of the active for the passive mood is that the subject is required to search in his memory for the past situation, as it originally presented itself to him, and to acknowledge or to disclaim its superimposition on the present. The appeal to his supposed total memory of his unconscious policies in satisfying his instinctual needs, or the needs derived from their frustration, is an appeal to him to understand his own behaviour as a whole, historically: and this form of understanding, the historical and autobiographical form, is taken

181

to be the fundamental form in the explanation of patterns of inclination and conduct. He may resist the appeal and his active exercise of memory may be ineffective. But this failure also will require an explanation in terms of a motive for refusal to remember, and will not be counted as evidence against the hypothesis of total memory itself. If a recurring pattern of feeling and behaviour stands out in an individual's history, and if its first, and only its first, occurrence is explicable by the operation of the instincts against the given resistance of reality, the later instances of the pattern can be traced back, through many complicating stages, to unconscious memories of this primitive occasion, to his first thoughts about it.

The whole weight of explaining, and of understanding, human behaviour is placed on the individual subject, as potentially an active, remembering being. Because of this, he can, to some extent, become rather more free and self-determining, through making an active use of memory in disinterring his own unconscious motives, and in acquiring a clearer view of present reality. This is a way to freedom that has no place in the psychology that rests entirely on the causal scheme, as this is applied also to physical things.

I stress the extended concept of memory, or of psychical traces, which is not a technical term of psycho-analytical theory, because I believe that the nearest point of attachment between the uncriticized, pre-analytical concepts of commonsense speech on the one hand, and the Freudian scheme on the other, is to be found exactly here. This is the natural place to build the bridge, because the crossing from common sense notions of personality, particularly of secondary disposition and character, to the theory of the unconscious mind is at its shortest at this point. Apart altogether from the much discussed dynamics of Freudian theory, and apart from clinical needs, we have here a general account of the formation of individual character, the claims of which must be recognized and discussed.

Spinoza and the Idea of Freedom

I believe that everyone who has ever written about Spinoza, and who has tried to interpret his thought as a whole, either has been, or ought to have been, uneasily aware of some partiality in his interpretation, when he turns once again from his own words to the original. Certainly this is my own position. When the study of Spinoza is reviewed historically, one sees that each commentator, unconsciously faithful to his own age and to his own philosophical culture, has seized upon some one element in Spinoza's thought; he then proceeds to develop the whole of the philosophy from this single centre. Spinoza as the critic of Cartesianism: Spinoza as the free-thinker and destroyer of Judaeo-Christian theology: Spinoza as the pure deductive metaphysician: Spinoza as the near-mystic, who imagines a level of intuitive understanding beyond discursive reason: lastly, Spinoza as the scientific determinist, who anticipates the more crude materialists, and the more crude secular moralists, of the nineteenth century: as the precursor of George Henry Lewes. All these masks have been fitted on him and each of them does to some extent fit. But they remain masks, and not the living face. They do not show the moving tensions and unresolved conflicts in Spinoza's *Ethics*. They remain interpretations that have been imposed from outside. They smooth over and cover up the opposing strains within the original thought. His writing has a hard, finished, unyielding surface. One can return to it again and again without ever being sure that one has penetrated to the centre of his intentions. He could only state; he could not loosely explain, or betray his intentions in an approximation. Yet I have the persisting feeling—I cannot properly call it a belief—that in the philosophy of mind he is nearer to the truth at certain points than any other philosopher ever has been. I do not therefore propose historical accuracy and historical justice as motives for returning once again to the original *Ethics* at one of its most difficult points. Rather I believe that there is something very relevant to moral and political philosophy at this time to be learnt from an entirely literal, unprejudiced, and uncondescending attention to Spinoza's idea of freedom. Perhaps his conception of freedom is after all a valid one; and perhaps we are now in a better position than our ancestors to find the true significance of it.

The two most obvious facts about Spinoza are the two most important facts in understanding his intentions: first, that his definitive philosophical work was justly called *Ethics*: second, that the supreme evaluative distinction finally recognized in his philosophy, other than the distinctions between true and false, and between adequate and inadequate, ideas, is the distinction between freedom and servitude. These are the terms, positive and negative, in which a man, and a man's life, his actions and passions, are to be finally judged. These are the terms in which a wise man reviews and criticizes his own conduct, his own emotions and attitudes, and it is by reference to this contrast that he will, if he is wise, make his own decisions. A man is wise in proportion as his thought at all times proceeds by active reasoning from premises that are well known to him as self-evident truths. These self-evident truths are necessarily available to him, as instruments for his enlightenment, among the many confused and inadequate ideas that he must also have. They are necessarily available to every thinking being, as the reflections in his thought of the universal and unchanging features of the natural order of extended things. His inadequate ideas reflect only his particular and temporary standpoint as one extended thing among others. If once he concentrates his attention on these timeless truths, independent of his own standpoint and perceptions, and argues carefully from them, he cannot help coming to the conclusion that human conduct has to be judged, and his own decisions made, by reference to this single standard, the standard of freedom of mind as opposed to servitude of mind; and he will unavoidably agree that the distinction between freedom and its opposite is the distinction between active reasoning, internally determined, and the mind's passive reception of ideas impressed upon it from without.

"He cannot help coming to the conclusion," "he will unavoidably agree that it *must* be interpreted"—here already there are the signs of necessity. As soon as we start to argue strictly, these and other signs of necessity will always enter in. As will be seen later, these marks of necessity, rightly understood and in the appropriate context, are the marks of freedom and activity of mind. The mind is active and free when, and only when, the argument is strict, when the conclusion of a passage of thought is internally determined by the thinking process itself. A man whose attention has been drawn to self-evident, primary truths, the terms of which he understands, will unavoidably follow a continuous train of thought and will unavoidably affirm the necessary conclusions. If he fully understands, he has no choice. If he has a choice, and if he can doubt and hesitate until he settles the matter by a decision, his conclusion will be determined, at least in part, by something that is external to the thinking process itself.

Some of these primary truths are concerned with the notion of cause or of explanation, in the widest sense of these words. In the widest sense of the word "cause," anything that is an appropriate answer to the question "Why?" gives a cause, irrespective of the category to which the thing to be explained belongs. The question "Why?" may, for example, be asked with reference to a belief, a human action, a human attitude or sentiment, the existence of a physical object, or the properties of numbers and geometrical figures. Anything that counts as an answer to the question "Why?" is an explanation, whether true or false, of the belief, action, attitude, sentiment, physical object, or mathematical property. In the vocabulary that Spinoza inherited, the word "cause" can be substituted for the word "explanation," without prejudging any questions about the type of explanation appropriate to these different cases. The distinguishing of different types, or categories, of causes, which is the distinguishing of different types or categories of explanation, has always been the proper work of philosophy, and of that reflexive knowledge that is peculiar to philosophy. Spinoza draws these distinctions between types of explanation in the *Ethics*, adapting an inherited scholastic vocabulary for his own purpose.

Let us assume the standpoint of an individual thinker, a finite mode, with his necessarily limited knowledge. Reflecting on the range of his knowledge, he will find at least one clear distinction: the distinction between an understanding of causes that is complete and self-justifying, and an understanding of causes that is not complete and self-justifying. There are ideas in reference to which the question "Why is it so?" receives a complete answer, in the sense that, in looking for the explanation, we arrive at self-evident truths, and definitions, in a finite number of steps. There are other ideas in reference to which the question "Why is it so?" leads us back along an infinite series of ideas, with no final and sufficient explanation to be found within the series, however long we continue. So much is common to Leibniz and Spinoza. They diverge when they specify the limits of application of the two orders of explanation, the complete and the incomplete. For Spinoza the fundamental difference between the two orders of causes is the difference between the series of eternal things and the series of things that come into existence and pass away at a certain time. There is no further difference between the two orders of

explanation which is not entailed by this primary difference. There is no ultimate contingency in the existence of
things in the common order of nature, no contingency im-
putable to a creator's free choice among logically possible
alternatives. The difference is only between that which is
eternal and that which is finite in its existence. The existence of things that are not eternal, and that occupy a determinate position in the time-order, can only be incompletely explained. There must always be an infinite regress
of causes required to explain why this particular thing
exists at this particular time. The existence of this thing was
contingent upon the prior existence of some other thing and
so on *ad infinitum*. No limit can be set on the universe of
individual things that come into existence and pass away.
But there are objects conceived as eternal things, about
which it does not make sense to ask when they came into
existence and when they will perish: numbers, for example,
or the whole of extended Nature, which can be referred to
as a thing, as *Res extensa*. About such things an explanation
can be given of why their properties must be ordered as
they are, an explanation that will terminate in self-evident,
primary propositions defining the nature of the objects referred to.

This distinction between the two orders of explanation,
the two kinds of answer to "Why is it so?", the temporal
and the non-temporal order, corresponds to Leibniz's distinction between truths of reason and truths of fact, and
also to familiar post-Kantian distinctions between analytic
and synthetic propositions. But it is a different distinction,
not the same distinction with a different label. Spinoza expresses the distinction, not only as a distinction between
different types of object, eternal things and finite things, but
also as a distinction between the ways in which any given
subject-matter can be studied. Whether we are inquiring
into human emotions, including our own emotions, or into

the nature and movements of physical objects, we can always, if we choose, look for the eternally valid laws that explain the variety of human emotions and the movements of physical objects. We can always regard the particular case of an emotion or of a physical movement, occurring at exactly this time and soon to disappear, as an instance, or illustration, of a constant, unchanging pattern. Such a pattern has its own ultimate explanation in the permanent structure of things. We can always regard the thing to be explained *sub specie aeternitatis*, without attention to the date on which it occurred, or to the standpoint from which it was observed, and not *sub specie durationis*, which would involve explaining its place in the time order that leads up to this particular occasion.

If we are interested only in ourselves and in our own environment, and therefore in the occurrence of the emotion, or of the physical movement, at this particular time, and if we wish to trace the causes in their historical sequence up to this moment, we will of course need to invoke the eternally valid laws in looking for the historical explanation of this particular case. But the interest is then an historical interest, and this is an interest that can never be finally satisfied. Some uncertainty will always attach to any historical explanation that we attempt. Some of the infinitely numerous factors, which should ideally have been mentioned, have always eluded us. We fall into error, and an error that has serious consequences in our practical activities, if we do not always bear in mind the intrinsic difference between the two types of explanation, the two orders of causes, the intellectual order and the common order of nature. We must always be aware of the incompleteness and necessary uncertainty of any historical explanation of things in the common order of nature. Intellectually, the error is to take some cause picked out from the temporal sequence of events and to concentrate our attention upon it as *the* cause, and then to suppose that we can know that, if only this had been different, which it might have been, the effect would never have followed. Then it will seem to us contingent that things happened as they did. But the appearance of contingency is due to the necessary limitation of our knowledge, to our incapacity to follow to its conclusion every path of investigation, where the paths are infinitely many. When we isolate some one cause as the sole object of interest, and think of it as something that really might have been different, we are simply failing to realize the infinite complexity of the connections between things in the temporal order. Practically and morally, the corresponding error will be to love or to hate with blind concentration the particular thing which, through weakness of mind, has become isolated in our thought from the infinitely complex network in the common order of nature. Instead of being detached and sceptical in reflecting on the infinite complexity of the causes, we shall be uncritically certain that we have identified the original good or evil within our own environment. We shall therefore for a time tend to act as if our welfare depended solely on the destruction or preservation of this particular thing. Our conduct will for a time correspondingly exhibit the same blind and helpless partiality, the same imaginative obsession with one thing, suggested to us by our environment, as the true cause of our present pleasure or suffering.

Most men spend their lives in an alternation between one object and another as the temporary object of desire or aversion, absorbed in their own partial view of their own environment, and unable to see this environment, and their own passive reactions to it, as formed by a concatenation of causes that extends infinitely in every direction. They have therefore no consistent plan, no stable and central direction of their interests. This alternation of desires, this fluctuation of the mind, is the state of fantasy, obsession, and unenlightenment. The mind is then to a greater or less degree disintegrated, in the sense that the succession of its states is not determined by the subject's own activity of thought. Their states of mind are only to be explained as more or less unconnected responses of their imagination to the stimulus of the environment, which evokes desires and aversions that have no adequate foundation in the subject's own directed reasoning. This condition of unfreedom, of slavery to the passions, is the equivalent in Spinoza of the heteronomy of the will in Kant. But it is not an enslavement of the will, but rather of the understanding. The remedy is the correction of the understanding and an appeal to its natural powers. The remedy is available to everyone who is able to reflect upon, and who never forgets, the two levels of explanation, the two orders of causes, and therefore the two kinds of knowledge which each man necessarily possesses. As long as a man is reflectively aware, whenever he thinks, of the nature of his own thought, as either actively directed towards eternal and demonstrable truths, or else as absorbed in uncriticized fantasies traceable to his own sensations and memories, he is not misled either in that which he claims to know with certainty, or in that which he considers desirable or undesirable, as good or bad. He will reflectively examine the reasons for his own desires and aversions, and he will distinguish those that are to be explained as the effects of events on his imagination, from those that are explained by an active consideration, independent of his own situation, of the tendency of an object to serve the purposes common to all thinking beings as such. Because he knows when he truly knows and when he only incompletely knows, he always knows when he has an entirely sufficient reason for his actions and attitudes, and when he has not. As he is by nature an active thinking being, he will prefer the type of explanation of things that is complete and intellectually satisfying when it is presented to him. As a body naturally tends to maintain itself, and restore itself, against the effects of the environment, so correspondingly a mind tends to assert its power of thought, and to prefer rational argument, whenever it is presented, to the passive association of ideas in the common order of nature. But we need to be awakened to the recognition and the use of the powers that our minds possess. This is part of the work of a philosopher, which includes, as in the example of Spinoza's own writing, exhortation, a call to reflection, alongside purely intellectual analysis.

Perhaps this picture of the free man as self-directing, as an integrated mind with a continous controlling reason, is so far a clear one. But the notion of freedom itself is still unclarified: what is the precise connection between a man's knowledge of the distinction between different levels of knowledge and his freedom in action? The connection is to be found in Spinoza's theory of individuals. Like every other identifiable particular thing in the natural order, a man tries in his characteristic activity to preserve himself and his own distinct nature as an individual, and to increase his own power and activity in relation to his environment. This trying (*conatus*), or inner force of self-preservation, is that which makes any individual an individual. Regarded as a physical organism, his overriding interest is to preserve his own stability as a distinct organism in relation to the physical environment. Regarded as a thinking being, his overriding interest is to preserve the coherence and continuity of his own thought against the flow of unconnected ideas which are his perceptions, sensations, and imaginations. The conatus of the individual, conceived as a physical organism, is the body's tendency to repair itself and to maintain itself in relation to the environment. The conatus of the individual, conceived as a thinking being, is the *vis animi*, which is the essential and natural tendency of the mind to assert active thinking and knowledge against the

191

passive association of ideas in imagination. The more the sequence of a man's own ideas can be explained without reference to causes outside his own thinking, the more active and self-determining he is, regarded as a thinking being. The more active and self-determining he is, to that degree also he can be more properly regarded as a distinct thing, having an individuality that sets him apart from his particular environment. The more self-determining and active he is, and the more free, in this sense of "free," the more he can be regarded as a real individual, as real as an individual thinking being.

Because a thing's reality as a distinct individual depends on its activity and freedom, Spinoza must take the word "free," rather than the word "good," as the fundamental term of evaluation. He is a scholastic and an Aristotelian in taking it for granted that praise and evaluation of a thing are necessarily an assessment of the degree to which it realizes its nature or essence in its activity. The nearer a thing approaches perfection in the activity proper to it, the more praiseworthy it is. He takes the virtue, objectively regarded, of any thing to be the same as the perfect realization of its nature. But, unlike Aristotle, he identifies the essential nature of any individual thing with its individuality, with that which makes it a distinct individual: and this is its power of self-maintenance in relation to other things. Its virtue is its power as an individual. A particular thing's nature or essence is its nature or essence as a distinct individual rather than as a specimen of a kind. Peter or Paul are therefore not to be judged as being more or less good men, that is, as realizing more or less completely the potentialities of their species. They are to be judged as more or less complete individuals, that is, as more or less distinguishable as active agents from the temporary influences of their environment in the common order of nature. A man's natural tendency or conatus is not to make himself a good or perfect specimen of his kind, to realize in his activity some general ideal of humanity, but rather to preserve himself, this individual, as an active being, who is, as far as possible, independent in his activity. He has achieved virtue, and succeeded in that which he necessarily desires, when, and only when, he is comparatively free and self-determining in his activity. He would be a perfect being, if he were perfectly self-determining, active, and free. His happiness, and enjoyment of action, do not depend on a choice of ends of action that he, as an individual, has to make and that he is free to make: the choice of whether to pursue the ideal of excellence that is proper to his species. In the last analysis, and speaking philosophically, there is no such choice of an ideal or end. Philosophically speaking, the choice is of the right means to an end that is already determined for him by his nature and appetites as an individual thinking and physical thing. The real choice is between the first step of reflection, preliminary to the use of his intellectual powers, and an undirected passive response to experience. His desires, as they emerge into consciousness, are determined by the thought of the causes of his pleasure and suffering. If the thought is confused, and is largely fantasy, he will pursue, *sub specie boni*, temporary ends, which, by the laws of his nature, must lead to frustration, instability, and suffering. Therefore he needs to be stirred to take this first step of reflection. His happiness consists in his sense of his activities as having their originating cause within him, and in his enjoyment of his own activity as unimpeded activity. He is frustrated, and therefore suffers, when his activity is not self-directed, but is rather the immediate effect of causes external to himself. The suffering is the loss of his sense of his own power and vitality as a distinct and active being.

The notion of an individual nature or essence may be found altogether obscure. We can, I think, still attach a sense to the notion of the essential characteristics of a species, and to the judgement of individuals as more or less perfect specimens of their kinds. But can we intelligibly speak of an individual or particular thing becoming more or less of an individual? Spinoza provides a criterion by which the approach to perfection of an individual *qua* individual is to be judged: the criterion is the degree to which the individual is active and self-determining. Any thing that is identifiable as a particular thing can be judged by this single criterion, irrespective of the kind to which it is allotted within conventional classifications. One may review the scale of the increasing activity and self-determination of particular things, and therefore of their increasing individuality, from physical objects of various orders of complexity, to living organisms, to human beings. Human beings, at the top of the scale, can be completely self-determining when their activity is continuous thought, with each idea following its predecessor in the intellectual sense of "follow" as well as in the temporal sense. At such moments —and the moments cannot be indefinitely prolonged—men rise above their normal human condition as finite modes.

In the ordinary vocabulary we conventionally classify things into kinds according to their typical human uses. Spinoza demands that, as moralists and philosophers, we should see through these anthropocentric classifications to the true individuality of particular things. When we group them into kinds, we should follow this single principle in differentiating the kinds: their characteristic power and form of self-maintenance as individuals. From the standpoint of the true natural philosopher, the natural order should be seen as a system of individuals within individuals, of increasing power and complexity, each type of individual differentiated by its characteristic activity in self-maintenance. The more fully we study and understand particular things, not as specimens of the conventionally recog-

SPINOZA AND THE IDEA OF FREEDOM

nized kinds, but as types of structure each acting and maintaining their identity according to the laws of the type, the
more we shall understand Nature as a whole. This is the
form in which natural knowledge, objectively valid for the
whole of Nature, is properly to be expressed. Psychology
as a science can be no exception.

There is one case in which each man is well qualified to
achieve such a true understanding of an individual: himself.
Starting from this secure example, he can work outwards
towards a true and objective understanding of Nature as a
whole. He will become dissatisfied with the conventional
classifications of things by their ordinary human uses, and
he will find a more objective and truly scientific principle
of classification in their various modes of self-maintenance.
Spinoza's objective study of the emotions, the outline of a
psychopathology, illustrates these principles. There are systematic connections, laws of unconscious memory, to be
found behind the conventional classifications of the passions. Systematic knowledge of these is the necessary first
step to self-knowledge.

It is now possible to state the connection between a constant awareness of the distinction between adequate and inadequate knowledge and the notion of freedom. We need
to apply the doctrine of the individual as essentially active
to a thinking being who is a person. For every belief that I
have, and for every claim to knowledge that I make, there
is an explanation of why I have this belief and why I claim
to have this knowledge. Every passion that can be attributed to me is a pleasure or a pain combined with an idea of
the cause of this pleasure or pain. There must therefore be
an explanation of my having this idea about the cause of my
pleasure or suffering. Suppose then that I am at all times
asking myself the question—Is the sequence of ideas that
has terminated in this idea a self-contained sequence that,
by itself, completely explains my idea of the cause? In other

195

words, was the conclusion reached by a rational process? Or must I mention ideas that are associated in my experience, but that are without intrinsic connection, in explaining my conclusion? Under these conditions of self-conscious reflection, I never affirm a proposition, or commit myself to a belief, without qualifying it as adequately or inadequately founded. If this condition were fulfilled, I could not be a victim of those passions that consist in the association of my pleasure or suffering with the idea of a particular transient thing, or person, in the common order of nature as its adequate cause. And when I say that I *could* not be a victim of the passion, the impossibility here is a logical impossibility. The unexamined links of association, which are necessary to the belief that is part of the passion, depend for their existence on my not being reflectively aware of them. As soon as I am self-consciously aware of them, I must then know that it is only through the fantasies engendered by my particular history that my present pleasure or suffering has become associated in my mind with the idea of these particular things or persons, which I now in consequence hate or love. If I actively inquire into the true causes of my pleasure or suffering, the passive association of ideas is broken, and the attention focused on the particular thing, or person, as the adequate cause is dissolved.

An emotion necessarily involves a thought of the cause or occasion of the pleasure or unpleasure, and it is in this sense directed towards an object. Spinoza's theory of the emotions represents them as states of pleasure or unpleasure, and of desire and aversion, combined with a thought of the causes, simple or complex, or occasions of the pleasure or unpleasure. To change the accompanying thought is therefore to change the emotion, and therefore to change the desire or the aversion that determines conduct. Suppose that I am angry with someone and am angry about something that he has done. To be angry is to be displeased and to be disposed to injure someone, together with the thought that he has been the cause of injury to me. When I consider my true interests as an active thinking being, and also examine a train of unconscious associations that leads to the idea of him as the original cause of my displeasure, and recognize their inadequacy, the passion of anger disappears. When I realize the contributing causes of my displeasure in my own unconscious memories and consequent dispositions, the idea of an adequate external cause disappears, and there is nothing left to be angry with. When on reflection I realize that no one external thing can be isolated as the cause of my displeasure, I not only realize my error in imagining a simple external cause of my state: I open the way to the activity of intellectual inquiry, regarding this particular case wholly as an instance of general laws. I thereby substitute the active enjoyment of my own powers of thought for the suffering associated with my imagination of an adequate external cause of my displeasure.

To interpret Spinoza as expecting emancipation solely from an intellectual understanding of causes is not entirely correct. It is equally incorrect to represent him as defining freedom simply as knowledge of the causes that determine my emotions and actions. Reason is the expression of my primary desire of self-assertion as a thinking being, of the urge to extend my own activity and freedom as far as I can. I am to the highest degree free when I am engaged in an intellectual inquiry, and when the subject of this inquiry is the order of my thought, as an instance of something that may be understood *sub specie aeternitatis*, and not as it is affected by particular causes in the common order of nature. My happiness then consists, first, in immunity from hatred of particular things, and from the other negative and depressive passions, an immunity that an adequate understanding of causes necessarily brings: secondly, it consists in the positive enjoyment of my own freedom *as* freedom, as the active exercise of the power of thought. These two necessary conditions of happiness, which may be distinguished in other philosophies, are inseparable, even if distinguishable, in Spinoza's thought. He is often represented as implausibly asserting that knowledge of the causes of suffering by itself brings liberation from suffering. This is a double over-simplification. First, the liberation consists in the substitution of a free activity and of self-assertion, which is as such enjoyable, for a passive reaction, which is as such depressing and frustrating. Secondly, in the definition of any of the passions the pleasure or suffering, and the thought of its cause, are indissolubly connected. If the confused thought, or imagination, of an external cause is replaced by thought in an intellectual order, an active emotion replaces a passion.

We may now ask whether, and with what qualifications, this idea of human freedom is still defensible, and whether it suggests the true grounds of our present interest in the freedom of the individual as the main end of policy, both in private and political affairs. Let it be remembered that a man is most free, according to Spinoza, and also feels himself to be most free, when he cannot help drawing a certain conclusion, and cannot help embarking on a certain course of action in view of the evidently compelling reasons in favour of it. He has a compelling reason for following a certain course of action when he knows with certainty that it will promote his power and freedom as an active thinking being, and therefore that it will promote his enjoyment of his own existence. Then he cannot hesitate. The issue is decided for him without any need for the exercise of his will in decision, exactly as the issue is decided for him when the arguments in support of a theoretical conclusion are conclusive arguments. The only difference between theoretical conclusions and practical decisions is that the latter are always governed by the agent's desire for his own good, rationally or irrationally interpreted.

198

When a man finds himself divided in mind between conflicting and inconclusive arguments, and between conflicting inclinations, he is, and feels himself to be, so much less a free man in his affirmations and in his actions. In such a case that which has determined his final decision, whatever it is, will be, at least in part, external to his own thought. In such cases some explanation could always in principle be given, a cause found in the common order of nature, for his deciding as he did. But it would not be a complete explanation of the right kind. He was moved to affirmation or action by something that was outside the rational sequence of thought. He was not entirely active and self-determining, but, at least in part, unknowing and passive in his motivation, since that which moved him to action was below the level of conscious thought. He was not altogether free in his decision, and he knows and feels that he was not, because he did not himself recognize its necessity. When some part of the explanation of my believing something, or of my doing something, is to be found in a cause unrecognized by my reason, and in something external to my thought, I had not sufficient grounds for my belief or action. If I have a full awareness of the adequate explanation of my affirming or acting, I necessarily have sufficient grounds for my affirmation or action. The knowledge of the necessity of affirming something, or of doing something, by itself converts an external cause into an inner ground of affirmation or action. If I know clearly why I believe something or why I am doing something, I also have my own sufficient reasons for affirming or doing. If I cannot completely explain why I reach the conclusion, and if I allow that there are other possibilities open to me, my conclusion, whatever it is, will have been motivated by something other than my own reasoning.

It should now be evident that the too simple question "Was Spinoza a determinist?" admits of no clear answer. The doctrine of the two orders of causes, the intellectual

and the temporal orders, by itself makes the question indeterminate—almost meaningless. But there is a question that
always lies behind any mention of "determinism" and that
certainly is worth asking: "Did Spinoza provide clear and
acceptable grounds for familiar moral distinctions? Or is his
idea of human freedom incompatible with the acceptance
of any familiar moral distinctions?" We cannot answer without considering the concept of morality itself: what kind
of classifications of men and of their activities are to be
counted as moral classifications, as resting on moral distinctions? There is no philosophically neutral answer to this
question. Following Kant, one may distinguish between the
moral and natural qualities of men on the basis of some doctrine of the will, which is taken to define the domain of the
moral. And there is certainly no place for any such distinction as this in Spinoza's thought. Or one may so restrict the
notion of morality that nothing counts as a moral judgement, or as a moral choice, unless the free choice of some
specific end, or specific standard, of human activity is prescribed, an end or standard that all men, as men, unconditionally ought to aim to achieve or to conform to. Within the
terms of Spinoza's metaphysical theory, there is no sense in
saying that men ought to be free, that they ought to be self-
determining, integrated in mind and constant in their desires, and actively rational, in an unconditional sense of
"ought." The unconditional injunction to them to pursue a
certain end implies that they have a choice among various
possibilities, and that they may make the wrong choice, unless they are enlightened by the moralist. Philosophically
speaking and in the last analysis, they have no such choice
of the ultimate ends of action. They are all, the virtuous and
the vicious, the enlightened and the unenlightened, in any
case trying to survive as active individuals and are trying
to assert their power and freedom as individuals. The only
question that arises, either in their own decisions or in

judgement upon them, is—"How completely are they succeeding in asserting themselves as self-determining individuals? How can they become more successful than they are in maintaining and extending their own freedom and activity?"

Of the ideally free man one can say that he will necessarily have certain virtues—for instance, the virtues of liberality and benevolence. In this sense there is indeed a standard or norm of conduct: that we can specify the dispositions that are inseparable from freedom of mind, and therefore we can specify the essential public and private virtues. Spinoza clearly explains in the Preface to Part IV of the *Ethics*: although the words "good" and "bad" indicate nothing positive in the things to which they are applied, we do indeed need to retain them in use, because (I quote) "we want to form for ourselves an idea of man upon which we may look as a model of human nature." This is part of the technique of self-improvement, a preparation for the life of reason. And he explains again in Part V that reflection upon maxims of virtue and wise conduct is a useful starting-point for the life of reason. But it is, strictly speaking, a misstatement, a philosophical error of the kind that occurs only in speaking to the unenlightened, to represent the virtues of the free, rational man as duties imposed upon us, or as appropriate matter for unconditional moral imperatives. There is no law, and therefore there are no duties, other than the natural law of self-preservation, which states that we try to extend our power and liberty as far as we can. How far we can, and by what methods of intellectual discipline, is the proper subject of any book that has the title "Ethics." Its conclusions are properly called the dictates of reason. Most of the duties recognized in conventional morality are in fact less rational foreshadowings of behaviour that would be the natural and unconstrained behaviour of a free man. He has his own adequate reasons for being a peaceful, friendly, just, and co-operative member of society. He may need to appeal to the myth of the moral law to persuade the mass of his fellow citizens to co-operate in civil society.

Some of the conventional virtues of civil society, those associated with renunciation, unworldliness, and repression, are not virtues but vices. They are signs of weakness and of failure in the individual's realization of his own vitality as an individual. They have been taken for virtues, when myths of a transcendent God and of another world have been taken seriously as metaphysical truths. Preoccupation with death, and with human weakness, and with the passage of time, rather than with the enjoyment of present activity, are the emotional counterparts of these false philosophies. In a well-known and significant paragraph (Scholium to Prop. x in Part v), Spinoza says that the attitude of the severe moralist, which issues in denunciations of the vices and vanities of man, and of the common conditions of human life, is always the mark of a diseased mind. Pathos and virtue are opposed to each other, because, for Spinoza, virtue is energy—in a rather more precise sense than Blake intended.

There is therefore a sense in which Spinoza is representing the study of ethics, in the then dominant Christian and Jewish tradition, as one immense error, as the pursuit of a harmful illusion. The illusion is that various goals or ends of human effort, towards which our actions might be directed, are open to us for decision and for appraisal, and that the discussion and comparison of the various ends of action is the proper subject-matter of ethics. The ultimate ends of action are not open for decision or discussion. They are fixed by the laws of our nature as mind-body organisms struggling to preserve ourselves against our environment. That which we generally take, in our ignorance of these natural laws, to be our own free decision between alternative ends is to be explained as the complicated working of these laws in our own individual psychology. They are laws governing increases and decreases of vitality in the mind-body organism, and, derivatively, of unconscious appetites and conscious desires. I am only self-directing and independent when I am actively studying the laws of nature themselves, free from any concentration of interest exclusively on myself and on my relation to other particular things. Unless I continually reflect in this detached, philosophical manner, my particular judgement of ends of action, of good and bad, will correspond only to my particular desires and needs, due to the complications of my particular environment, and to the fantasies that have arisen from this history. I am deceived, if I do not discover the element of fantasy, and of unconscious memories, in my original judgements of value. Moral argument, that which replaces the traditional free discussion of ends of action, should be an attempt to bring to light, and to recognize, our own motives and their sources, and thereby to make our pursuit of our own safety, and the enjoyment of our own activity, fully self-conscious and therefore fully rational.

It is at least possible that Spinoza is right in his opinion that traditional ethics is the pursuit of an illusion, and that gradually, in the course of years, he may be shown to be right. But for him of course this conclusion was not opinion, but knowledge. Nor did he think that it required, or could receive, confirmation from further observation and scientific inquiry. I am assuming a view of his philosophy, and of philosophy itself, which was not his; the view that a philosophy such as his, which began with a claim to final truth demonstrable by a priori argument, is to be judged now as a speculative anticipation of truths that may gradually be confirmed by scientific inquiry, and by accumulating human experience. The confirmation, if it comes, will not be like the confirmation of an empirical hypothesis. It will not be direct confirmation, which leaves one with no reasonable alternative other than to accept the hypothesis as true. Rather the confirmation would be that some notions closely resembling Spinoza's key notions become widely accepted as peculiarly appropriate in studying and in evaluating human behaviour. New psychological knowledge might fit better into this framework than into any other, and psychologists themselves, and those who must now be directly or indirectly influenced by them, might come to employ concepts closely akin to Spinoza's. Certainly anyone who altogether rejects Spinoza's naturalistic standpoint, and anyone who has some religious and transcendental ground for his moral beliefs, would remain unpersuaded: and, given his premises, justifiably so. But those of us who have no such transcendental grounds may at least pause and consider the possibility that much of our habitual moralizing about the ends of action is altogether mistaken. Certainly we should not deceive ourselves by dismissing Spinoza as the kind of determinist who allows no possibility of deliberate self-improvement, as if this were the dividing line between him and the traditional moralists. It is not. An unprejudiced reading of the introduction to the *De Intellectus Emendatione*, and of Part v of the *Ethics*, will show that it is not. The dividing line is his theory of individuals maintaining themselves as individuals and of the mind and body as the two aspects of a single organism; and this line can be traced back to his nominalistic logic and to his philosophy of nature.

I have elsewhere suggested that there is an illuminating, and more than superficial, resemblance between Spinoza's and Freud's conception of personality. The more closely one considers this resemblance, the more clearly it appears to be traceable to common philosophical beliefs, which lie far below the surface of a shared terminology. That simple, misleading question "Was Spinoza, was Freud, a determinist?" has to be put on one side, and for the same reason, in both cases: that determinism, as a label, is associated with a particular model of the type of explanation to be aimed at in individual psychology and in the assessment of character; and this is a type which was certainly not theirs and which they had no interest either in accepting or rejecting. A determinist, as this label is commonly understood, has the single idea that any human behaviour is to be explained by well-confirmed natural laws which, taken together with a statement of initial conditions, exhibit the behaviour, whatever it may be, as always in principle predictable. This is not the kind of understanding, and of self-understanding, that is proposed by Spinoza and Freud.

Let me briefly list their points of agreement. First: there is the "economic" conception of the mind: that any individual is a psycho-physical organism with a quantity of undifferentiated energy that appears in consciousness as desire and, below the level of consciousness, as appetite. This is the instinctual energy that must find its outlet, however deformed and deflected it may be by its interactions with the environment. Desires and appetites are projected upon objects, as objects of love or of hate, in accordance, first, with the primary economic needs of the organism, as objects promoting or depressing its vitality, and, secondly, upon objects that are derivatively associated, through the complex mechanisms of memory, with increase or depression of vitality. Following this conception of a person's undifferentiated energy of self-assertion, Spinoza's account of passive emotions, and of the laws of transference that govern them, is very close to Freud's mechanisms of projection, transference, displacement, and identification, in forming the objects of love and aggression. Second: that the way towards freedom and self-direction is through the recognition of the inadequacy of the causes with which an individual associates his pleasures and sufferings. A man's discrimination between good objects and bad objects will be explained to him as imaginative projection upon reality of unconsciously remembered incidents in his personal history. Third: the purpose of such an explanation is to give him an overriding interest in the objective order of things, an interest independent of his own fantasies and of the passive association of ideas. The recall to reason is a recall from fantasy, and from the attachment to past experience through unconscious memories, towards an active and present enjoyment of his energies. He therefore becomes free to direct his mind as he chooses to its proper objects, instead of endlessly and helplessly repeating patterns of pursuit and aversion that originally established themselves below the level of his consciousness. Fourth: in his original state of uncriticized passive emotions, based upon fantasy, and the projection of his conflicts on to external objects, a man necessarily follows contrary and violently conflicting inclinations, and not a stable and consistent policy. Taken as a whole, his behaviour, in realizing his own desires, is therefore self-defeating. He is in this sense a divided and disintegrated personality. Freedom consists in the integration of all his desires and aversions into a coherent policy, the policy of developing his own powers of understanding, and of enjoying his active energies.

The point of philosophical interest here is the conception of mental causation which in turn determines the conception of freedom as the proper subject of ethics. For both Spinoza and Freud, the starting-point was the individual who, although part of the common order of nature, has to assert his individuality, his activity as an individual, against the common order of nature: in later, un-Spinozistic language, to assert the self, as agent, against the not-self, the external reality which resists him. His only means of achieving this distinctness as an individual, this freedom in relation to the common order of nature, is the power of the mind freely to follow in its thought an intellectual order. Then the flow of his reasonable thought and his reasonable action is predictable with greater certainty than when his thoughts and actions were determined by causes external to his own thinking. Spinoza and Freud alike argued that it is the common condition of men that their conduct and their judgements of value, their desires and aversions, are in each individual determined by unconscious memories. This is the nature of the passions—that their objects can be explained only from knowledge of unconsciously remembered satisfactions and frustations in the individual's history, and not from the properties of the objects themselves. The future activity of a reasonable man is predictable on the basis of his present activity, while the future of the man who is a slave to his passions is to be inferred only from the fantasies that he formed in the remote past. When a man's thought follows the objective order of things in nature, he is, and knows that he is, for a time an autonomous individual, asserting his own power and independence of mind. I repeat "for a time." For neither Spinoza nor Freud were optimists. Freedom is at the best only intermittent and partial, and the general condition of men, as parts of nature, is one of fantasy and of passion determined by unconscious memory and therefore by conflict and frustration. But Freud's was certainly the deeper pessimism. Attending to the evidence of fact, he found no reason to believe that the mere force of intellect and of reflection could by itself open the way to self-knowledge, and therefore to freedom of mind. And one traditional form of philosophical writing, which still survives in Spinoza, is disappearing from our literature: the exhortation addressed to reason, the call to reflection on the right way of life, which used to be the preface, as in the *De Intellectus Emendatione,* to intellectual analysis.

Spinoza's philosophy can be construed as a metaphysical

justification of individualism in ethics and politics. In so interpreting him, we only follow his design of his own work, which has never, I think, been treated with sufficient seriousness, largely because the attention of political philosophers has been concentrated on the more crude and inapplicable metaphysics of Hobbes. Whatever may be our judgement on the metaphysical premises from which it was deduced, Spinoza's theory of the passions is indeed a justification for taking the freedom of the individual as the supreme goal of political action. The now prevailing liberal conceptions of freedom, based on an empiricist philosophy, leave a mystery: why is the individual's exercise of choice, free from outside interference and threats of force, the supremely valuable activity of a man? Mill himself drew his answer from his utilitarian philosophy. The freedom of the individual was not for him a supreme and absolute end, but rather a means to the general progress of mankind. The individual's freedom of choice is a means to diversity and experiment, and diversity and experiment are means to the discovery of the most desirable forms of life. There is nothing in this philosophy that requires that the freedom of any individual is as such to be respected before all other things. Perhaps a revived doctrine of natural rights could give a sense to the absolute, as opposed to the conditional, value of the freedom of the individual. But no sense is given to the notion of natural rights within the empiricist philosophies of this time. If every man is by the law of his nature as an individual trying to assert his own power and freedom, in Spinoza's sense, in his thought and action, there is indeed a natural basis for the insistence on freedom as the supreme value in politics, as also in personal morality. The pursuit of any incompatible end will only lead to conflict and violence.

To return to the starting-point, it is, I think, at least possible that Spinoza has presented the outline of a defensible conception of individual freedom as the ultimate value in politics. In the *Tractatus Theologico-Politicus*, particularly in Chapter 20, he undertakes to show both that a civilized social order, based on freedom of thought and toleration, is a necessary condition of the use of reason, and therefore of the individual's fulfilment and enjoyment of his active powers: also, and more important now, to show that violence and social conflict are the projections into the external world of conflicts of passion within the individual. The first demonstration is in its conclusion, though not in its method, a commonplace. The second is not. We continue to speculate without conviction about freedom and social co-operation in the traditional terms of political philosophy, without any serious attention to the psychopathology of the individual, and as if all the discoveries in clinical psychology in the last fifty years had never been made. And this is, I think, why political philosophy seems stagnant and lacks conviction, except as an interpretation of the past. It has lost contact with the revolutionary and relevant moral science of its time. It is contrary to reason, and contrary also to John Stuart Mill's own principles in philosophy, that we should still cling to Mill's definition of freedom, when the philosophy of mind upon which he based it is discredited. We thereby preserve the letter, and lose the spirit, of empiricism, and of the liberal beliefs that were derived from it.

A Kind of Materialism

I shall discuss a philosophy of mind to which I will not at first assign an identity or date, except that its author could not have lived and worked before 1600. He is modern, in the sense that he thinks principally about the future applications of the physical sciences to the study of personality. As I expound him, I hope that it will not at first be too easy to tell whether or not he is our contemporary, whether indeed he is not still writing today. I attempt this reconstruction as a way of praising a philosopher, who has not, I think, been at all justly interpreted so far, and this seems an occasion for praise: but also because it may be one way of seeing some often neglected implications of materialism, as a doctrine of personality. I believe that this philosopher's doctrine, rather freely interpreted, may be the best introduction to clear thinking in this area.

My philosopher starts from the assumption that the acquisition of verbally expressed knowledge by human beings, and their ability to form articulate beliefs, are features of human behaviour that must be studied in the same way that any other capacities of living organisms are studied. We must look for the observable, and therefore for the physical, mechanisms that are involved in the exercise of these capacities, exactly as we would if we were trying to understand any other features of the behaviour of organisms of a specific type: e.g. the migration habits of a species, or their ability to recognise places and positions, or to communicate with each other. In such cases we think that we have explained a specific capacity of the creature if we discover the physical mechanisms involved in the normal exercise of that capacity. Then we may also try to understand the value of such mechanisms for the survival of the species and in preserving its peculiar way of life.

Certainly we can anticipate that the physical mechanisms associated with advanced thought, of the type that is peculiar to human beings, must be immensely complex, relative to our present knowledge. In all probability physical structures of a kind that we cannot now even begin to envisage are involved in the acquisition of linguistic and mathematical skills, in the exercise of memory and of the imagination, and in the formation of complex sentiments and mental attitudes: in all those processes that we may subsume, loosely, under the heading of thought. Indeed the word "mechanism," which I have introduced, may be thought misleading, in so far as it is associated only with types of physical process that are already discriminated within physics. The word must be understood more generously, as potentially standing also for physical structures, and for types of physical process, which are not yet recognised, or even envisaged, in contemporary physics. My philosopher specifically provides for this open-endedness in what we are to understand here as falling under the heading of physics.

He criticises his predecessors and contemporaries because, in their studies of the acquisition of knowledge by human beings, they have left no evident place for this kind of explanation. They have founded their theories of knowledge upon alleged distinctions between types of proposition —for example, between necessary and contingent propositions—without trying to relate these distinctions, in turn, to any observable mechanisms that are presumed to be at work at different levels, or in different types, of thinking, and of language use. This is because these philosophers could not bring themselves consistently to view human beings solely as one kind of natural object among others. Under the influence of inherited moral and religious ideas, and of their natural pieties and sentiments, his predecessors had always kept some powers of mind in reserve, treating these superior powers of thought as if they transcended the natural order, in the sense that they are not to be understood in terms of the observable mechanisms, which the exercise of them involves. They seem to have assumed that those powers of mind, which are the conditions of any organised knowledge of natural processes, cannot themselves be made the objects of such knowledge.

Previous philosophers had certainly been impressed by those discoveries in the physiology of perception—and particularly of vision—which show the mechanisms used in the acquisition of the most elementary knowledge of the physical world. But they have generally stopped short of allowing for the possibility of analogous discoveries in the physiology of thought of other kinds, and in the physiology of the sentiments. They drew a line that was to divide the autonomous exercise of the power of thought from the acquisition of knowledge by the use of the sense-organs, and therefore by the use of the body as an instrument. My philosopher is determined to be entirely consistent in his naturalism, in the sense that he will not admit any discontinuity in principles of explanation. Rather he argues that the known mechanisms employed in the formation of the most elementary perceptual beliefs give a clue to the understanding of human powers of thought at all levels. If we have an adequate understanding of the relation between thought and bodily processes in perception, we will have a secure basis for interpreting the mind-body relation quite generally.

My philosopher starts then within the tradition of the hard classical materialist, of Lucretius and Hobbes, a tradition that is once again alive today after a period of contempt and obscurity. He sees that most philosophers have wished to fence off an area of inquiry into human performance in which scientific explanation of a standard pattern will be out of place and which shall belong to philosophy alone. He claims to understand the sentimental roots of this fear of the unlimited possibilities of psycho-physical explanation. His theory will show why this philosophical resistance, with its emotional overtones, is to be expected in the natural constitution of the species.

Against the classical materialists, he argues that none of them had followed through to the end the implications of their thesis; and this is because they have not asked themselves the question that a serious moralist will unavoidably ask. Crudely put, this question is—"Suppose that a man is once convinced that all the distinct operations of his mind are embodied in distinct bodily processes, which have their explanation in the terms proper to physics: suppose also that he already has some of the required detailed knowledge of the physical embodiments of his own thought: how will he then interpret and evaluate, in the light of this detailed knowledge, his own thoughts and sentiments, together with the conduct that seems to express them?" Materialists have not persistently asked themselves what it would be like actually to *be* a materialist, in the serious sense: not simply of affirming an abstract thesis in the classroom, but of actually living and acting with some of the specific knowledge that a materialist claims must be obtainable. What would it be like to apply this exact knowledge, once obtained, to oneself, every day, in forming one's own attitudes, sentiments, and purposes? When this question is pressed, it seems that classical materialism turns into a doctrine which the materialists will not recognise as their own.

Their doctrine of personality has been lopsided, and finally incoherent and not plausible, because they omit themselves, active, scientifically well-informed, reflective materialists, with continuing appetites and interests, from the picture that they give of the mind-body relation. My philosopher is particularly skilful in shifting attention back and forth from the consideration of persons as active observers of the physical world to the consideration of them as also observed objects, with their bodies in a dual role, as both purposefully used instruments of exploration and also as observed objects. In distinguishing between different levels and kinds of knowledge, he first thinks of persons as intricately designed instruments, which register and record changes in their environment. But he also recalls that they are instruments internally determined to use themselves to explore the world, guided by the stored knowledge and beliefs which they happen at any time to possess about the situation and capacities of their own bodies. He therefore insists on the dependence, at any given time, of a man's interests and purposes upon his knowledge of his situation, and of his knowledge of his situation upon his interests and purposes. He describes very vividly this circle of dependence in which we are caught. At first sight the circle seems to exclude the possibility of any planned improvement in understanding and control of the kind that interests a moralist; for it seems that the output in knowledge and purposive behaviour must be wholly determined by the inputs from the environment, together with the internal structure of the organism. His problem as a moralist is to indicate a possible point of issue from this circle; and this he does by considering the reflexive forms of thought that are involved in even the most elementary processes of perception.

Even in the most elementary perception, a man knows that, as an observer of a world of objects, which includes himself, he has to make allowances for his own physical situation and bodily state and dispositions, and for the particular standpoint from which he happens to be observing the world. This process of making allowances for the limitations and distortions of a contingent point of view is part of the process by which any observer disentangles the apparent order of things, as it first presents itself to him, from that which he will finally count as the real order. As a perceiver, physically interacting with the environment, he is able in his thought to make these allowances, and to correct his first impressions, and so to distinguish the apparent, from the real, arrangement of objects around him, only because he also has the thought of moving, and of making relevant changes in his own body, with a view to noticing the effects of these changes upon his prior impressions. His body, including his sensory apparatus and brain, is for him the instrument that registers effects, which at the same time are associated with perceptual beliefs, only because he has actively used his physical equipment, his body, with the prior thought of arriving at true beliefs about the causes of these effects. In the most elementary perception, I am always, and usually without conscious reflection, making corrections for the changeable situation of my own body and angle of vision, as I believe them to be, and for the changeable state of the sense organs and of the organism generally. My perceptual beliefs are always arrived at by some conscious or unconscious reflection on the physical transactions that are involved in the perception, as I believe them to be in the particular case. And the higher levels of knowledge, dignified as science, are distinguished by the care and thoroughness with which the limitations of the standpoint and physical equipment of observers are tested and allowed for, in constructing a more inclusive, and less egocentric, model of the natural order, which includes the observer.

Even in the most developed natural science a residuary allowance has to be made for the limitations which the physical position of human observers in the universe imposes: also for the limits set by their sensory equipment, and by the structure of their brains, as instruments of thought. My philosopher constantly insists that our systematic knowledge of the external physical world, and of our own specific constitution, both depend upon a limited range of physical interactions with the environment. We must always remember that the physical instrument, which is the body and the brain, is highly selective in its responses to external causes, and that, correspondingly, human beings are limited also in the range of knowledge of the natural order that is accessible to them. The natural order will always extend far beyond our powers to discriminate and to understand. But the more we learn about the laws governing the observable physical universe, the more we are in a position to learn about the mechanisms of the human body and brain, and therefore about the specific structure, and the limitations, of the instrument itself.

As in elementary perception, so in the physical sciences as a whole, there is a reflexive, or feed-back, process. We shall read back discoveries in physics into an enlarged physiology; and we can make allowances for the limits set upon our physical theories by the mechanisms that embody our habits of discrimination and of thought, as more and more is learnt about these mechanisms, and about how far they might be improved.

Classical materialists, my philosopher implies, could give no coherent account of how perceptual beliefs are formed, because they had not clearly distinguished the physical mechanisms of perception from the perceiver's reflection on, and consequent use of, these mechanisms. We all know that changes in the body, or in the intervening medium, will be associated with an immediate disposition to different perceptual beliefs; but the beliefs will not actually change, and the dispositions to believe will remain latent, if we know at the time that the unchecked disposition is associated only with changes in the intervening medium, or in the perceiver's brain and sense organs. This power of self-conscious reflection upon the mechanisms associated with our first impressions, and the making of thoughtful allowances for our particular standpoint, are as much part of the innate endowment of the species as are the sense-organs themselves. It is natural to evaluate in thought, consciously or unconsciously, the first perceptual impressions that we receive, and the initial beliefs that we form; it is natural to us to move and to change the angle of vision in testing initial beliefs, guided in our thought by the hypotheses that we form about their causes.

Suppose then that we think of all thought, and not only the formation of perceptual beliefs, as entailing the more or less reflective use of a physical mechanism. We are to suppose that every specific sequence of thought is associated with a specific sequence of physical changes in the body, in the same way that a perception of something red is associated with a physical transaction, when I am looking at something red. In this respect all thought, even of the most abstract kind, is to be thought of as a kind of perception. The difference between different kinds of thought is a difference in the nature of the physical transactions involved. In ordinary perception there is an interaction with the immediate physical environment, while the physical mechanisms involved in more abstract thinking are causally independent of the subject's immediate environment. The physical mechanisms of thought that remain to be discovered are presumably to be found principally in the brain, and in association with some of the sentiments, also in the whole nervous system. The self-conscious materialist, at all times applying his thesis to himself, believes that the physical instrument of his thought, not less than his sense-organs, functions in accordance with physical-chemical laws which will be more and more understood. In proportion as the instrument's specific functioning is understood, he will think of himself as able currently to make further corrections in his thought, and to allow for causes of abnormal functioning in particular cases. At a relatively crude level, we do in fact make allowances for the variations of those attitudes and sentiments, which we associate with known variations in our physical state: that is, we dissociate ourselves from an initial attitude, or sentiment, which we at the time take to be associated with a bodily state, which in turn is largely attributable to causes that are unconnected with the ostensible external object of the thought or sentiment. The self-conscious materialist thinks of his own reflections on the various causes of his thoughts, and of the associated physical states, as always modifying the original thoughts. He will at every moment think of his changing beliefs, desires, and sentiments, and changes in the direction, or topic, of his thought, as associated with changes in just one physical object, his body. In reflecting on the order of physical changes associated with the intentional order of his thoughts, he is at the same time correcting the thoughts themselves; and this activity of correction also has its physical embodiment.

At a very elementary level, and unsystematically, one already knows something of the bodily mechanisms associated with some kinds of thought, with some kinds of emotion, with some memories, with some desires and fears, with some attractions and repugnances. But one has only the kind of rough and pre-scientific knowledge of the bodily mechanisms of one's thoughts, desires, and sentiments which a primitive man may have of the mechanisms of perception. As a primitive man, or a child, does not know in any detail how the eye, nerves and brain function in vision, so a materialist does not know in any detail how his brain functions in other kinds of thought. He knows that his power of thought is embodied in a physical instrument, and that if the condition of the instrument is grossly changed, as by drugs, the power of thought is grossly changed also. He knows that he may try to concentrate his thought, and to exercise his memory, and that he may also deliberately leave his thoughts to stray and allow himself to daydream and to imagine. But he does not know in any detail *how* he does these things, in the sense of knowing the fine structure of the physical processes employed. As a materialist, he is sure that when he sets himself to remember, or to solve a problem, a physical process has begun, just as it has when he sets himself to explore something with his eyes. If the fine structure of the process were known, some of the conditions of the mechanism's malfunctioning would also be known, and he would be interested in a technology that would improve the instrument of thought, as we have improved our powers of vision.

At this point the self-conscious materialist meets the challenge of the classical, or crass materialist, who suggests that descriptions in physical terms of bodily processes and bodily states are, in the last analysis, the only finally correct descriptions of a person's activities and states. The classical materialist suggests that those states that would ordinarily be described as having such-and-such hopes and fears, desires and aversions, beliefs and doubts, would be better described, if the relevant exact knowledge was available to us, in terms of associated brain states. For present purposes I need not review the many well known difficulties in formulating this kind of materialism: I am concerned only with an argument peculiar to the self-conscious materialist. He replies that the new specific knowledge of associated brain states will modify the thought of the knowing materialist, who will reinterpret his psycho-physical states by reference to this new knowledge of physical causes. He will put his new knowledge to a use in checking and directing his own thought, as a skilled listener applies his knowledge of acoustics in his listening. The materialist who is trying to solve a scientific problem will not think of an account of the brain processes that embody his process of thought as a substitute for the thought itself. He will still be thinking and expressing his thought, when he knows in more detail how the thinking is done, as an observer still needs to think, when he knows how the perception is done.

A man may indeed, for some purposes, substitute an account of associated bodily processes for an account of a process of thought, when he is observing another person or reviewing his own past activities. Then he does indeed have the choice of whether to describe the subject's activity in terms of associated physical processes, which are to be explained in terms of physics, or in terms of the subject's thoughts or intentions, which are to be explained by other thoughts and intentions, in accordance with the laws that govern connections of thought. But he has no such choice when he is himself doing the thinking, and the known physical processes involved become the instrument of his thought, as he evaluates its reliability: this is the point that the example of perception immediately suggests. From the standpoint of the thinking subject, who knows which physical structures and processes embody which particular powers and processes of thought, the physical structures and processes become usable means of directing and controlling thought, as the fallible eye is the means of directing and controlling vision.

Let us suppose that he knows that his capacity to be angry and to be frightened is embodied in a liability to specific chemical changes in his body, as he knows also that his capacity to remember words resides in some structures in his brain, and that his capacity to enjoy certain rhythms in music is embodied in some known properties of his nervous system and brain. When, observing his friend's conduct, he becomes angry, he will evaluate his first angry thoughts about his friend in the light of his belief about the causes of this psycho-physical state. He will distinguish the case in which his anger is principally attributable to peculiarities of his own preceding psycho-physical states from the case in which his anger is a standard, even if unenlightened, mode of perception of its ostensible object, his friend's behaviour. We already make these discriminations, as a condition of employing the concept of anger, and in distinguishing one state of mind from another, principally by reference to its type of cause or occasion. But we now make the discriminations by typical causes very roughly and intuitively; and the ordinary vocabulary of distinct intentional states and emotions needs to be refounded on a more systematic psycho-physical theory, which would show both the mechanisms involved and their function in preserving the organism.

The philosopher whom I am expounding called therefore for a radical and difficult conversion in men's inner life through this new understanding of the mind-body relation, starting from sense-perception as the clue to the relation between thought and physical processes. In pre-scientific societies, and in childhood, men could, and still can, misinterpret their perceptions of the sun, perceptions that depend upon the same optical equipment in all men; the misinterpretations occur in so far as they are ignorant of all the physical mechanisms, and psychological associations, involved in the formation of their first ideas of its size and distance. They could not correct these first impressions, as we now can, in the light of a more coherent physics, which explains why the sun looks small to us and what its size and distance must be. There is an intelligible sense in which their impressions of the sun, and of its size, could be said to be the same as ours. Since the physical mechanisms associated with the formation of the primitive thought of the sun as small are the same in all of us, we can still recognise in ourselves the vestiges of a thought of the sun, when we look at it, as being smaller than we now know it to be. But this thought is immediately cancelled, or bracketed, by our thought of the physical transaction associated with its formation. The primitive thought remains only as a first impression, immediately cancelled by collateral knowledge. There is also a good sense in which a primitive man, or a child, sees the sun differently from us, when he looks at it and sees it hanging there in the vault of the heavens: he sees it differently, in spite of having the same sensory equipment, because, using collateral knowledge he thinks of it differently. The physical cosmos, in the thought of the primitive man, or of the child, clearly has a quite different shape and dimensions. More particularly, the observer is altogether out of scale in relation to the natural order of which he is a part: this is the primitive egotism, and anthropocentrism, from which the theory of knowledge and the physical sciences will together liberate us.

In the psychology of the sentiments, another Copernican revolution is needed. Not only are we largely ignorant of the complex physical processes in which our thought is embodied and, particularly, of that thought which enters into our emotions and our attitudes to others: but the emotions themselves, once they occur, reinforce and prolong this ignorance. Under the influence of a passion, we do not think of that passion as a psycho-physical phenomenon issuing from a complication of causes, internal and external. We typically confuse our unexamined love or hatred of someone with a veridical perception of his amiability or hatefulness. We fall into a kind of naive realism in respect of the objects of our attitudes and sentiments, leaving our conceptions of the objects uncorrected by calm and persistent thought about complex causes. While a man's pleasure or suffering lasts, he will think only of the apparent cause and object, real or notional, with which the pleasure or suffering happens, for internal reasons, to be immediately linked in his thought. He does not stop to interpret, and to correct, his first impressions of the cause of his pleasure and suffering by a more systematic understanding of how this first impression has been formed, in accordance with laws, both psychological and physical. Lacking the necessary collateral knowledge, he is like the child or primitive man who does not question his first impression of the sun. He does not detach himself from his first reaction, by persistently asking why he has come to feel and think as he at first does, and by finding the just balance between internal and external causes.

But a self-conscious materialist must in consistency take this first step of detachment, if he seriously believes what he claims to believe. He must think that the immediately singled out external cause, and the singled out external object, of his pleasure or displeasure, of his desire or repugnance, are, at best, one set of factors among many in a complex interaction. He cannot remain an ordinary naive realist about the relation of his own emotions to their objects, when he reflects on the unexplored complexity of internal psycho-physical factors which enter into any intentional state. In our ordinary vocabulary, every enjoyment, desire, or sentiment has a notional object, and the sentiments are distinguished principally by the subject's own thought about the cause of his pain or pleasure. Within the order of the subject's first, uncorrected thought there is a primitive explanation, which he has ready, of why he enjoys, and why he thinks desirable, those particular objects. This thought about the sources and nature of his own state of mind is open to his own criticism in the same way that perceptual beliefs are open to criticism. The first impression naturally occurs, but can be no less naturally modified by collateral knowledge. When he reflects on how his belief about the external cause was formed, his original thought of a simple cause will be cancelled, as the primitive impression of the sun is cancelled; and his state of mind, and particularly his attitude to the offending person, will have changed also, merely as a consequence of this reflection. He may still have disagreeable feelings, and may recognise a tendency in himself to attribute these feelings to his friend's behaviour, just as the observer's first impression of the sun remains. But as his thought about the causes of his own feelings, are corrected, the nature and direction of his emotions, and his consequent dispositions to act, will change also. For his reflective thought about his own sentiments, and his reflective interpretation of its cause, and his identification of its object, always have to be included in any adequate account of his final psycho-physical state.

The serious materialist, who has some systematic knowledge of the bodily changes associated with changes in his sentiments and attitudes, will always be complicating those diagnoses of the causes of his own states of mind that first suggest themselves to him. Observing other people as psycho-physical organisms, and knowing how this or that sentiment of theirs has been formed, he will think of their sentiment as alterable, either by an alteration in their physical state, or alternatively, by an argument that convinces them that their thought about the causes of their own states of mind is erroneous, or that it is at least inadequate and over-simple. After a more adequate causal analysis, it may be clear that the presumed object of their sentiment is not the real object, and that the sentiment must be differently characterised. But in the subject's own case these two independent methods of correction collapse into one. If I seriously try to correct my own sentiments and attitudes by physical operations, and not merely for the sake of experiment, I must *already* regard my present physical state as an obstacle to adequate thought. I am in the same position as the man who thinks that his senses are deceiving him and who thinks that he knows how they are preventing him from seeing things as they are. In these cases, the subject's first thought has been corrected by another thought.

A change in my thoughts about the causes and nature of my psycho-physical states modifies these inner states themselves; for the emotions and sentiments are in part distinguished, in the common vocabulary, by the subject's thought of the cause and of the object of the pleasure or suffering that he feels. In the typical situation in which I might take a drug, with the intention of removing the fearful thoughts which I believe to be unrealistic, or inappropriate to their object, I have already in my thought discounted, or bracketed, the fearful thoughts, together with the consequent dispositions to act. I am then like the man who, inspecting an object, changes his position in order to see the thing as it is, from what he takes to be the correct angle of vision: he moves his body, or strains his eyes, to produce a physical effect, guided by a thought of what the standard position of observation is. Then he evaluates the effect in his own changed impression. When I come to think of my fears of some object as causally independent of the properties of the object, I have bracketed, or cancelled, the fearful thoughts, as I bracket, or cancel, my first impressions of the sun. The sun remains its present size whatever I think about it; but my psycho-physical state ceases to be simple fear, if the thoughts of danger, which enter into the fear, are at the same time cancelled by the thought that the imagined danger is an illusion. My sentiment is then at least a more complicated one, and is no longer just fear of this specific object. The subject's psycho-physical state has been changed in virtue of his reflection upon its sources.

My self-conscious materialist argues that the relation between a man's thought and sentiment, and the physical state that embodies it, is in these ways too close to be counted as a causal relation, or as analogous to the relation between two physical states, one of which adequately explains the other. It is precisely the point of materialism to assert a much closer relation between processes of thought and physical processes than is implied in most of the idioms of ordinary speech. My philosopher is a genuine materialist in the narrow sense that he asserts that every change in the state of the organism, which is a change in thought, is also a change in some bodily state, and usually in the principal instrument of thought, the brain. From the standpoint of an observer, a person's bodily and mental processes are each reflections of the other, with neither of them privileged as substance to shadow. According to one possible criterion of identity, the same process in the organism, which for the subject is his thought or sequence of thoughts, may also be observed and described, by an observer, as a physical state or sequence of physical states.

If, being a moralist, you succeed in changing someone's thoughts and sentiments by your arguments, there will be associated bodily changes also. If, being a doctor, you operate directly on the physical mechanisms of his thought, there will be an associated change in the sequence of his thoughts. A brain surgeon may selectively prevent his victim thinking what he would otherwise have thought, and turn his thought in another direction, provided always that the surgeon's work is not complicated by his victim knowing at the time what the surgeon is doing, and how he is doing it.

But the subject's own power to change his attitudes and sentiments resides first in his thought about his thoughts and about their causes. His limited power and freedom to change his psycho-physical states depend on his power to bring more systematic knowledge of their causes to bear on his own particular case. If I ever come to know what is happening, physically speaking, in my brain when, for instance, I try to recall a name, I would then think of myself as using this particular piece of apparatus, just as I now think of myself as using my eyes when I look for something; and I would think of correcting abnormal conditions and postures of the instrument of non-perceptual thought, as I now make allowances for, and correct, abnormal conditions of the instrument of vision. When a man now uses his power of thought, in forming his beliefs and expectations, in imagining, in changing his sentiments and attitudes, he is employing the still largely unknown mechanisms in which these powers are embodied. And he even now knows that he is. A trivial example: Suppose, for example, that he knows that a thought that he is about to fall is associated with a change in some region of the brain, he will use this knowledge in making allowances for abnormal stimulations of the mechanism—for example, from an experimenter's electrodes. The first thought that he was about to fall would remain, but immediately be cancelled by reflection on causes, and therefore the actual belief that he would have had, if he had not known about the cause of the associated physical transaction, will not remain. According to the self-conscious materialist, this power of reflection, this perpetually turning feed-back process, which constitutes human thought, must itself be embodied in physical structures, which are involved in all conscious thinking.

You will perhaps say that his is a very peculiar kind of materialism—scarcely materialism at all—that allows so much for the power of reflection: and I will still reply that he who currently applies the thesis of materialism to himself, in his own thinking about himself, and with some of the knowledge that materialism presupposes, will not easily avoid this peculiarity. From the standpoint of a scientific observer, a running commentary on the subject's successive states might equally truthfully be cast in terms of physical changes or in terms of a sequence of thoughts. The choice between the two kinds of description depends upon the observer's interests and purposes. But the subject identifies his own contemporary activity with the connections of thought and intention which are all the time being checked and changed by his second-order thoughts about them. For the subject who is thinking, the sequence of thoughts and of intentions, and of thoughts about thoughts, and so on indefinitely, seems, at the time, to have priority over, and to explain, the sequence of physical changes which embody them: yet, he knows that, objectively regarded, the two aspects of his activity are equally associated; and that each sequence is explicable in its own terms.

You will have recognised here the apparent incoherence in Spinoza's thought—for it is of course about him that I am speaking—with which all commentators have contended: even his earliest correspondents. Spinoza seems both to assert that every idea is united with a particular modification of the body, and also to assert that, in reflection, ideas can be made the objects of other ideas up to any level of complexity. I think that he indeed accepted both these propositions and that they are consistent with each other. Whatever my belief, attitude, or sentiment is, I have some limited power to reflect on the causes and the nature of this contemporary psycho-physical state, and, by reflection, to change it; for if I change my conception of what my attitude or sentiment is, and of how it has arisen, the attitude or sentiment itself is thereby changed. According to the hypothesis, this power of reflection is itself embodied in an internal physical structure, not yet known, which is the vehicle of peculiarly human thought. Therefore it is not pointless, or inconsistent, for Spinoza, the moralist, to urge men to recognise their powers of reflection, and not passively to allow their beliefs and sentiments to be formed as the effects of transient causes uncorrected by their own power of thought. It is no more pointless, or inconsistent, than it is to ask a man to check carefully, using all his collateral knowledge, before deciding on the shape and colour of an object, to ensure that his senses are not deceiving him in the particular case. Yet, in postulating this power of reflection, Spinoza sets no limit on the possibilities of scientific explanation of psycho-physical states. He infers only that there is a peculiarity in the application of scientific explanations to contemporary thoughts, attitudes and sentiments: namely, that the changes in the subject's contemporary knowledge of, and beliefs about, the cause will modify the effect. My bodily states at any time can be understood as the independent effects of physical causes. But the thoughts that they embody, and therefore my sentiments, are thoughts about the nature and causes of my psychophysical state. For this reason the crass materialist is mistaken in his belief that a man's thoughts and sentiments might be adequately explained by reference to associated bodily states alone. As the example of perceptual belief shows, a person's belief about the causes of a change in bodily state determines the content of the thought that finally issues from that change. The order of thoughts can only be adequately explained by the rational and associative connections peculiar to thoughts, and physical states by their connections with other physical states in accordance with the laws of physics.

The classical materialists are wrong in supposing that the two orders of explanation could properly be reduced to one. They have the illusion that this reduction is possible, because, when writing philosophy, they write only from the standpoint of scientific observers of men. As observers of external realities, they will naturally look to the physical order of explanation, the only one that is then accessible to them. Meanwhile they forget that, as they observe, their own thought involves thought about its causes, and that its changes have to be explained in these terms.

This is, I think, the sense, or point, of Spinoza's so-called double aspect theory of personality, which I am representing as a modified materialism; he had arrived at it, I believe, by looking for the true moral implications of the Classical, or Epicurean, materialism revived by Hobbes and Gassendi. He asked himself what a scientific materialist, given an extended physiology, and an exact knowledge of the mechanisms of thought, would then do to improve his way of life. First he would use his new knowledge of physical interactions in reinterpreting, and therefore in reforming, his own beliefs, sentiments, and interests. Secondly, he would think of a new technology, which might improve his power of thought, as he has improved his capacity to see things invisible to the naked eye. I think that Spinoza thought that the reduplicative, or reflexive, nature of human thought was associated with some still unknown complexity of physical structure, analogous to other stages in the order of physical complexity, such as the occurrence of living organisms. Cartesians and common-sense dualists do not envisage discovery of the physical mechanisms of thought, corresponding to those of perception, because we do not yet know, in Spinoza's words, what the body is capable of doing by itself: they have built a philosophy upon the basis of this ignorance of physiology. Therefore Spinoza believed that systematic cure of defects of personality, and particularly of the destructive passions, is, on one side, a medical problem, demanding operations on the physical mechanisms involved, as the care of defects of vision and of hearing is a medical problem. On the other side men have to be persuaded by argument to refer their own thoughts and sentiments to inborn standards of rationality, and to look further and more systematically for the causes of their beliefs and attitudes. Powers of mind are no less, and no more, open to training and improvement than the powers of the body; and there is no a priori reason why appeals to reason and to scientific understanding should be either more, or less, useful than physical methods of controlling destructive passions.

It follows that we should never ask whether a type, or a particular specimen, of human behaviour, or of feeling, are finally and properly to be explained by physical, or by psychological, causes, as if this was a proper exclusive disjunction. The question can be given a sense if it is interpreted as an inquiry about the means of explanation available to us within our present knowledge. But as a programmatic dispute about the long-range future of psychology, it is senseless, a mere waste of energy, on Spinoza's hypothesis. To understand the semi-conscious and unconscious connections of thought in the imagination is no more, and no less useful, as a contribution to knowledge than is an understanding of the brain states and processes which embody them. But from the standpoint of a person determining what his own present states of mind should be, there is a very significant difference: a person's contemporary reflections on the causal links between his ideas will immediately modify the ideas themselves, while his contemporary knowledge of, and beliefs about, the causes of physical states of his body do not by themselves modify these states.

Our language is still so thoroughly dualistic and Cartesian that it is very difficult to grasp, and to hold on to, the alternative model that Spinoza suggests. It is natural to us, studying other persons or our own past, to pick out bodily changes as causes of changes in states of mind; and the double aspect theory does not deny, and could not plausibly deny, that many such partial causal connections are known to us, and that we act upon them every day. If the bodily mechanisms are damaged, thought is impaired; and if a thought is suggested to the mind, the associated physical mechanism is equivalently affected. Spinoza only denies that such causal connections as these ever constitute an adequate explanation either of a physical state or of a thought, in the sense in which the occurrence of one physical state, or of one thought, may constitute an adequate explanation of another, in accordance with the laws of physics and with the laws of thought.

I freely admit that I have been free in my interpretation of Spinoza. But I take myself to have been expanding Prop. 22 of Book I of the *Ethics*: "The human mind not only perceives the affections of the human body, but also the ideas of these affections."

231

Sincerity and Single-Mindedness

I shall argue that sincerity is a dubious, uncertain ideal, and that it is very difficult to attain. It is not something obvious and simple, and it is not true that we all know what it is. And the argument involves a general point about the peculiarities of psychology as a science.

The knowledge that one can properly claim to possess of mental states and of mental processes has some peculiar features, which distinguishes it in important respects from the knowledge that one can properly claim of physical states and of physical processes. These peculiarities emerge most clearly, as one would expect, when one considers knowledge claims in respect of the higher mental states, and particularly the sentiments and attitudes. The points that I shall make have a quite general application to intentional states—all the way from believing that p to being horrified that p. Many philosophers, following Wittgenstein, have stressed the fact, which originally appeared almost as a discovery, that the commonplace vocabulary which we use from day to day in labeling the sentiment, passions, attitudes of ourselves and of our friends, in political argument, and in serious gossip, is a vocabulary that embodies a rudimentary, and pre-scientific theory, of human behaviour. The concepts that we ordinarily employ to classify and to distinguish our sentiments, passions, propositional attitudes are explanatory concepts, explanatory in relation to behaviour. They serve, among other things, to correlate standard recurring types of situation with standard recurring patterns of behaviour as expected responses to these situations. There are very good reasons why this should be so, reasons that are to be found in the conditions under which the psychological vocabulary must be learnt in the first place, and in the social purposes which it serves in the control and manipulation of persons. All this seems to me true and important, an achievement of recent analysis. But I draw from it a moral which is not always drawn: that once these social necessities, determining the norm of our psychological vocabulary are recognized, one proper work of philosophy is to explore ways of recovering for attention those phenomena of the inner experience which are partly, or even wholly, left out of account in the commonplace explanatory scheme.

There are those who, for moral and also for temperamental reasons, subscribe to the well-known phrase of a moralist, "Il ne faut pas se regarder vivre," and who find something morbid and enervating in the pursuit of accurate self-knowledge, of finer discrimination, and in the indulgence of just this curiosity. This saying seems to me unacceptable. Although no one will deny the necessities of conjugation, that my coming to see that I am horrified that p cannot be altogether unlike my coming to see that you are horrified that p, the first person singular of the present tense of psychological verbs—I hope, I fear, I wish, I believe—does seem to me supremely interesting, in respect of the intimacy of the knowledge that is claimed.

However we try to make new psychological discriminations, and to recover unnoticed experience, whether under the guidance of a full-fledged theory or not, we must in any case indulge in self-watching; and one ideal of health and sincerity—proclaimed in the formula "One must not watch oneself living"—is against self-watching. Your watching should be directed to the external world of objects and of other persons. I think the moralist meant that it is a bad thing from the point of view of happiness, which he thought depends upon a certain degree of naturalness and spontaneity; and naturalness and spontaneity are, in this context, thought to exclude self-watching, which cannot be expected of concept-lacking animals; and animals are the model of naturalness. Other self-watching French moralists have made just the same point about their self-watching countrymen: Stendhal, for instance. "Be natural: be like the Spaniards or the Italians: just feel as you feel, and act as you are disposed to act. Do not watch yourself feeling, or you will no longer know what you really feel; and finally, you will scarcely feel anything at all. If you watch your feelings, and wonder what they are, they will become a cerebral invention, a kind of posturing to yourself. You will no longer be sincere: your impulses will cease to be impulses, and you will confuse what you think you ought to feel with what you actually do feel. And this is vanity, the disease of the soul to which we Frenchmen are peculiarly prone." I am not translating, but putting words into Stendhal's mouth. Much earlier La Rochefoucauld had remarked that people are never either as happy or as unhappy as they think they are. Vanity again: they exaggerate, because a mediocrity of feeling is something that they do not like to confess to themselves. And of course there are many people who would never have been in love had they not heard so much talk about love: again there is a confusion between that which the current vocabulary suggests that it is proper to feel and the feeling that arises naturally and spontaneously, the feeling that is there without our having watched it grow and without our having labelled it. This is the case for naturalness, for looking outwards, and not inwards. It is one common ideal of sincerity or integrity; but I think it is probably a false ideal. My reasons for thinking this are to be found in the peculiarities of reflexive knowledge, that is, of the knowledge that a man has of his own contemporary intentional states. There is another ideal of sincerity, or integrity of mind, in substance that which was proposed by Spinoza, and which, I think, rests on a more tenable account of self-knowledge.

234

Watching is, among other things, a way of coming to know, and it will be helpful, as an introduction, to contrast watching a change in one's state of body with watching a change in one's state of mind. Whether a change in the state of my body is watched by me or not will not in general make any difference to the change. The attentive observation of physical happenings normally, and with certain disquieting and marginal exceptions, has no effect on the physical happenings; it does not by itself alter them. The physical object watched is entirely independent, since the true nature of the object, and its properties, can be established in a variety of other ways, and by different observers from different points of view. No one observer is a privileged observer. The French writers whom I have just quoted evidently believed that watching one's own states and processes of mind will in normal cases change them from what they would have been if unwatched. They believed that the attentive watching here does typically become a kind of interference: that a man may become very unhappy, only because he has after reflection started to think of himself as being very unhappy. The diagnosis of the state, when it is the object's diagnosis, has contributed to making the state what it actually is. And then his unhappiness will be, they think, artificial; and of course they contrast artificial with natural, the latter being good, the former bad. The kind of situation that they have in mind is that of the man who watches himself falling in love, or who watches himself grieving for someone now dead, and who thereby converts what might have been a sentiment that has arisen of its own accord, and in the natural course of events, into a form of sentimentality. He has turned his attention away from the external object of his feeling to his feeling itself; and this change of interest, inwards and away from the external object, is the beginning of sentimentality. It is as if the subject himself, by his attention, is himself creating

235

or sustaining the feeling, rather than allowing it to be created or sustained by its external object.

Of course I will not deny that there are situations which may be described in these terms. But they make up only a special sub-class of the total range of cases in which a man's coming to know, or changing his opinion about, what his state of mind is constitutes a change in his state of mind. My suggestion is that it is a common characteristic of the higher mental states, and of all the intentional states, that the subject's belief about the explanation, and therefore about the nature, of his contemporary state of mind is always one of the factors that determine what his state of mind actually is. Intentional states of mind—hope that p, anger that p, fear that p, belief that p, shame that p, horror that p—are not independent objects, which remain unchanged by the subject's changing views of their nature. The subject's watching, and the conclusion of his watching in some discrimination of what his state of mind is, will be constitutive elements in his state of mind. Any observer, or candid friend, who wishes to know what his mind is, will need to know, among other things, what he, the subject, thinks that it is.

The best possible evidence, available to any observer, that the subject has a certain feeling about a matter that concerns him, or that his attitude is so-and-so, or that his sentiments take such-and-such a form, is that the subject himself is quite sure that this is a correct account of the matter, and that he is sure after reflection, the question having been raised—"What is my attitude, what do I *think*, or feel about this." This is not to imply that the subject is not liable to error on these matters, that he may not in various ways be deceived, or deceive himself. He may discover for himself that he is wrong, or it may be evident to others that he is self-deceived and insincere in his professions, even though he does not realise it. He is the authority, but he is

236

a fallible, deceivable authority. There is no question of the form, "How do you know?" but there is the question "Are you sure?"—there is no question of the source of the knowledge, because the grammar and topic together show that he is the authority but a fallible one. He does not *need* to use inductive argument, or to consider the evidence of behaviour. But he can be defeated in his claim to know what his attitude or sentiment is. This is an aspect of the fact that these concepts are standardly employed in an explanatory role, in relation to behaviour; the evidences of behaviour may be discordant with the subject's avowals.

But his claim to knowledge still has authority just because his *thought* of his state of his mind as having a certain cause, and therefore being of a certain kind, is one of the factors which determines what his state of mind actually is. If he thinks of himself as feeling guilty about something, or ashamed about something, or angry about something, or as being interested in something because it has such-and-such properties, he may sometimes be wrong: but the fact that he has this conception of his own state of mind will be one element in his state of mind. He cannot, so to put it, be merely wrong or wholly wrong: if he is in some way confused about his state of mind, or self-deceived, then his state of mind must be a complex and confused one.

He will himself discriminate between different possible accounts of his present state of mind by reference to the occasion and circumstances which explain it: for example, he will distinguish between the three possibilities—that he likes to think that p is true, that he hopes that p is true, and that he believes p is true—by reference to the conditions on which, as he supposes, his favourable attitude to p depends. His conception of the explanation of his thought that p must be entered into any account that is given of what his thought is—whether it is a hope, a liking to think, or a belief. Suppose that the subject professes to believe that p, and a

237

friend, while being sure that he is not simply lying, has evidence that his profession is insincere, and that he is self-deceived, and that a better account of the matter is rather that he hopes, or likes to think, that p is true, rather than that he actually believes that it is. Then the observing friend must still include the fact that the subject believes that he believes that p in the account of the subject's state of mind: it would be misleading *simply* to describe him as hoping that p is true. Such an account would omit what could be called the intentional element—namely, that the subject takes what is really his hope that p to be a belief that p, and that he is ready, or disposed, to assert that p in the relevant circumstances. In arriving at a true, and in this case complex, account of the subject's state of mind in respect of p, the notional explanation of his favourable attitude to p has to be included as well as the real explanation. One can see the necessity of this, if one reflects on how the proposition, which is the object of his sentiment, emotion, or attitude, is specified: the subject's thought of the cause of his state of mind must be indicated in specifying the object of his hope, anger, or fear; and we will specify the object of his hope or horror, as he sees it, even when we believe that he is in part, or wholly, self-deceived, in the account that he gives of what he hopes for, or is horrified about. Once again, there is of course a great variety of ways in which a man may be in error in his conception of the object of his hope, or horror, and in some cases we may make a simple correction in his account, without needing to mention what his original formulation was. For instance, we will do this when the error was a trivial error in the description that he uses, or in the names; but where his thought of the cause and of the object is interestingly and importantly wrong, the more complex account will be needed.

Consider another example of a state of mind that is in itself philosophically interesting, because of the place that it may be given in ethics: the sentiment of regret. Regret is a sentiment, and it is something that one can be said to feel. So the question will arise of the diagnosis of some feeling that one has: is my feeling properly a case of regret, or of something else? One can be more or less sincere in the regret that one expresses, without the intention to deceive, in public words or in one's diary; and, in addition, there can be a mood of sentimental regret, cultivated and sustained. Regret is a mode of unhappiness, or unpleasure, conjoined with a thought about the past. He who regrets something typically thinks that something that he has done, or that he has suffered, or something that has occurred, constitutes a mistake or a loss. He might express the fact that he regrets something that he has done by saying that he is unhappy about his action, and unhappy in a particular way: namely, in that particular way that is distinguished by his thinking that the action, which was the occasion or cause of the regret, was a mistake, and a mistake that entailed some loss. As a mode of unhappiness about the past, regret, like any other sentiment, is distinguished from its many close rivals —shame, remorse, guilt, disappointment and many others— primarily by the precise content of the accompanying thought. "I am not ashamed of what I did: even less do I feel guilty about it. But I do regret it deeply." He who says this has clarified his thought and thereby has clarified his feeling. He has determined the nature of his unhappiness about the past more specifically. Looking back to a sentiment, which he no longer feels, he might similarly say to himself: "What I felt at that time was not really shame, or guilt, but simply regret for what I had done." He has made clear to himself, presumably by calling on his memory, what he thought at the time and therefore what, more precisely, he then felt. He has explained his past unhappiness, or unpleasure, by a reference to a thought about his situation.

His thought, as he recalls it, need not have been explicitly or clearly formulated in his mind. Thought here could be no more than a vague imagining, or an unquestioned assumption. In some cases of regretting an action, it might be misleading to call the thought of loss and mistake a belief, just as it would often be misleading to call an expectation a belief; his thought of loss might have been below the threshold or articulateness and explicitness which the word "belief" implies. But if he regretted, he had the idea of loss, even if the idea was not a fully explicit one, and even less was formulated by him at the time.

Even persons of the same culture, and using the same language, may greatly differ in the degree to which they are liable to feel unhappy in specific ways about things in their past, as they may greatly differ in their liability to guilt, shame, and remorse. Their liability to experience these various modes of unhappiness will in part depend on their liability to think of the past in certain specific and sometimes competing terms—in terms, for instance, of loss, or of moral wrongdoing, or of judgment and responsibility. If a man were genuinely convinced of some forms of fatalism or determinism, he would be expected, for this reason alone, not to feel some of these sentiments about his past actions. We might even, not unreasonably, take his not having some of these sentiments as a test of the *sincerity* of his expressed conviction of the truth of fatalism. We may say to him "If you were *sincerely* convinced of the truth of fatalism, it would be quite impossible that you should at the same time also feel remorse about your conduct: you *can* only, and at the most, feel regret, the kind of regret that one feels when a misfortune strikes one."

The answer might be that men may, and commonly do, cling to incompatible propositions at the same time; and in such a situation there may be no simple and true answer to the question "Is he really and *sincerely* convinced that fatalism is true?" If the subject himself is ready to affirm, after reflection, that he is convinced of the truth of fatalism, and if he is trying to be accurate, then it cannot be altogether false that he is convinced of the truth of fatalism; even though it may not be the whole truth either, as may be shown by the fact that he has thoughts (or ideas), and therefore has feelings, which would otherwise be counted as good grounds for believing that he is not convinced of the truth of fatalism. If his state of mind is one of confusion, any truthful account of his state of mind must reproduce that confusion. The subject himself, when he is questioned about a contemporary state of mind, will normally be more interested in clearing up the confusion in his own mind, rather than in giving a truthful account of the confusion as it has hitherto existed. As soon as he becomes aware of the confusion in his mind, he must admit, if he is to be truthful, that he does not yet know what he believes and what he feels about the matter in question. He knows only that he is inclined towards incompatible ideas about his past, as explaining his present state of mind, and therefore towards incompatible, or at least towards different, sentiments. There is as yet no clear answer to the question—which of these conflicting thoughts, and consequent feelings, is really his? The state of a man's body cannot be confused, although it may be confusing, in the sense of difficult to discern. But his state of mind may be one of confusion, with the consequence that only inclinations to incompatible states of mind in respect of the same object can be truthfully imputed to the subject.

Descriptions of states of mind, of beliefs, desires, and emotions, are liable to a kind of indeterminacy which has no parallel in description of physical states. Even such forms of question as "Does he believe that p is true?" and "Does he want p to be true?" may on occasion require an answer which, in the interests of accuracy, have to be in the form—"It would not be true to say that he does and it would not be true to say that he does not"—and without the suggestion that the concepts of belief and desire need to be made more precise. The indeterminacy is necessary to the ordinary explanatory use of the concepts. Insofar as the subject is confused and uncertain, when he asks himself what he believes, what he wants, and what he feels about something, his actual beliefs, desires, and feelings are confused and unformed also. It may not be simple and entirely true either that he hopes that p is true, or that he believes that p is true.

Suppose that a man is uncertain about what he feels about some past action of his, although he is sure that he feels very uneasy and very unhappy, or, as one might say, that he feels badly about it. He puts to himself, in all honesty, the question—"What is this feeling that I have? What is my attitude? Is it embarrassment, or guilt, or some kind of shame, or is it just regret, the feeling that something of value has been lost?" He is looking for a diagnosis, and for an explanation of his felt uneasiness. While he is unsure of the correct diagnosis himself, and while he is still putting this question to himself, at least his conscious feeling has not crystallised into one of these determinate forms. No one can truthfully attribute to him one of these determinate sentiments yet. He still has to make up his mind what he thinks, and therefore, in more specific terms, exactly what he feels, apart from just feeling unhappy. And this making up of the mind is, in many typical cases, like a kind of decision, being a conscious adoption of a specific attitude towards something in his situation which he picks out as both justifying and explaining his unease. But crystallisation may on other occasions be more a discovery than a decision; prompted by the suggestion of another, he might for the first time find in himself some thought, with its accompanying desire, which had been causing his unease and thereby

242

influencing his behaviour. He may bring to the surface of his mind a thought about his situation which had been repressed and excluded from his consciousness, and which would immediately indicate one diagnosis as being correct as an account of his sentiment up to that moment. When this thought of his is brought to consciousness, it is open to his criticism and is liable to be either endorsed or repudiated. His coming to know what his sentiment about his past action is, as he makes up his mind what he thinks about the action, is at the same time the crystallisation of the conscious feeling.

When he is in doubt about what he feels about his past, he is aware of just this possibility of self-deception and illusion. Perhaps he had concealed from himself, or had not admitted to himself, the strength of his feeling. He is matching words, with all their conventional uses and associations, to the confused phenomena: what counts as being *very* unhappy, or what is to regret something *intensely*? Or perhaps he had repressed, or half repressed, some image or fantasy of the past which has to be counted as an element in his state of mind: or perhaps he had not noticed some feature of his behaviour or expression which was obvious to observers, and which was an effect of a deep conflict in his mind, which he had not admitted to himself. In some typical situations of private and public life anxiety about the manifold possibilities of self-deception is certainly not out of place. Someone else may urgently, and for the most practical reasons, need to know precisely what his feelings are, and it may be very difficult for the subject to give an account that is at once clear and complete. My suggestion is that it may even be *impossible* at certain times to give an account that is at once simple and complete, just because his state of mind is one of confusion and conflict. To be sincere, he must convey the confusion in his sentiments and attitudes, and refuse the determinate alternative.

243

The problem of error and corrigibility in avowals of intentional states, and therefore the problem of sincerity, is a confusing one, just because recognising what one thinks, feels, or wants, is apt to be wrongly assimilated to recognising and identifying an independent physical object, where an independent object is something that can be observed by different observers from different points of view, and will change its appearance, but not its real properties, as the point of view changes. The real properties of the object remain the same, whatever the perspective from which it is viewed. But to become sure, by reflecting, what one's sentiment about or attitude to something, is one way, even the typical way, of forming, or bringing into existence, that state of mind; yet it is also true that in becoming sure what one's state of mind now is, one must also recognise facts about the past, and protect oneself against self-deception, and against the neglect of observable fact. "Observable fact" here includes those thought-revealing features of expressive behaviour which an observer might notice; but even more important are the circumstances in which the unhappiness and its accompanying thought originally occurred. If I have overlooked, or misconceived, the circumstances, I shall be in part deceived in the account that I render to myself and to others of what my state of mind is; but this false thought is an element in the state of mind, as finally formed.

Insincerity is typically a gap between what I am disposed to say about myself and what I am disposed to do. If it is true that I regret a mistake, it must normally be true that I have some disposition, however ineffective, to avoid a repetition of the mistake. I may discover or notice to my surprise that, when the appropriate circumstances occur, I have lacked, and am still lacking, any sufficiently strong disposition; so my conscious thought is without its natural expression in a tendency to act. And this is one typical situation in which I shall say that my expressions of regret are not, or have not been, sincere, because there is this confusion and this conflict between my thought and my practice. Following this scheme of thought linked to disposition, I shall then infer that I must also think of the action in some other way, perhaps as in some ways admirable, though without realising that I have also this other view of the past. Prompted by noticing features of my behaviour over a period of time, I may for the first time formulate, and make conscious, a repressed thought about my past, of which the actual behaviour was the expression. I may use the record of my conduct, just as a candid friend might, as a clue to the presence, now or in the past, of beliefs or wishes that I may have concealed from myself, or that are otherwise masked or overlooked. So the confusion and conflict is still a contradiction in thought, which has as its consequence, and as its evidence, a confusion both of feeling and of disposition. As soon as I realise that I have no disposition to avoid the repetition of mistake, I may question whether I do entirely regret the action, whether this is really my thought about it; and for the word "entirely" here, "sincerely" could be substituted. The insincerity that is revealed in a gap between what a man is disposed to say about himself—that is, about his sentiment or attitude—and what he is disposed to do is still itself a confusion of thought. "I sincerely regret that p" is to be construed, in parallel with "I sincerely believe that p," as claiming entirety of mind and the absence of contrary thoughts in respect of p.

The ideal of sincerity, in a context of this kind, amounts to the ideal of undividedness or singleness of mind. My *statement* that I regretted the action could be an honest one, in the narrow sense that it was not *intended* to deceive either myself or others. One may use "sincere" as a predicate, not only of statements, but also of states of mind; the regret that I feel might not be sincere regret, because of

245

the dividedness of mind, the conflict between the conscious thought revealed and the unacknowledged ideas that explain some features of my behaviour and expression. If sincerity is interpreted as undividedness of mind, and if to be sincere in regretting, or to be sincere in one's despair, is to feel these things with one's whole mind, then "watching oneself live" may be, not an obstacle, but rather a necessary condition of sincerity. I say "may be," because the conclusion only follows given one further assumption: that there are less than conscious thoughts, and consequently less than conscious dispositions, which may be in conflict with the thoughts, accompanied by pleasure or displeasure, which are fully conscious. On this assumption self-watching is always necessary as a precaution against an unrecognised conflict or confusion of thought; on this assumption it always makes sense for a man to ask himself "Am I sure that the attitude, the thoughts and the consequent dispositions, which I am ready to acknowledge as mine, really are the whole of what I think and feel about this matter? Or is it the case that, if I adopt the standpoint of an observer of myself, I will discover other, and contrary, thoughts and dispositions which I recognise as having been present, although unacknowledged?"

The ideal of sincerity as mere naturalness, which I have been criticising, depends upon the assumption that the emotions, which arise in the natural course of events, as I interest myself in external objects, are immediate data of consciousness, easily legible. I fall in love: I become jealous: I regret my actions: I fall into despair. I become aware of these things happening to me in the natural course of events, and I am to look for the explanation of these occurrences in a combination of external circumstances and of my acquired and innate dispositions. According to this picture, it is a corruption of consciousness to question too persistently the account of my feelings that immediately suggests itself to me; for watching and questioning interferes with the natural flow of feeling, and is a kind of morbidity. But I am suggesting that one is driven to reflection upon causes merely as a condition of distinguishing in one's own experience the various sentiments which are much more complex than simple occurrences of pleasure and displeasure. Following Spinoza, I am placing alongside Hume's assimilation of belief to the sentiments a contrary assimilation of the sentiments to beliefs and imaginations—crudely, beliefs and imaginations about the occasion and cause of a felt pleasure or displeasure, or of a perturbation of feeling of some kind. Only insofar as I have a belief, or some kind of idea, about the occasion and cause of the pleasure and displeasure that I feel can I experience, and be aware of, a complex intentional sentiment which is either regret, or shame, or embarrassment, or guilt about something, or which is boredom, or depression. All these concepts are explanatory concepts and allege an explanation of the phenomena when they are applied in a diagnosis, whether by the subject himself or by another. When the notional explanation of the feeling—that is, the explanation that the subject gives to himself—is changed, the state of mind is changed also, whether or not the original notional explanation was correct; secondly, when the notional explanation diverges widely from the true explanation, the true account of my state of mind must be a complex one, which exhibits this confusion. If my belief or assumption about the cause of the feeling is displaced by an argument that shows me that the belief or assumption about the cause is unfounded, my sentiment will change also. Although I may continue to feel unhappy when I think of my past action, it will not be true that I regret the action, if I no longer think of it as a loss or as a mistake. If my unhappy feeling was associated with a less than conscious idea about the past, an argument against feeling unhappy about the action might seem to me convincing; but it might still leave the less than conscious idea untouched, and therefore there would be conflict and confusion of mind. "Are you really sincere in disclaiming regret?" as opposed to "Are you being honest in what you say?" not only requires me to make sure that my explicit thought is not in conflict with some unacknowledged or repressed idea; in this process of making sure, my state of mind is liable to change, insofar as my beliefs about it, and its causes, are changed.

A more cautious version of Spinoza's ideal of a free and undivided mind is now not so difficult to justify, or at least to explain. To study contemporaneously my own emotions and attitudes, and their causes, with a view to determining why they are as they are and therefore what they are, is to acquire reflexive knowledge, in Spinoza's terminology. It is also a kind of action upon one's own states of mind; for in discriminating more exactly what my contemporary sentiment is, I in effect form and focus my state of mind. To ask myself questions about my own present states of mind is both to examine my ideas about the source of my feelings, as well-founded ideas or not, and at the same time submit to the test of sincerity—are these ideas the only ideas that I have of the object, and of the source, of my feeling, or are there others which I have repressed, or have not acknowledged? Without the habit of this dual inquiry, I should be more liable than I am to be in a state of conflict, which will be revealed in conflicting dispositions, a tendency to do something and then to undo it. Such a state of conflict is in itself painful and something that everyone will wish to avoid.

For these reasons I do not see how Chamfort's dictum can be defended. The ideal of naturalness of feeling, uncorrupted by reflection, is for us an unattainable one, once we have built up a sophisticated vocabulary of intentional states, of emotions, sentiments, attitudes. The very elaborate vocabulary of sentiments and attitudes is a vocabulary for self-watching persons; we experience the sentiments, and have the attitudes, *because* we have theories about the sources of our own feelings: and the theories are built into the vocabulary of the sentiments, which one may use very selectively, just because one does not wish to be committed to all the commonplace explanations implied by it.

Within this Spinozistic scheme one can still give an account of what sentimentality is, and of why it is a corruption of consciousness, and a form of insincerity. The man whose regret or despair is a sentimental regret, or a sentimental despair, is the man who thinks of his own state of mind, however disagreeable in itself, as a praiseworthy or an agreeable fact about himself. He does not *only* regret his action, he does not *only* experience the unhappiness that is accompanied by the thought that there is nothing to hope for; he also takes pleasure in the thought that these are his thoughts and therefore are his sentiments. Sentimentality is a further form of the doubling of self-consciousness, of the mind's tendency to turn back upon itself in reflection. It is incompatible with any integrity, or undividedness, of thought and feeling. For the sentimentalist his own sentiments are playthings in which he takes pleasure; they do not occupy his entire mind, and they are for that reason light and feeble. A strong and sincere sentiment is one that, for good or for ill, occupies the subject's mind fully, and that displaces competing thoughts and dispositions. But it does not follow that a sincere sentiment must be natural, spontaneous and unreflective, as the French moralists seem to imply. It *may* be natural, in the sense that the explanation of the sentiment is principally to be found in external objects and in innate dispositions of the subject, and not so much in the subject's own conscious reflection: but it need not be, and generally will not be, in one usual sense of "natural."

Perhaps there do exist ideal Tolstoyan men whose sentiments and attitudes form themselves immediately, unconditionally, and all in one piece, and who are almost incapable
of any anxious dividedness of mind or concealed complexity, and of whom we can say "He believes what he believes" and "He feels what he feels" and who has no reason
ever to be unsure whether his attitudes or his sentiments
are what he believes or assumes that they are. He would be
a man who would not need to take seriously in his own experience the contrast between psychic appearances and
psychic realities. Most of us are not like that, and the ordinary use of the psychological vocabulary shows that we are
not. A natural feeling, which is also a strong and sincere
feeling, is a passion; and the ethics of romanticism represents the man of passion as the ideal of the sincere man of
undivided mind. But the ethics of romanticism only with
difficulty avoids contradiction and turns very easily into an
attitude of irony, as Stendhal showed; for the cultivation of
strong and sincere passions, as a policy—"espagnolisme,"
as Stendhal called it—requires either a restraint of intelligence, or a kind of self-consciousness that amounts to sentimentality. How can a man watch for, and endorse, his own
moments of spontaneity and natural passion without an
ironical awareness of his own duplicity? The answer is that
he can do this only in fiction, by creating a representative
of himself.

As we have gradually over the centuries invented for ourselves an elaborate vocabulary to discriminate shades of
sentiment, and as these discriminations continually complicate the range of feeling to which we are liable, it is now
humanly impossible to reverse the process and to discard
the thought that informs the sentiments. And if there
were such a thing as moral progress, it might partly consist
in an increased sensitiveness to such discriminations between the sources of, and reasons for, pleasure and unhap-

piness: as well ask that, in the interests of naturalness, one should forget the more refined discriminations between kinds of action that are now built into the vocabulary and that must now enter into practical intentions.

What exactly is being claimed in respect of contemporary knowledge of one's own sentiments—e.g. the sentiment of regret—and what exactly is the contrast with contemporary knowledge of one's own physical states? I will summarise the stages of the argument in separate propositions.

(1) The more sophisticated states of mind, specifically the sentiments and emotions and attitudes, are distinguished from each other in the common vocabulary partly by the cause, or occasion, of the occurrence of the affect, or perturbation, which may be e.g. a feeling of unease or unhappiness, and partly also by the subject's belief about the cause or occasion. For example, regret is distinguished from remorse and guilt in this way, and embarrassment is distinguished from anger and shame in this way. The third factor that enters into the discrimination is the expected behavioural expression of the intentional state, with its specified object, which supplies evidence that the subject's thought is, or is not, of the kind that is imputed to him, or that he imputes to himself. Evidently the subject is in a peculiar and special position when he is assessing his own present state of mind, quite different from that which he assumes when he is considering what can be truthfully said about his own past sentiments, or about the sentiments of another, past or present.

(2) If the subject changes his opinion about the explanation of one of these contemporary states of mind, he changes his opinion about what his state of mind is.

(3) If on reflection I become sure that I do regret something that I have done, then at least regret is one element in the state of mind that can be imputed to me, even if other, and contrary, attitudes can also be truthfully im-

251

puted to me, of which I am unaware. If after further reflection I am no longer sure that I do regret the action, and when I come to think that my attitude towards it must be quite differently characterised, then it cannot be true, while the uncertainty lasts, that my state of mind is *simply* one of regret; under these two conditions, my state of mind either must be unformed or must be one of conflict and confusion.

I am not denying that it makes sense for someone to say about me: "Although he would, or does, deny that he regrets the action, and with no intention to deceive, he does really regret the action" or "He does regret it, although he does not yet realise that he does." The fact that such sentences have a use is sufficient to establish that an honest avowal of a sentiment or emotion is very far from being incorrigible, and that there is a place for forms of insincerity. The very fact that I may be uncertain about the correct characterisation of my state of mind shows that there is a place for my being deceived, and that there are possible observations which would establish that an opinion of mine about my own state of mind is not true.

The form of words "Although he does not realise it, he does regret the action" represents the state of mind as one of half-formed or confused regret, and not simply of regret unknown to the subject. It is a necessary condition of the truth of "He simply regrets the action, without qualification" that, if the question were raised, he would think that this was his attitude. We can infer from the fact that, when the question is raised, he is unsure whether he regrets it or not, that either the truth about his present sentiments is more complex, or that he does not yet regret the action.

From these three propositions we can infer the following conclusion: If I became convinced that the perturbation that I now feel, in association with the thought of some action of mine as a mistake, has an adequate explanation in some third factor, which is not causally connected with my present thought of the action, it will no longer be true that I regret the action. While I thought of the action as a mistake, and while I explained my present perturbation as due principally to this thought, I thought of my perturbation as a case of more or less intense regret. If I now come to believe, and if it is also true, that my perturbation has a quite different explanation, into which the memory of the action does not enter at all, then it was never the whole truth that I regretted the action, and it has ceased even to be part of the truth. Of someone who feels unhappy when he thinks about his action, and who thinks that his action was a mistake, and who attributes his unhappiness to this thought, we are bound to say that, among other things, he regrets his action, even if his causal, or quasi-causal, judgment is at fault, and even if this is for this reason an incomplete account of his state of mind. But a change in his causal beliefs will entail a change in his state of mind.

A more familiar example may make the same point. A man may be listening to music and at the same time, unknown to him, receiving a physical stimulation which produces a state of exaltation and pleasure; if the stimulation stops, the exaltation and pleasure would stop also. The man may think that he is enjoying the music intensely, and, although this is certainly not the whole relevant truth about his state of mind, it is not entirely false either; it is not entirely false, just because he believes it to be true. He listens to the music as the source of his pleasure, and, because of this, we *can* say that the stimulation, which ordinarily causes just pleasure, on this occasion causes him to enjoy the music. But as soon as he ceases to believe that the music has any connection with his pleasurable state, we shall have less inclination to say that he is enjoying the music, because in *his* thought there is now no association between the music and the enjoyment. The difference in the specification of the object of the enjoyment depends upon the subject's belief about the cause of the enjoyment.

Once the subject has considered the question "Is your state of mind correctly characterised as such-and-such?" either he has a true belief about his state of mind, or the answer must be that his state of mind is one of confusion or conflict in the respect inquired into, and there is no simple yes-or-no answer to the question. So he who says "Although you think that you believe that p is true, you do not really believe it: you just hope that it is" accuses his interlocutor of a confusion, or conflict, of mind in respect of the proposition p. Just as a non-trivial mistaken belief, after reflection, about the correct characterisation of the object of one's desire makes that desire a confused one, so a mistaken belief, after reflection, about the correct characterisation of what one's attitude, or what one's sentiment is, makes the attitude or the sentiment a confused one. It will readily be conceded that, if I have a radically mistaken belief about the correct description of the particular action which I say that I regret, identifying it by an incorrect description, there will often be no simple answer to the question of whether I regret that action, correctly described, or not. It will also readily be conceded that a correction of the radically mistaken belief will entail a reconsideration of what my sentiment is. The same indeterminacy will apply to ascriptions of sentiments as to the identification of the objects of the sentiments. In both cases the process of forming a belief about, or of coming to know, what one's state of mind is cannot be held apart, in the mind of the subject, from the formation of that state of mind; the two processes overlap.

A contrast may illustrate the point. Suppose a question is raised, not about my present sentiments, but rather about my present psychological needs, where the end to be achieved is my happiness: the question is "Does he need to be consoled?" and not "Does he want to be consoled?" Insofar as the word "need" does not generate any kind of intentional context, there is no reason to say that a change in the subject's own opinions about the correct characterisation of his present needs will by itself constitute a change in his needs. An observer is in as good a position to determine the subject's needs as the subject himself, provided that they both possess the relevant information about a man's normal needs, and about the particular case. The subject's diagnosis is to be tested for truth in exactly the same way as any observer's diagnosis; it has no peculiar authority. This remains true, even if in a particular case the subject's opinion about his needs is a causal factor which to some extent determines his needs; whether there is this causal relation in a particular case will have to be discovered experimentally. But we do not need experiment to decide whether a man's changing opinion about whether or not he wants to be consoled will affect his actual desires in this matter; we know that it will, just because the terms in which he would think of, and would describe, the object of his desire, if the question were raised, cannot be altogether omitted from any complete account of his desire: this remains true, even if his opinion is mistaken, and even if his state of mind is therefore one of confusion.

There is no reason whatever to deny that, given an intentional state of mind, we can always look for adequate causal explanations of the occurrence of that state, already identified under a certain description, which we will hold constant throughout the inquiry. The scheme of scientific explanation by covering law is no less applicable to these psychological phenomena than to any other natural events. Paradoxes only arise—the paradoxes of which Spinoza took advantage—when we reflect on the methods of inquiry by which causal explanations are normally arrived at, and, secondly, on the use that is normally made of them, once they are discovered. Often, in the course of a causal inquiry, one will vary the various relevant antecedent conditions and wait to see whether there is a hypothesized concomitant variation in the independently identified effects. If my argument is correct, this experimental method is applicable to intentional states of mind, only under very definite restrictions and within certain limits. If the subject is required to report the varying effects of different stimulating conditions, as he normally would be, he cannot both know what the particular experiment is, and report the effect, without this knowledge of the stimulating conditions affecting the ensuing state of mind. Secondly, the subject cannot use knowledge of the causes of his intentional states, which he may have acquired, to plan what his sentiments and desires are to be, exactly as he may use knowledge about the causes of his sensations and of his physical states; for again his knowledge of how the state of mind has been brought into existence will by itself change the ensuing state of mind from what it would have been without his knowledge.

This is one reason why we so persistently suspect that psychology, as an applied science concerned with the sentiments, beliefs, and interests of men, has different prospects from physics. Even if physical causes were found to explain some sentiments and interests, as they occur, the subject's knowledge of the cause will lead him to view these sentiments and interests differently, and, in virtue of this change, his sentiments and interests will actually be different. As we raise questions about the nature, and therefore about the origin, of our own states of mind, and watch them changing in response to changing circumstances, our states of mind themselves are changed by the theories that we form about their origin. My changing beliefs about the presence or absence of an infection in my bloodstream will not by themselves change the chemical situation: but my changing beliefs about the origins and nature of my sentiments will change the sentiments themselves.

256